Mission-Shaped Evangelism

Related titles from Canterbury Press

Night Vision: Mission Adventures in Club Culture and the Nightlife
Jon Oliver   978 1 85311 956 9
'. . . full of stories which tell of Christians being salt and light in a culture where people desperately need to experience the flavour of God in their lives.' *Andy Hunt, DJ*

Fresh Expressions in the Sacramental Traditions
Rowan Williams, Brian McLaren, Steve Croft and others
                                978 1 85311 973 6
'This book should inspire, intrigue and invite fresh energies into a new phase of Christian outreach that is both contextual and true to the faith of the church through the ages.'
Fresh Expressions website

Evaluating Fresh Expressions: Explorations in Emerging Church
Edited by Martyn Percy and Louise Nelstrop
                                978 1 85311 816 6

www.canterburypress.co.uk

Mission-Shaped Evangelism

The Gospel in Contemporary Culture

Steve Hollinghurst

CANTERBURY
PRESS

Norwich

© Steve Hollinghurst 2010

First published in 2010 by the Canterbury Press Norwich
Editorial office
13–17 Long Lane,
London, EC1A 9PN, UK

Canterbury Press is an imprint of Hymns Ancient and Modern Ltd
(a registered charity)
St Mary's Works, St Mary's Plain,
Norwich, NR3 3BH, UK

www.scm-canterburypress.co.uk

British Library Cataloguing in Publication data

A catalogue record for this book is available
from the British Library

978 1 85311 842 5

Typeset by Regent Typesetting, London
Printed and bound in Great Britain by
CPI William Clowes, Beccles, NR34 7TL

Contents

Part Three Mission-Shaped Evangelism in the Twenty-First Century

Preface

For the researcher no subject is ever closed, no idea proven, no investigation finished and thus no book ever truly completed. When I set out to write *Mission-Shaped Evangelism* I didn't anticipate the new questions it would raise for me and the new research it would generate, all of which made the material grow and the writing time lengthen. And then of course new data kept appearing and others were constantly adding their material to the questions I was seeking to address. I need to thank those at Canterbury Press who had patience with me through all of this and the subsequent editing and rewriting. I also very much want to thank my colleagues at the Sheffield Centre for all their support and encouragement, and at times some gentle badgering to finish. In particular I want to thank our assistant researcher, Claire Dalpra, who followed up contacts, found helpful material and read and provided feedback for me on the first draft, which led to a number of helpful changes. Most of all I want to thank my wife Anne who put up with me writing this in much of my and therefore our spare time for the last two years.

This is thus not a definitive statement on evangelism for our time and culture; it is part of an ongoing discovery of what that is. I hope, however, it is both a useful assessment of where we have been, the issues we face and some signposts for the journey forward. I found doing the research that this book entailed both challenging and inspiring; I hope you find it the same. As I finish the book, it is the ancient Christian Festival of Lammas, the celebration in parts of the Northern Hemisphere of the first fruits of the harvest. Like many European Christian festivals we share this with a growing contemporary

Pagan community, and as such it provides a snapshot of the cultural situation in which we seek to share the Christian faith. Our predecessors who brought the Christian faith to Europe nearly 2,000 years ago made much of such connections in order to create indigenous expressions of faith. I believe we are called to recapture this in our own age for the same reason. The first fruits are but a sign of the full harvest to come: tentative, uncertain, yet full of promise that the Lord of the Harvest is at work. This is not a bad picture of where we are in recovering a mission-shaped evangelism, following the increasing failure of approaches geared to a fading Christendom. I often find myself trying to find these first fruits of God's missionary work in our culture in the hope of discerning from them the harvest to come. The fields may not yet be white for harvest, but the workers are already needed to enter the new landscape of our emerging global culture. We have much yet to discover from God on the journey, but we are called as people of faith to travel as Christ's Body into that world, not sure of our destination, but trusting in the one who leads us there and sees it long before we do.

Steve Hollinghurst
Lammas 2009

Introduction

In writing this book a number of people, perhaps not surprisingly, have wanted to know what lay behind the title *Mission-Shaped Evangelism*. Since the publication of the *Mission-shaped Church* report[1] there has been a tendency to refer to all sorts of things as 'mission-shaped'. This is partly due to a desire to create the kind of mission engagement with contemporary society the report advocates. However, there has also been a tendency to turn the label into a rather meaningless branding exercise. The *Church Times* in November 2004 illustrated this rather well with a St Gargoyle's cartoon in which the vicar 'even had a mission-shaped sausage dog'. My use of the 'mission-shaped' label relates to the cross-cultural mission agenda of the report, which I hope will yield lasting fruit after the fad has passed.

So why *Mission-Shaped Evangelism*? The story of the *Mission-shaped Church* report begins with *Breaking New Ground*,[2] a report on church planting in the Church of England written ten years earlier. Amid concern from some it gave a cautious green light to church planting in the Church of England. The *Mission-shaped Church* report stems from observing such church plants over the intervening years, noting a move from plants like the sending church to a great diversity of 'fresh expressions' of church, seeking to respond to cross-cultural mission situations in the UK. Implicit in the report is an assumption that evangelism will be part of 'mission-shaping' churches, but the focus is cross-cultural church planting rather than an all-encompassing understanding of mission for today's Church. For this reason, John Hull is right that it does not fully examine what happens to the gospel when it is inculturated, or the possibility that the gospel is already present in the culture before the missionaries arrive.[3]

A number of Hull's criticisms are about the nature of evangelism. He also complains that the report doesn't celebrate religious diversity but instead implies 'proselytizing activity'.[4] For Hull this connects with his application of Raimon Panikkar on Christendom, Christianity and Christianness.[5] Panikkar argues that these phrases characterize different periods of the Church's mission, and that today we should adopt a non-creedal personal spirituality he calls 'Christianness' which welcomes religious pluralism.[6] Hull connects each phase to the prominence of particular biblical texts. The Great Commission of Matthew 28 is seen as emblematic of 'Christianity' viewed as an expression of faith geared to colonial expansion. The conversion of those of other faiths is thus viewed as a mistaken expression of colonialism. However, neither the report nor Hull's critique fully explores the nature of evangelism in a multifaith and multicultural society. Such an exploration is essential if we are to know what type of mission we expect to shape our church.

In 2005 the UK Evangelical Alliance published a report on the state of evangelism in Britain. They found it to be in a state of flux, with potential polarization between those who saw evangelism as proclamation only and those pursuing more developmental approaches with an emphasis on presence. They noted that there was not much big crusade meeting evangelism like that of Billy Graham, once seen as defining evangelism. They were concerned that increasingly people felt less able to speak about their faith in a multicultural, multifaith society and felt that available resources no longer connected in a changing, postmodern culture.

Ironically, as their review was coming to an end in 2004 the EA cancelled the national evangelists' conference, a long-established event, due to a lack of participants. Against such a background it is not surprising that the evangelist can feel they are a dying breed, and dwindling numbers mean that several other events and organizations are struggling to be viable.

Introduction

The tensions the EA report mentions are present as some seek to explore new approaches to evangelism and tackle Hull's point about how the gospel might be altered by the process of inculturation. Particular understandings of the gospel message and evangelism are ways different groups within the Church use to define themselves, especially those who identify as evangelicals. The questioning of these areas by some is therefore matched by a desire in others to preserve their heritage. A good example was the controversy long-standing evangelist Steve Chalke caused when he attacked penal substitution[7] as the understanding of Jesus' death, suggesting a more corporate Kingdom focus as opposed to a focus on individual salvation.[8] In the USA similar controversy surrounds the work of Brian McLaren,[9] accused by many evangelicals[10] of embracing too uncritically postmodern culture and becoming a relativist. Contemporary debates around culture and mission and evangelism are not just dividing evangelicals; Christians from Catholic, liberal and charismatic traditions are equally divided by attempts to reshape faith in line with issues raised by cultural change.

Many of those involved in mission thinking today have been influenced by the work of the late David Bosch.[11] Drawing on the paradigm theory of Thomas Kuhn as adapted by Hans Küng, he argues that mission has historically been shaped by shifts between epochs of history.[12] Christian mission cannot be anything but incarnational, responding to its time, place and culture. This incarnational approach to mission would now be considered mainstream by many missiologists and is that taken in the *Mission-shaped Church* report. For Bosch, just such a major shift began in the latter part of the twentieth century from the modern to the postmodern era.

Bosch describes[13] how at times of transition from one epoch to another people become divided between champions of the emerging world-view and defenders of the old. The champions of the new feel that the scales have fallen from their eyes and they can't understand how they ever saw the world in the old way. The defenders of the old immunize themselves against the new with deeply emotional reactions, feeling that their whole world is threatened. All of which sounds like a description of some of the debate surrounding *Mission-shaped Church*, the writings of Chalke and McLaren, and a number of other issues that divide the Church.

Traditionally mission was seen as something that happens abroad when entering foreign cultures; evangelism was seen as what the Church does at home, in 'Christian' countries. One can see why evangelism was not shaped by the concerns of mission within western countries that considered themselves Christian. This understanding is challenged when the culture radically changes due to the kind of paradigm shift Bosch describes, especially when this shift undermines the assumed place of Christianity. Bosch characterizes the distinction between mission abroad and evangelism at home as between mission to the 'not yet' Christian and evangelism to the 'no longer' Christian. He suggests that this distinction is breaking down as 'Christian' nations now have 'not yet' Christians and non-Christian nations have 'no longer' Christians.[14]

Home evangelism needs to become an expression of cross-cultural mission. We need a 'mission-shaped' evangelism, recognizing that some approaches to evangelism are not in fact 'mission-shaped'. This may explain why the vast majority of those our current evangelism reaches come from the dwindling minority who have church backgrounds.[15] Paradigm shifts in culture take decades to work through; we do not yet have a clear picture of where we are going, and so there is an element of the 'prophetic' about some of this work, which is always risky! However, the situation we face, especially in Europe, does not allow us the luxury of waiting. If this were not challenging enough, Bosch reminds us[16] that Christianity seeks not only to be relevant to the present but to maintain its roots in the past. It is incarnational in diverse cultures and ages because God became incarnate in just such a way in Jesus. However, as followers of Jesus the incarnation of faith must not break continuity with the Jesus who both founded that faith in history and sustains it today. Further to this, in a world in which culture is increasingly global it makes sense to ask global as well as local questions about the paradigm shift Bosch refers to. Does it affect the mission situation beyond Europe or not? What are the implications for a globalized view of mission as 'from everywhere to everywhere'?[17]

Mission-Shaped Evangelism draws on material used in talks and training sessions I have been doing in Britain and abroad over the past six years as Researcher in Evangelism to Post-Christian Culture at the Church Army Sheffield Centre. This, however, is the first time that these threads have been drawn together in such a way, and I hope that in doing so further insights can be offered and a wider and more detailed discussion fostered. My intention is to offer an overview of the issues in our culture we need to face, and apply mission thinking to these; exploring what the 'good news' is in our emerging culture so we can move beyond the current 'crisis' and be effective in evangelism in the twenty-first century.

Notes

1 *Mission-shaped Church*, Church House Publishing, 2004.

2 *Breaking New Ground*, Church House Publishing, 1994.

3 John Hull, *Mission-shaped Church: A Theological Response*, SCM Press, 2006, p. 26. I note, however, that Hull himself acknowledges on pp. 12–13 some discussion of these themes on pp. 86–108 of the report.

4 Hull, *Mission*, p. 13, see also pp. 11–12.

5 Hull, *Mission*, pp. 29–30.

6 Raimon Panikkar, 'The Dawn of Christianness', *Cross Currents*, Spring/Summer 2000 (online at www.aril.org).

7 This basically states that Jesus was our substitute in suffering a death penalty that we should have faced because of our sin. For many evangelicals this would be seen as central to a biblical understanding of Jesus' crucifixion, as argued forcefully by John Stott in his influential *The Cross of Christ*, InterVarsity Press, 1986.

8 Steve Chalke, *The Lost Message of Jesus*, Zondervan, 2003.

9 Brian McLaren's ideas are expressed in a number of books like the trilogy of novels that began with *A New Kind of Christian*, Jossey Bass Willey, 2001, or the non-fictional *A Generous Orthodoxy*, Zondervan, 2006.

10 The classic critique would be D. A. Carson, *Becoming Conversant with the Emerging Church,* Zondervan, 2005.

11 David Bosch, *Transforming Mission,* Orbis, 1991.

12 Bosch, *Transforming*, pp. 181–9.

13 Bosch, *Transforming*, p. 185.

14 Bosch, *Transforming*, p. 410.

15 See John Finney, *Finding Faith Today*, Bible Society, 1992.

16 Bosch, *Transforming*, p. 187.

17 This is how CMS, once a foreign mission agency, now describes its activity; in a similar way BCMS changed its name to BCMS Crosslinks to emphasize that mission no longer runs from the West to the rest.

Towards a Mission-Shaped Evangelism

The *Mission-shaped Church* report offers two crucial insights. First, that the UK is now largely a foreign mission field where the lessons of foreign mission need to be applied. Second, it offers a process it calls 'double listening' as a key tool in mission. My intention is to use these insights in assessing evangelism in our contemporary context.

Applying the lessons of foreign mission

Along with David Bosch, a number of others have contributed to a growing understanding of cross-cultural mission. The ideas of two in particular, Vincent Donovan and Roland Allen, influenced the *Mission-shaped Church* report. In the Foreword to the revised edition of *Christianity Rediscovered*[1] a discussion of how Donovan's insights from mission among the Masai in Africa might apply to 'the tribe of teenagers in the USA' is reported. This contributes one of the most oft-quoted statements used in *Mission-shaped Church*: 'Do not try to call them back to where they were, and do not try to call them to where you are, beautiful as that place may seem to you. You must have the courage to go with them to a place neither you nor they have been before.'[2]

Traditional evangelism to the 'no longer Christian' is effectively calling people back to where they were, which is where the evangelist is now by showing just how beautiful that place is for both the evangelist and their audience. Donovan realizes that evangelism to the 'not yet Christian' cannot be like this. Where the evangelist is, as beautiful as it seems, stems from the incarnation of the gospel in the evangelist's culture. This indeed is a good place to call others to who share that culture, but actually not the place to call people to from different cultures. Rather the evangelist not only calls those to whom she witnesses to travel to a new place, but she must journey there herself, because the expression of faith that emerges from that new context will not be one the evangelist is used to.

Allen, writing early in the twentieth century, is critical of how mission led to the dependency of new Christians on foreign leadership and models of faith and church. He emphasizes instead the need to let God's Spirit guide new converts to discover how Christian faith is expressed correctly in their own culture rather than let European missionaries decide this.[3] Missiologists often refer to this as 'inculturation', justified by the incarnation of God in Jesus. The *Mission-shaped Church* report, using Jesus' image[4] of the grain of wheat that falls into the ground and dies but in doing so produces much fruit, describes cross-cultural mission as 'dying to live'. Similarly, it uses Philippians 2 in which Jesus' incarnation is described as taking on the form of a human servant obedient to death, from whence he is raised up by God as another description of this. This paints cross-cultural mission as a radical process of death to the familiar expression of faith in the old culture, incarnation of the missionary in the new and the coming to birth of something fresh, like Paul's description[5] of the human body 'sown' in death possessing a new body at its resurrection. Gospel and church need to grow up into an indigenous plant from a seed planted by the missionary within foreign soil, rather than as a transplant from the missionary's own culture, hence the need for what the report calls 'fresh expressions of church'.[6]

Finally, missiology sees all mission as God's, the *missio Dei*. Our mission is a part of and dependent on what God is doing. Very often we behave as if evangelists make people Christian. Instead, as Rowan Williams said at the Anglican church planting conference in 2005, 'mission is seeing what God is doing and joining in'. The mission of God begins in the very nature of God as Trinity in mutual self-giving, out of which comes creation. In this way God's mission encompasses the work of God in creation through to the new heaven and the new earth. This means that mission is far broader in time than God's work in Jesus of Nazareth and far broader in scope than human salvation.

Double listening and cross-cultural evangelism

As Allen realized, the only place one can see how Christianity is faithfully expressed in any culture is from within that culture. For this reason *Mission-shaped Church* offers an approach it calls 'double listening',[7] which it describes in the following terms.

> For church-planting, listening to both contemporary cul-
> ture and to Church tradition is vital. The planters – here
> understood in the simple generic sense of those involved in
> the starting and sustaining of further and fresh communi-
> ties of faith – carry with them an existing understanding of
> the faith and of the Church. They do not come with empty
> hands, but the next task is to have open ears. Attention to
> the mission context, or listening to the world, comes before
> discerning how the inherited Christian tradition works with-
> in it. Mission precedes the shape of the church that will be
> the result, when the seed of the gospel roots in the mission
> culture. Listening to the context of the world shapes what
> emerges. Then the second aspect of double listening validates
> it, through connection with the faith uniquely revealed in the
> Scriptures.[8]

This process helps us avoid the opposite pitfalls of cross-cultural mission; on the one hand failing to incarnate the gospel in the new culture, rendering it irrelevant, on the other allowing its contours to be dictated by the new culture so much that it ceases to be the Christian gospel at all.

It is important to note that missionaries do not come empty-handed. They carry a message they believe will be worth offering in this new context. They also come with their own cultural glasses through which they will tend to view the new context and with preconceived ideas about 'how to share the gospel' formed in their own culture. This is why it is crucial that 'double listening' begins not with the message the missionary brings but with listening to the culture in which the missionary now is. Unless this is done, and done with a thoroughness that enables the missionary to stand in the shoes of those he seeks to communicate with, the missionary will simply proclaim the gospel as if they were still in their sending culture. They end up like the tourists who insist on speaking their own language and simply speak louder and slower if they're not understood. This approach unwittingly weds the gospel message to the culture of the missionary. People in the new culture then either reject the gospel because they reject the missionary's culture or they accept it because they are also accepting the missionary's culture. Converts are then likely to be discipled into the missionary's culture. The effects of this are not hard to find; in some places the desire to become western, seen as gaining power and prosperity, has led to an acceptance of Christianity as part of westernization. In others we find people wearing western clothes purely to go to church, which is a building copied from American or European architecture.

The process of listening to the culture that the missionary finds herself in will vary according to the distance from that culture to her own. Someone used to doing mission among young adults in one city may find themselves quickly at home among young adults in another. However, differences in income, race, religious background, leisure activities, musical taste and relationship patterns, as well as locality, will all mean that one group of young adults does not totally share the culture of another. We need to listen to a culture before seeking to offer the Christian faith within it. We cannot assume that people share our culture and circumvent this.

The next phase of double listening is to the tradition one

brings. If one has listened well to the local culture at this stage, the Christian tradition can be heard as it might be from within that culture. It is at this stage that the missionary begins to find ways to communicate the gospel to people within the perspective of the new culture. At this point the missionary will find that some aspects of the faith connect well with the local culture; others will need to be reinterpreted. Here we have to take on the challenge of communicating effectively while remaining faithful to the tradition.

In reality the process is not as neat as this two-stage model suggests. There is constant interplay between both parts, but the key is to ensure that there is real time to listen to the culture before shaping the gospel within each context. This may be quite lengthy: foreign missionaries speak sometimes of not even beginning to communicate the gospel effectively until they have lived in their new culture for about seven years. We cannot assume that missionaries in once-Christian countries may not also find places within their own nations that require this kind of time commitment. This is one reason why it is so important to approach such areas as foreign mission fields. If we do not, we are likely to deem the mission a failure through simply expecting 'results' far too quickly. Those who fund mission in the West seriously need to grasp this lesson. The practice of giving 'seed-corn' funds to start up mission over short periods of time, or placing missionaries with three- or even five-year contracts, won't work in many of these situations. We will need long-term projects in the new 'foreign mission fields' of the once-Christian nations of the West.

Much of the thinking behind 'double listening' in *Mission-shaped Church* was formulated by my colleague George Lings at the Sheffield Centre. In the time since the report's publication he has noticed a tendency to view double listening as listening to the world and listening to God. He emphasizes that this is a misunderstanding. It is a process of listening to the culture and to the Christian tradition, and God can be expected to be heard speaking in *both* places. The missionary does not take God into the situation; God is already at work there. What the missionary brings is the Christian tradition, and seeks to make connections between that and what God is already doing. This assumption will be questioned by some theological approaches and I will return to this later in the light of what we can learn from the Christian tradition about cross-cultural evangelism.

The rest of this book follows the pattern of double listening. Part 1 explores our contemporary culture, or cultures; Part 2 looks at the Christian tradition with regard to cross-cultural mission, leading to Part 3, an approach to evangelism and the gospel message in our age in continuity with the Christian tradition.

Notes

1 Vincent Donovan, *Christianity Rediscovered*, SCM Press, 2001.

2 Donovan, *Christianity*, Preface to the 2nd edition.

3 Paul's missionary methods and ours from D. Paton and C. H Long (eds), *The Compulsion of the Spirit: A Roland Allen Reader*, Eerdmans, 1983, pp. 10–22.

4 John 12.24–26.

5 1 Corinthians 15.36–38.

6 *Mission-shaped Church*, pp. xii, 30, 90.

7 *Mission-shaped Church*, pp. 104–5.

8 *Mission-shaped Church*, p. 104.

PART ONE

Listening to God in the Cultural Context

2

The Collapse of Christendom

The tale of the fishing community

Once upon a time there was a large lake, and on its shores lived a fishing community. They had become expert at fishing the lake and knew exactly the right kind of boat to use, the right nets to cast, and where and when to cast them. So, they thrived for many generations. However, after a while they noticed that their catches began to dwindle, and then some days they caught nothing at all. They began to be anxious and wondered what was going wrong, as they had kept faithfully to all they knew about fishing and worked hard to put it into practice. They decided to investigate.

Now earthquakes were not unknown in this area and indeed a large one had happened a few years before. As they investigated, they found that the earthquake had thrown up a cliff, diverting a river that had fed the lake with fresh water several miles in a new direction. They decided they would sail down it to find where it now went. Having navigated the river's new course, they found it opened out into a strange new lake they had never seen before. Moreover, round this lake were some of the weirdest people, fishing in a way they had never seen before. Not one of them was fishing properly with a boat and a net; instead they were using all sorts of strange methods and were landing catches of the strangest fish. They decided to see if they, too, could catch some. So they put their boat onto the lake, sailed out and lowered their nets but caught nothing. So, they tried the other side, and behind and in front and every trick they knew, but they still caught nothing

Dejected, they went back home and called a meeting and the whole community discussed what to do. Some said that it was clear they would never get fish from the new lake and would simply have to keep fishing the old one; after all, there were more fish in it yet, perhaps still enough to last their lifetime. Others suggested that if they waited long enough, perhaps another earthquake would divert the river back again and solve the problem. However, others said they had to face the fact that the old lake would soon have no fish and they had to find a way to fish the new lake or the community had no future. What were they to do? What would you do, for indeed this is our story, the story of the church in Britain at the start of the twenty-first century.

Collapsing church attendance and a 'non-churched' people

The fishing story is illustrated by Figure 1. The lower line shows monthly attendance in British churches by age using the figures from the 2005 Church Census.[1] The top line shows for those over 15 in 2005 what percentage had attended church monthly or more when they were under 15 themselves. This splits the population into three different groups: 9 per cent attending church or Christian youth clubs at least monthly; 26 per cent who used to attend when they were under 15 and no longer do, who I refer to as the 'de-churched'; and finally 65 per cent who did not regularly attend under 15, who I refer to as the 'non-churched'.[2]

Research by John Finney[3] found that 76 per cent of those who came to faith as adults had a church background. This means both that future church attendance is predictable largely on current childhood attendance, but also that much of our current evangelism is effective largely with those who have been raised with an understanding of the Christian message and regular experience of church. Our fishing is geared to the lake populated by those raised in a Christian country and we are experienced at catching its Christendom fish. However, since

Figure 1 Church attendance 2005

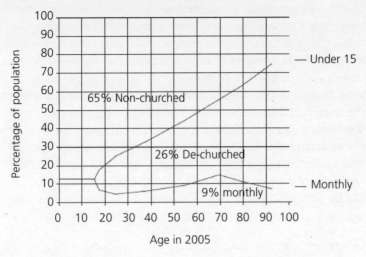

the early twentieth century the church has been losing children at a rapid rate. This means that the de-churched population is both ageing and shrinking in size; indeed, it has fallen by about 15 per cent[4] since the last Church Census of 1998. At present it looks as if the trend of falling youth attendance will continue. However, even if rates of attendance by under-15s stopped falling we would still see a gradual fall in the de-churched population over the next 50 years as it ages and dies.

If the church is to break out of a pattern of long-term decline leading to attendance rates that mirror those of the minority faith communities it must be able to successfully evangelize those in the growing non-churched population. Here reality is slightly better than the fishing story paints it. Finney's survey shows that 24 per cent of adult converts came from this group. We are catching some fish from the new lake, but we clearly find this much harder than fishing from the old one. Finney found that those who came to faith from non-churched backgrounds very rarely responded to evangelistic preaching or at mission events. Most could not say when they became a Christian; they had simply done so gradually over a period of time and then came to a realization of what had happened. In terms of the fishing story it's as if the few fish coming into the stock pond from the new lake are somehow arriving without being caught by the fishing community first. This is the opposite of the normal experience for those who had church backgrounds, who largely responded to mission events and could name the time and place they did. This alone suggests that our mission events and current approach to evangelism are geared to those with church backgrounds, who were of course the majority of the population until partway through the twentieth century and had been so since the establishment of Christianity as the faith of Britain a thousand years earlier.

This analysis is open to a number of questions. Surveys that ask people what their church attendance is often show much higher figures. For example, that done recently for Tear Fund by Research Matters[5] records monthly church attendance at 15 per cent of the population and suggests figures for the de-churched of 44 per cent and non-churched of 41 per cent,[6] significantly different from the Census figures. What then is the true picture? First, there is good reason to believe that neither set of figures is accurate. The Census counts people attending church on a particular Sunday; it cannot tell us about the church attendance of those not present on that day. When one considers foreign holidays and days off sick alone one can see that even a committed weekly church attendee is unlikely to be in a British church 52 weeks of the year. Someone missing five to ten Sundays a year might well be a weekly churchgoer but actually not be in church for 10–20 per cent of Sundays, one of which might have been Census Sunday. It is not unreasonable therefore to assume that the Census figures might be missing about 15 per cent of regular churchgoers. The Tear Fund data, though, suggests that 45 per cent were missing on Census Sunday, and very high figures of past attendance too. However, surveys do not measure what people actually do but their memory or perception of what they do. In the United States until recently head counts have rarely been done and survey figures relied upon. In 2005 a survey by the Barna group (a major Christian research unit in the USA) recorded 47 per cent in church on an average Sunday. The American Church Research Project took head count figures for weekly attendance and found only 17.5 per cent in church. The same seems true for other countries.

The 'real' figures for regular church attendance simply can't be accurately determined from the evidence we have. If we allow for about a 15 per cent error in Church Census figures we would have a figure for monthly attendance of 11 per cent, a de-churched population of 29 per cent and non-churched population of 60 per cent. These are likely to be close to the accurate figure. However, even if the Tear Fund figures are correct, and I think it is unlikely, the shape of the graph is still the same: the de-churched are predominantly over 50, and the 'old lake' is still shrinking. Whether or not the 'old lake' has a few more fish in it only changes the time it will take to empty unless that trend can be reversed.

There are also questions about the story itself. New Christians are not in fact like fish but become members of the fishing community themselves, increasing those catching fish. Actually, even if the number of those fishing increases it will have little effect on catches; the problem is not too few fishing but too few fish to catch in the old lake. The only possible effect of more being caught is to deplete the lake faster. The only ways to change the fortunes of the fishing community are either restock the old lake or learn to fish from the new one.

Could the old lake be restocked? That is, could the decline in childhood church connection be reversed and in time lead to an increasing de-churched as well as church-attending population? But where are the extra under-15s going to come from? A stable church attendance relies on a culture in which people send their children to church because they themselves were sent. It seems to be the case that adult church attendance was often lower even at the height of Christendom in the UK.[7] However, those who went to church as children have in the past sent their own children even if they rarely went; it was part of the culture to do so. Increasing the number of children raised in church is thus governed by the decision of parents to raise their children this way. Other approaches are effectively evangelism for non-churched children.

Figures show that 16 per cent of babies born are baptized as infants in the C of E, yet about 5 per cent of under-15s are monthly attendees, so clearly there is room to raise more of those having infant baptisms in the church. Indeed I was once a youth worker in a church that used baptisms of the children of non-church-attending families in this way. The church simply assumed that the family meant to keep the promise to raise the child in the faith; the church maintained contact with the family and when the child reached the right age told them it was time for the child to attend the children's programme in line with their baptismal promises. This was successful, and over time many of the parents started coming to church too. However, even such an increase in children raised in church relies on the Christendom model of infant baptism,[8] the numbers of which halved in the Church of England in the 15 years prior to 2005[9] and are still falling. Unless this changes, seeking to draw in baptized children is only a short-term opportunity.

Children's work and schools work are other ways to influence the faith content of a child's upbringing. But at what point is this influencing the world-view in which a child is raised and at what point does it become evangelism to a child already holding a post-Christendom approach? Is parental support essential for childhood religious activity to be part of a Christian formation for that child? Clearly the example of baptisms above shows that parents do not have to be active church attendees themselves for church involvement for their children to prove a gateway to being raised in the Christian faith. However, this relies on their parents having a sufficient link to Christendom to have their babies baptized and send them to church activities. Some have argued that the UK's state-funded church schools might effectively raise children in the Christian faith. I remain to be convinced that this is so if there is no support from the family and no connection with church beyond the school gates. It would be interesting to survey the beliefs of children attending church schools to assess what effect schools have compared to secular schooling. My suspicion is that the answer is very little.

It looks as if we can only raise 'old lake' children from 'old lake' parents. Research by the Barna organization in the United States reinforces this point.[10] Adults who had attended church as children were three times more likely than those who didn't to attend as adults and twice as likely to send their own children. The shape of the graph of falling church attendance by under-15s in the UK suggests that the same applies here; once some people stop sending their children to church the decline picks up speed as those who weren't sent are more likely not to send their own children.

The Church can no doubt do more to nurture Christian understanding in the children of parents raised in a Christendom model, both church attendees and de-churched. However, even if the rate of decline in the de-churched, 'old lake', population might be slowed, it probably can't be reversed. The key to the Church's future is developing evangelism that enables the non-churched to come to faith.

Does Church decline mark the end of Christendom?

Even if Church decline is significant, this is not on its own proof that Christendom has come to an end. Christendom is a cultural phenomenon and thus also about the political power of the Church, the pervasiveness of Christian belief in society and the identification of people with their Christian heritage. Is there an argument for the persistence of Christendom alongside collapsing church attendance?

In the 2001 UK Census nearly 72 per cent of the population ticked the box declaring their religion to be 'Christian'. Whatever people meant by this, most didn't go to church regularly. Grace Davie has coined two phrases for this phenomenon: 'believing without belonging' and 'vicarious religion'. The first notes that people belong to little these days, churches included, but they still have many of the beliefs of the past. Though over time creedal beliefs fade, some residual beliefs remain. The second suggests that people still want churches to be there for them at times of life transition or crisis. They are also still interested in clergy as public figures representing a certain set of 'values'. In this way churches are religious 'on their behalf' and there for them when needed.[11] In both these ways people identify with Britain's Christian heritage, but don't normally go to church or share the more defined beliefs and practices of those who do. Is this Christian identification strong enough to mean that *Mission-shaped Church* is wrong to conclude that Britain is effectively a foreign mission field?[12]

The collapse of Britain's Christian heritage

An example of 'believing without belonging' might be persistence of belief in God. However, Figure 2[13] shows how our understanding of God is changing over time, from belief in a personal God to a life force more like in the *Star Wars* films.

The European Values Survey suggests something similar for the period 1981 to 1999 and records these different beliefs by

Figure 2 Belief in God

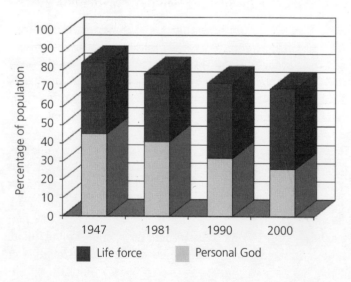

age, allowing us to see that the shift away from belief in a personal God occurring over time is also occurring as we move from older to younger generations. Belief in something 'out there' that might be called 'God' persists; Christian belief in a personal God is falling. If this is 'believing without belonging' it is increasingly not connected to the Christian faith.

What then of people's continued affiliation to Christianity? This might indicate a level of Christendom as 'vicarious faith'. In many Northern European countries this notion is given more substance by the membership of most of the population through the payment of a church tax. Nothing like that happens in Britain, but vicarious faith might be measured by looking at people's use of the church at key points in life and their willingness to identify themselves as Christians. Figures 3 and 4 show, however, the declining rates of both infant baptisms in the Church of England and church weddings across all the denominations.

There are clearly some who seek out the church for baptisms and weddings who would not regularly attend, but the numbers are falling and hardly suggest a strong persistence

Figure 3 Infant baptism in the Church of England 2007

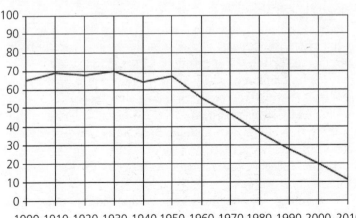

Percentage of births by year

Figure 4 Church weddings 2007

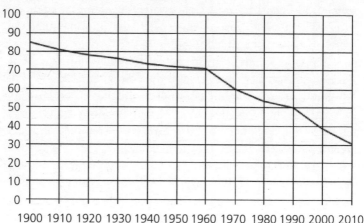

Percentage of marriages by year

of Christendom. There is a further question of how much the use of the church in this way by younger adults is actually an attempt to please parents and grandparents who are more likely to have a Christian background. Church weddings and infant baptisms may decline as much as two generations behind church attendance.

If 72 per cent of the population claimed to be Christian in the 2001 UK Census, is this something that is likely to be maintained, or the last element of Christendom to fade? The question on religion was new in 2001 but survey data in Figure 5[14] shows that this too has been falling since 1990.

The 2001 Census also indicates that this fall is likely to continue by showing how affiliation is declining among younger sections of the population, as seen in Figure 6. The little 'blip' in the line reflects children being recorded with their parents' affiliation.

By comparison, the European Values Survey shows this decline in both 1981 and 1999. Figure 7 shows not only that this decline is accelerating from a minimal effect to a significant

Figure 5 Christian affiliation in the UK

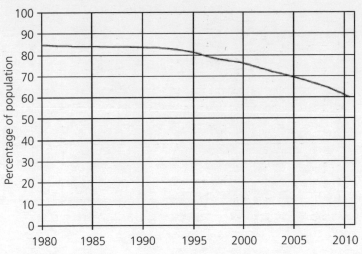

Figure 6 Christian affiliation in 2001

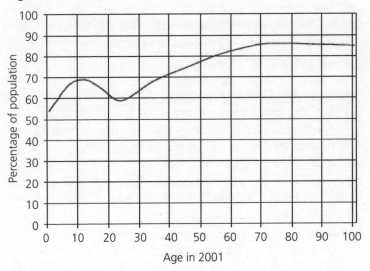

Figure 7 Christian affiliation

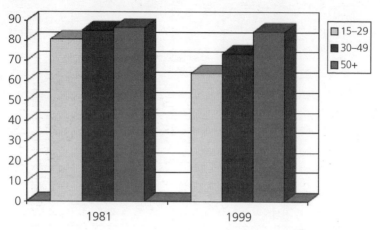

one in the 1990s, but also that generations are growing less religious as they grow older. This clearly suggests that the age profiles in the UK Census represent a fall in affiliation to the Christian faith from generation to generation and thus a falling rate in the population as a whole well into the future. It would be surprising if the 2011 Census didn't record a Christian affiliation of under 60 per cent.

The four generations of the collapse of Christendom

Callum Brown[15] emphasizes the role of women as agents of Christian identity in families. I also note from my own experience that many who brought babies for baptism in the 1990s were prompted by Mum or more often Grandma. These four generations in many ways represent four phases of the collapse of Christendom.

I think that Figures 8–11 show that 'believing without belonging' and 'vicarious faith' are not signs of the persistence of Christendom in spite of falling attendances, but stages in its decline. If 'believing without belonging' might definitely apply

Figure 8 Builders (born 1920s–1930s) in 2005

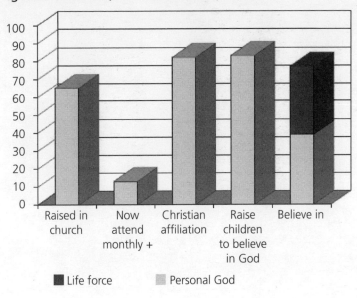

Figure 9 Boomers (born 1940s–1950s) in 2005

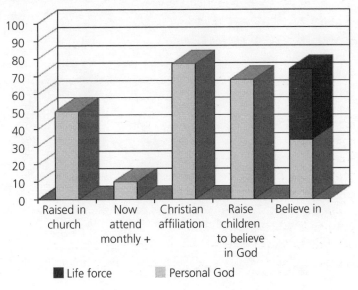

Figure 10 Generation X-ers (born 1960s–1970s) in 2005

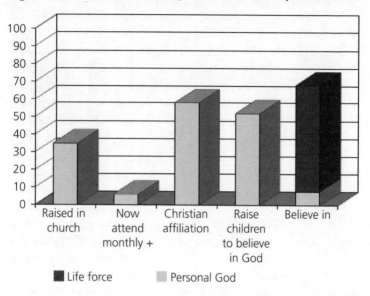

■ Life force   ▨ Personal God

Figure 11 Generation Y-ers (born 1980s–1990s) in 2015?

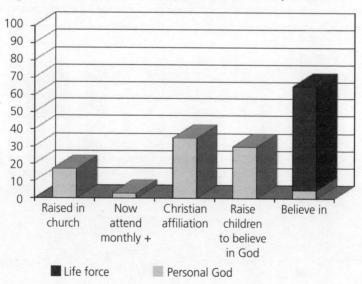

■ Life force   ▨ Personal God

to the 'builders', it is starting to shift away from Christian belief in the 'boomers' and has almost totally done so by generation Y. If 'vicarious faith' might well describe the boomers, and has some persistence in generation X, this too has almost gone by generation Y. There is a clear pattern: a steady erosion of childhood attendance over several generations leads to beliefs shifting away from the Christian tradition and less and less desire to raise children as Christians with some level of vicarious faith remaining. Identification with the Christian faith is the last thing to fade. By the middle of the twenty-first century, unless things change, a Census is likely to find about 25 per cent of the population claiming Christian affiliation, and less than 3 per cent attending church regularly. Of course, things may change for all sorts of reasons, including attempts to reach the non-churched inspired by things like the *Mission-shaped Church* report; indeed, there are signs in the 2005 Church Census that this is already making a difference. However, I think it is safe to assume that Christendom is well and truly lost and the idea that Britain is a Christian nation can no longer be taken seriously even if bits of its Christian heritage seem to have some continuing influence. The Church is facing the task of the re-evangelization of a no longer Christian nation, a task perhaps shared by many of the churches in the western world.

Notes

1 This can be found in Peter Brierley, *Religious Trends 6*, Christian Research, 2006.

2 The terms 'de-churched' and 'non-churched' are those preferred by the *Mission-shaped Church* report over the rather ambiguous term 'un-churched' that is often used. This latter term could be and often is applied to either group, hiding the very different ways these two groups of people seem to respond to evangelism.

3 John Finney, *Finding Faith Today*, Bible Society, 1992.

4 That is, from 30 per cent of the population to 26 per cent.

5 *Churchgoing in the UK*, Tear Fund, 2007.

6 The survey actually has further brackets, based on less frequent

church attendance, a church fringe and those belonging to another religion, so in order to make a comparison, irregular church attendees and fringe have to be added to the de-churched group and those of other religions to the non-churched group. Evidence from a whole range of surveys suggests that the views and beliefs of irregular churchgoers are closer to those of non-churchgoers and that monthly attendance is probably the best marker of whether or not someone should be considered 'churched'. The Tear Fund survey, however, does offer a useful grading of those with connections to the church.

7 For a discussion of attendance patterns in the last few centuries see Robin Gill, *The Myth of the Empty Church*, SPCK, 1993.

8 The Church of England's established role means that it is likely to be the place non-attending parents go, if anywhere, to have children baptized or dedicated. The exception is where older family members come from a different church tradition and expect their new infant relatives to have the ceremony appropriate to their own tradition even if the new parents are non-attendees.

9 C of E official statistics, 2001 and 2005.

10 2005 religious data from www.barna.org.

11 Grace Davie, 'From obligation to consumption', in Steven Croft (ed.), *The Future of the Parish System*, Church House Publishing, 2006.

12 *Mission-shaped Church*, pp. xii, 40, 90, 107.

13 From the *Soul of Britain* report, ORB, 2000.

14 Mori 1992–2007. I have included the 1981 figure from EVS, but in the 1990s EVS and Mori are almost identical so this inclusion offers little margin of error and helps show the recent nature of the collapse of Christian affiliation.

15 Callum Brown, *The Death of Christian Britain*, Routledge, 2001

3

Cultural Change and Post-Christendom

From modern to postmodern?

The idea that we are moving from modernity to postmodernity is not without controversy. It seems to me that much of the debate is between the approaches of different academic disciplines and between those who want to stress a shift away from modernity and others who wish to see us entering a different phase of modernity. This is further complicated by the advocacy by some of postmodernism, a philosophical system often applied to the understanding of truth and communication, and the observation of postmodernity as a description of culture.

The move from the medieval to the modern was marked by a whole range of thinkers contributing to this changing worldview. The contribution of postmodern thinkers suggests a similar phenomenon. So in literary theory Derrida and others have stressed how texts can be deconstructed to reveal meanings that challenge their apparent surface understanding and further how texts once written get separated from their authors and come to mean what the reader believes them to mean. Baudrillard charts the collapse of communism as the dying gasp of modernity and the globalization of capitalism as a shift to a de-centred world in which reality exists on TV screens and computers, which present us with manufactured images that forever point to other images, signs that never signify anything real. Rorty charts the passing of the 'myth' of a common humanity, replaced by a new tribalism in which small-scale cultures can celebrate their own diverse identity. Foucault exposes how the idea of a common humanity has been a mode of oppressing and rejecting the different and nonconformist, challenging concepts of morality and sanity as having any meaning beyond human power games. Irigary explores the 'void' so exposed as a place of discovering the feminine as 'other', in contrast to a modernist feminism that wanted to stress the lack of difference between men and women. Lyotard famously sums up post-modernity as a 'suspicion of meta-narratives', that is, stories that claim to explain the way the world is. Common themes are the move from the universal to the particular and from the objective to the subjective.

Others, especially in the social sciences, have sought to stress the current culture's continuity with modernity. So for Anthony Giddens we are in Late Modernity, a shift caused by a rapid acceleration of technological change creating the experience of 'ridding the juggernaut' in society.[1] Zygmunt Bauman speaks of Liquid Modernity, stressing the shift of goods and services from mass production to niche designer marketing, and thus the shift from being producers to consumers.[2] Arguments for such views are often bolstered by stressing the similarity of postmodern culture with ideas expressed by the Romantic movement and Nietzsche in the late nineteenth century. However, this seems to ignore the fact that both these were based on a strong critique of modernity. The Romantics sought to break away from the world of objective rationalism and industrialization to allow expression of subjective feeling and a celebration of nature. In this they foreshadowed the subjective turn in the twentieth century. In other ways the strong belief in universal values derived from a common human nature, evident in the writings of Emerson, for instance, shows the persistence of elements of modernist thought.

Nietzsche's critique is more thorough. The 'mad man'[3] makes the point well. Humanity's attempt to replace God with human morality has unseen consequences; without God there is no horizon, the earth is unchained from its sun, there is no up or down. Indeed, without God there is no objective point from which truth or morality can be determined; everything becomes subjective. As he argued elsewhere, the search for truth had uncovered that there was no truth and indeed the real world was simply a myth.[4] For Nietzsche this deed of humanity in 'killing God' is in fact liberating, something to be celebrated that frees human individuals to rise above the herd.

Yet the mad man's message is not grasped by his hearers; he has come too soon, he declares. In this recognition, the mad man challenges reference to Nietzsche as some form of proof of post-modernity's continuity with nineteenth-century modernism. It is a thought ahead of its time. It would not be until the latter half of the twentieth century that such ideas would have echoes in the theologies of the death of God, and the theories of postmodernism. As Callum Brown observes,[5] the argument for a continued modernity goes hand in hand with an agenda that wants to see religious decline as a long-term process that started with the rise of rationalism in the seventeenth and eighteenth centuries. Instead, he argues that Christianity didn't really collapse until the twentieth century, with the 1960s as the key period that marks the beginning of the post-Christian age, a collapse that is a product of postmodernity and not modernity at all.

It is worth remembering that the shift from the medieval to the modern, Enlightenment world also took a long time to work through. From the fifteenth century it can be seen emerging in the Renaissance with the rediscovery of Classical thought and the rise of a classically inspired, though still religious, humanism. The invention of the printing press is also crucial to the shift towards modernity, as are the beginnings of empirical method in science and philosophy with thinkers like Francis Bacon in the sixteenth century. In many ways the founding statement of modernity comes from the seventeenth century, with Descartes' 'I think therefore I am' centring human identity within rational thought. During the same century William Harvey, consciously inspired by Descartes, would investigate the way the body's circulation worked and change our perception of the heart from the centre of being to a machine that pumped blood. Other heirs of Bacon and Descartes, like Newton, Kant and Hume, would lay the foundations of modern thought and technology, leading to a social revolution, the founding of western democracy and the industrial revolution. Throughout all of this, the central shift was from a society derived from divine order and revelation mediated through church and state to a society in which the rational, individual person was at the centre and became the arbiter of truth. A position pointed to in the Renaissance was grounded in the writings of sixteenth-century thinkers, established with the overthrow of monarchy in the seventeenth and eighteenth centuries and from then held sway into the late twentieth century. Indeed rationalist thinkers in our own day remind us it has not entirely passed.

Parallels can be drawn with the shift to postmodernity. It is pointed to in the Romantic movement and Nietzsche, grounded in the writings of postmodernism and established in the collapse of communism, leaving capitalism to spearhead an increasingly global consumer culture. Technologically the computer plays a similar role to the printing press, signifying not the fixed rational world of modernity but the virtual world of postmodernity. If this parallel holds true, then by comparison the shift to postmodernity is happening at about twice the speed of that to modernity; it also is still in its early days, and this should suggest some caution in expressing any understanding of exactly how a postmodern world will be.

Cultural change and the end of Christendom

Baudrillard dates the beginning of postmodernity to the collapse of the student commune in Paris in 1968. How key this was to the collapse of communism as a modernist ideal in the West can be debated, but it fits with other studies and surveys that point to the important part the generation who came to adulthood in the 1960s play, those often called the 'boomer generation'. This generation in Britain is the first in which the majority don't have church backgrounds. Callum Brown places the start of the post-Christian era at 1963, marking the point when women's liberation led to the turning away of women from Christian identity, and thus the loss of their influence in socializing British children into faith. I am not convinced that the process can be pinned on this factor alone, but statistical analysis does suggest that loss of childhood socialization into faith was crucial in the decline of Christendom.

While the majority of those born between 1900 and 1940, and thus who came to adulthood before the key 1960s period, were raised within a culture that socialized people into Christianity, they themselves increasingly broke the pattern by not socializing their children into the faith. The process, therefore, cannot be entirely the result of women's liberation in the 1960s. It is also worth noting that the 2005 Church Census shows that one of the major stories of the past 15 years is falling attendance by women, but among those aged under 45, born in the 1960s and after, rather than the generation who became adults in the 1960s and 1970s. The role of women in church attendance looks significant, in particular in raising children in the faith, a conclusion supported with good documentation by Crockett and Voas,[6] but it can't be narrowed to the boomer generation.

There are several key factors at work in the two generations prior to the boomers. With the nineteenth-century move from the village to the city, social structures based on extended families and stable communities, with the church at the centre of rural life, collapsed, leading to much looser connections between adults and urban churches. While most still sent their children to church, the new urban pattern of childhood churchgoing suggested a belief that faith was for children and something grown out of, at best part of a 'good Christian upbringing' but beyond its moral legacy of little value to adult life.

I think Brown is right to argue that this factor has been greatly overplayed in the secularization argument; urbanization over several centuries did not seemingly lead to the collapse of church attendance, though we can chart a slow decline from the 1850 Church Census through to the 1940s with increasing attendance in the 1950s. Childhood attendance had its high watermark at the end of the nineteenth and into the early twentieth century, so this crucial factor comes later than the major urbanization of modernity. What does seem to have happened, however, is what Brown calls the feminization of the church,[7] in which women became the chief adult church attendees and the source of childhood socialization into the faith.

Another legacy of the industrial revolution was the rapid growth of mechanization and technology, which led to an increasing optimism that science could usher in a utopian future, especially marked in the generation prior to the boomers. This raised expectations especially in the 1950s and 1960s that by the twenty-first century science and technology would have eradicated disease and poverty, people would have increased leisure as machines took over the chores of daily life and work, and a colonization of space would mean that every family had their own jet car, wore space-age clothing, ate food in the form of pills and took holidays on Mars. In many ways the collapse of this vision is another part of the shift from the modern to the postmodern, but those who shared these dreams were perhaps also strongly influenced by the secular humanist values of the producers of the science and technology that lay behind them. If social structures suggested church was for children, secular humanism would suggest its beliefs were also childish.

This powerful combination does not seem to have led to people surrendering belief in God, but probably contributed to an increasing distance between personal belief and church attendance. For many, 'being a good Christian' took on a very secular form in which morality was informed by a Christian heritage but belief became something private and personal. My own experience as a minister taking funerals for many from this generation reinforces this notion. It was the norm to be told that the deceased 'didn't go to church but was as good a Christian as the next person'. Is it perhaps then surprising if such people increasingly questioned whether to send their children to church?

As John Finney's research showed, the privatized faith found in those raised in Christendom but no longer participating in the church can be revived into public profession, as indeed happened for some, for instance during the Billy Graham crusades of the 1950s. Brown notes that the period between 1945 and 1960 saw strong social pressure for women to return to the traditional role of wife and mother, to boost the population after the war and enable returning soldiers to find work. This in turn seems to have been a factor in increased adult and childhood church attendance during this period, creating a temporary small upturn in the slow downward trend over the twentieth century.

Another factor affecting the first two generations born in the twentieth century in Europe must, of course, be the experience of two world wars. For many, confidence in a God who ordered the world was severely shaken by the horrors experienced. What kind of a God could be believed in after the Somme or Auschwitz? If people didn't stop believing in God altogether, the existence of the God of the established churches of Europe, the one who supposedly ordered the world and was 'on our side', certainly seemed doubtful.

Postmodern culture as a foreign mission field

A lot of Christian material on postmodernity seems either to celebrate it as something that liberates us to express faith with more diversity and creativity, or to attack it because it undermines Christian proclamation of the truth. In that postmodern societies in many western nations seem to also be post-Christian or at least post-Christendom, it is understandable if postmodernity is viewed as a threat to Christianity. However, deciding whether Christians should be 'for' or 'against' postmodernity is not helpful, or indeed possible; there is no 'culture neutral' place from which to make such a decision. Rather, the challenge is to find out how to be Christians within an increasingly postmodern culture, and that is a task that requires the process of double listening. Christians need to discover what in this culture they wish to affirm and what they wish to challenge, but this can only be done effectively from within a postmodern Christian community. What, then, are some of the key elements of the shift from modernity to postmodernity, and what do they say to Christians seeking to be effective cross-cultural evangelists?

From text to hyper-text

One of the key inventions that helped usher in modernity was the printing press. Books became available to all who could read and were quickly spread far more widely than when they were copied by hand. This greatly aided the interchange of ideas that fuelled the rapid growth of science. However, it didn't provide a total democratization of the ability to publish. Many people could access and thus debate ideas that were once restricted, but few could actually distribute their own ideas with ease in the printed media. This led to the creation of new elites who controlled access to the printed word.

Printing led to the formation of a definitive but growing body of knowledge, with those controlling publication ensuring quality. It is from this that we get the idea of 'believing what we see set down in black and white'. For Christians it revolutionized access to its key text, the Bible. Prior to this, few owned one and those who did needed to read Latin or Greek to understand it. Printing enabled Christians to have a 'personal biblical faith', no longer reliant on the teaching of the church hierarchy.

In late modernity scholarship was opening ancient texts to new analysis as scientific method sought to answer questions about authorship, historical accuracy and composition once left to tradition. This led to a growing rejection by some of traditional approaches to the Bible in a quest to replace its accounts with historical and scientific truth. The postmodern approach to texts would raise doubts about the value of such a quest by casting doubt on such concepts of truth. For the postmodern thinker, studying the text became an interaction between subjective readers and a free-standing text no longer tied to its compositional context or author. In such thought, texts no longer relate to underlying facts but legitimately have differing interpretations. Indeed, the very act of 'putting it down in black and white' created this separation in a way that a living interactive oral tradition did not. Further to this, the politics behind the composition of a text came to be a subject of concern. Texts that survived were viewed as representing those who had power and so interpreters wanted to ask whose voice was excluded and what opinions had been rejected in the process of writing.

All of this has important implications for any attempt to base Christianity on authoritative texts, whether they be the Bible or creeds or theological writings. The very postmodern view that Gnostic writings represented the original teaching of Jesus and that the official tradition was a later rewriting, deliberately reflecting the views of the Roman Church after the conversion of Constantine, is one of the reasons so many people found Dan Brown's *Da Vinci Code* plausible. If some wanted to recover a 'Gnostic Jesus', others wanted to make him a mainstream Jewish prophet with no intention of founding the Christian faith. In this version St Paul, emerging from his victory over the Jewish followers of Jesus, is accused of inventing the traditional church view written into the Gospels well after the much earlier Pauline letters. Such ideas stem from serious academic publications that most people have not read, but the media has enabled them to enter the popular consciousness. Added to this is a belief that 'you can make the Bible say whatever you want it to', so that appealing to the Bible as authoritative is actually an attempt to bolster what is in fact merely a personal opinion. Indeed, anyone who seeks to uphold traditional Christian interpretations looks like someone actually continuing the tradition of those who have oppressed the truth for their own political ends. Such challenges are not unique to Christianity in a postmodern culture; they are, for instance, part of the 'image problem' faced by Islam. By contrast, the kind of faith favoured by postmodern people will either not be text-based or have texts that are considered inspirational but not authoritative.

The internet is the postmodern counterpart of the printing press, creating several significant changes from the printed word. The use of computer screens to read internet-based material tends to limit the size of what is likely to be read to at most a few pages. In many ways the length of what is written and the time taken to compose it can be seen as measures of how 'definitive' a text is viewed as being; the magazine article might represent a work in progress or an observation offered for discussion, a large hardback book on the other hand suggests an attempt at the 'last word' on a given subject. As such the transition from the printed word to the internet is a move away from definitive statements in favour of temporary ones. This is enhanced by the ease with which internet text can be altered, removed from context or deleted. Someone's opinion posted on a blog site can end up being forwarded around the world as part of a supposedly now factual account. Internet myths are born this way and many still seem to cling to modernist notions of the reliability of the published word, even when those words are part of an email chain that has no regulatory body to check its accuracy.

If the ability to publish was limited in the age of print, it is now open to anyone with access to a computer. This still excludes many in the world's population, of course, but has radically increased the likelihood of the 'ordinary person' getting their material into the public domain. The increase in speed of both composition and distribution greatly increases the volume of material produced; freedom to publish may not be matched by the likelihood of being read! Further, quality control is almost impossible; on the one hand it may now be much easier to receive unofficial communication from people in war zones or under the control of totalitarian regimes, but on the other the publishing of opinions that society might feel should not be aired cannot be prevented.

Christians communicating using this media are going to find it very different from what they are used to. I was amused by some recent attempts at 'virtual churches' which recreated online the architecture of a traditional church and offered 'normal' worship, and were then upset when members of the congregation felt they could enter the pulpit and preach. Traditional church architecture is designed on the model of one leader and many led, so the congregation sit in rows facing the leader. The leader is the only one expected to issue instructions and the only one allowed to preach. Congregational input is limited to the reciting of texts, spoken or sung, as directed by the leader. Internet communities simply do not work this way. All will expect to 'preach' and make suggestions; in a sense a virtual church is made up of different leaders and no congregation, save perhaps for an unknown number of 'lurkers' whose presence on the sidelines is not perceived but who may be forming their opinions of faith based on how the action is going.

From the story to my story

One of the characteristics of modernity is the quest for over-arching explanations of the way the world is. For the Christian the Bible acts as the grand narrative, explaining the sweep of world events from creation to new creation, exposing the realities of the human condition and showing how to relate properly to God and thus overcome the problems that beset us. Modernity, however, offered many competing versions of the 'big story'. It might be the communist understanding of world history as class struggle, or an evolutionary story that explained life on the basis of genetic survival, or others. If these were often conflicting accounts, the idea that such an explanation was to be sought was not questioned.

In postmodernity there is great distrust of grand narratives, hence Lyotard's oft-cited description of postmodernity as a 'suspicion of metanarratives'. This suspicion stems from an awareness of the use of power. The suggestion that a particular story can be the framework for everything looks rather like an attempt at domination by those who are promoting it, telling others they have to live according to that story's dictates. For this reason, appeal to the Bible as the proper authority to live by for all people is seen as an illegitimate attempt at domination. This is also true, however, for similar appeals made by others who see a particular view of the world as authoritative. In contrast, if the big stories are suspect, the personal story is celebrated, and indeed story form is preferred to isolated information as the mode of communication. People want to tell their own stories; they don't want to be told they belong in someone else's story. This privileges the personal testimony and this is as true for a Christian's testimony as any other, if not offered as superior.

From experts to individuals

Modernity highly valued specialists and experts. In many ways the Christian evangelist or minister was an expert in the sphere of faith, and at times like marriages and deaths people would simply expect the minister as the expert to run the show. The journalist, the academic and especially the scientist were also seen as experts; people trusted them and followed their advice. People today no longer trust the experts as they once did. Imagine, for instance, your reaction when a scientist comes on TV to refute rumours of the dangers of eating a food product and tells you it is perfectly safe. Few would simply assume that the expert must be right. Many will want to know who is paying them for their opinion; indeed a number will assume the food must be dangerous, or the scientist wouldn't have denied it. This suspicion is connected to the way the claimed knowledge of the expert places them in power over you and makes you liable to be manipulated by them. Added to this is a mistrust of the motives that lie behind this attempted manipulation; is the scientist's main interest your health and safety, or is it their own reputation, or the reputation of the company who makes the food product? Needless to say, recent history has shown that such fears are not unfounded.

The Christian expert will come under the same suspicion. Public pronouncements on morality or justice, or appeals to 'become a Christian' will not automatically be viewed as motivated by concern for others. The suspicion will be that these are simply attempts by Christians to force the public into actions that serve the interests of the church. This view is bolstered by media stories reminding everyone that the church is in decline and desperately needs new members, and their money, to keep the show on the road. There is also a widespread fear of 'brainwashing cults'. A consequence of this is that a number of people believe that listening to evangelists is dangerous because you might be brainwashed by them, or that the food served during Alpha course sessions is drugged to make you susceptible to appeals to become a Christian. All of this makes it increasingly difficult to run the classic evangelistic event based on an upfront speaker; they are likely to come across as someone who can't be trusted. The increasing spread of TV evangelism adds to this perception. People don't want anyone to tell them what to believe, they want to choose their own beliefs.

From rationality to virtual reality

One of the founding statements of modernity is Descartes' '*cogito ergo sum*'; I think therefore I am. In modernity the essence of humanity was rational thought, and in many ways a person is seen as being 'their mind', with their body as a machine they inhabit and control. This view of humanity influences not only the concept of self-identity but also the approach to medicine, ethics, sexuality, gender, life after death and what society treats as valuable.

Graham Cray has suggested that the postmodern equivalent should be 'Tesco *ergo sum*'; I shop therefore I am.[8] If in modernity my rational mind was my identity and the body was something it inhabited, in postmodernity it is my identity I inhabit. As such it is not something fixed, but an outward form I choose to present. I tell you who I want you to think I am through my consumer choices, the clothes I wear, the place I live, the car I drive, the music I listen to and the people I hang out with. This is nowhere more so than on the internet where I can be anything or anyone I want with a virtual identity. Behind this there is some concept of 'self' that I am seeking to express but this can be experimented with until it 'feels right'. Equally the identity that feels right may vary according to circumstances, so I am a different person here than I am there.

In modernity rational thought was key to understanding; in postmodernity experience and emotions are more important.

There is also a far more 'embodied' and holistic approach to reality side by side with the fluid self-identity, and this is why holistic medicine has become so popular. In this approach the mind is increasingly seen as the place not of rational thought and analysis, but of consciousness and awareness, something grasped rather than something worked out. Further to this, while rational thought is not totally rejected it is suspected, blamed for mind–body dualism and the assertion of truth in terms of black-and-white answers. This in turn is seen as contributing to intolerance, possibly the worst sin in the post-modern world-view. In this world everything has blurred edges and is not fixed but fluid.

The logic of consumerism

If for Baudrillard the collapse of the 1968 Paris commune ush-ered in the postmodern period, with the end of communism as a dream among radical westerners, the collapse of the Berlin Wall in 1989 marked the resultant victory of western capital-ism. Capitalism, of course, is initially a product of modernity, but in the last half of the twentieth century it changed from a system based on production to one based on consumption as the shift from the modern to the postmodern occurred. One of the signs of this has been the move from mass production to designer production, from everyone having the same cheap product to everyone choosing 'their look'.[9]

The 'consumer logic' running through the cultural shifts mentioned above is a key element of postmodernity. Just as I choose my look by putting together different designer com-ponents, I similarly choose my values, my lifestyle, my beliefs, my way of seeing the world. None of these is taken as a given, and overarching world-views that insist that certain things should be taken together as a package or not at all are resisted as being attempts to deny the right to choose. This is also seen in a move from modernist politics, in which people supported large-scale political philosophies and parties, to postmodern politics centred on single issues that individuals care about.

Religion is approached in the same way; hence a turning away from traditional religions that offer overarching packages of belief towards a self-assembled collection of beliefs that could come from any tradition. In a similar vein, Nick Spencer noted in *Beyond Belief* that non-church people treated God as a consumer service provider, someone whose 'job' was to address particular problems and who would be assessed according to his performance on these.[10] The classic problem of why God doesn't prevent suffering is treated in much the same way as one would react to a hospital that had a poor record of treating heart patients.

From facts to experiences

In modernity things that are claimed to be 'true' are seen as facts, provable by scientific experiment and logical argument and true everywhere at all times. In postmodernity truth is centred on personal experience, especially *my* experience, but the experience of others I know or have seen on TV or read about in the paper or on the internet is also respected. Because my experience and your experience may differ, the classic postmodern phrase 'that may be true for you but it isn't for me' makes sense. In this way truth becomes relative and no longer universal. It is not that everything is viewed as only being applicable on an individual basis; we expect the many gadgets and machines that have become essential to our lives to work and do so universally. What we no longer do is assume that the universe operates the same way, or that questions of philosophy or ultimate reality have universal answers.

A reassessment of science and the scientist and the pride of place they held in modernity has followed. Not only is the scientist now an expert not to be trusted, but science has been reduced to the level of provider of innovative technology rather than answers to life's big questions. This is partly due to disenchantment with the dream of scientific progress already mentioned. The scientific utopia is no longer believed in and people are looking elsewhere for the answers to the big questions, if they are looking at all. Added to this, science itself has become stranger. The nice linear certainties of Newtonian mechanics have been replaced by Einstein's theory of relativity, chaos theory, wave particle duality and Heisenberg's uncertainty principle. Most people, of course, will have no detailed knowledge of these, but may have heard the names and have some notion that they stand for an approach to science that says at the level of the very small or the very large, all that rational linear stuff doesn't seem to hold true.

If Christianity is understood as a total world-view claiming to be universal, it will be opposed in postmodernity. One of the reasons there is a loss of confidence in evangelism is that the old-style 'let's prove it's true' approach increasingly doesn't work. But can Christianity be incarnate within postmodernity authentically? Something that I think offers pointers and indeed challenges to us is that while Christianity has been losing influence in postmodernity, other forms of spirituality are making a comeback.

Notes

1 Anthony Giddens, *The Consequences of Modernity*, Polity Press, 1991.

2 Zygmunt Bauman, *Liquid Modernity*, Polity Press, 2000.

3 Friedrich Nietzsche, *The Gay Science* (1882, 1887), ed. Walter Kaufmann, Vintage, 1974, para. 125, pp. 181–2.

4 *Beyond Good and Evil* (1886) and *The Twilight of the Idols* (1888).

5 Callum Brown, *Death*, p. 195.

6 A. Crockett and D. Voas, 'Generations of Decline', *Journal for the Scientific Study of Religion* (2006) 45(4): 567–84.

7 Brown's usage is not the same as that in some recent articles suggesting the church has become feminine and off-putting to men. Indeed, Brown's data and that of the Church Census would suggest that recently the church has been less and not more attractive to women.

8 Heard by the author at a conference in the mid-1990s. Tesco being the major British supermarket chain.

9 In this much at least I agree with Baumann.

10 Nick Spencer, *Beyond Belief*, LICC, 2004.

4

The Rise of the New Spiritualities

This chapter partly draws on my unpublished master's thesis, 'Christ and Post-Christian Spirituality', and on material published in *New Age, Paganism and Christian Mission, Equipping Your Church in a Spiritual Age* and *Coded Messages*.[1] I do not intend to repeat the specific focus of these publications on evangelism among spiritual seekers and practitioners, and recommend these to you if you wish to explore that further as well as a complement to this chapter. Rather I want to explore the 'New Spiritualities' as part of the overall picture of culture after the collapse of Christendom and how this affects evangelism to the population as a whole. With studies from Scandinavia, the former communist states of Eastern Europe, Catholic Europe, North and South America and Australia as well as the UK, this area may also be significant for exploring how far the British situation is mirrored elsewhere.

Postmodernity and spirituality

Elements of popular culture often give us clues to what is happening at other levels of society. This I believe is true of the rise of the New Spiritualities. In any major bookseller you will find two separate sections on religious and spiritual subjects. One of these will be labelled Religion and contain subsections for the different major world religions; this section is shrinking. Far larger and growing is a section with a title like Mind Body Spirit, containing books ranging from yoga to tarot, self-help, meditation, witchcraft, water dowsing, and many more.

In 1999, taking into account sales in Christian bookshops

as well, books in the Mind Body Spirit category outsold those on Christianity and were about the same as the sales of books on all the traditional world religions combined. The 'shifting of the shelves' in high street bookshops and the struggles of Christian bookshops since suggest that the balance is heading in the direction of the New Spiritualities.

Television is also interesting; in the USA and the UK there has been a growth in both drama and documentary programmes with New Age, Pagan or supernatural themes. Examples of drama include *Buffy the Vampire Slayer*, *Hex*, *Charmed* and *Sabrina the Teenage Witch*, all portraying positive imagery of females with special powers; *Supernatural*, with its charismatic demon-hunter brothers who use occult practice rather than faith as their weapon, in spite of this being set in mid-town USA; *Medium* and the much darker *Afterlife*, with female mediums as the key characters, portrayed both as genuine and able to help others; and one of the most fascinating, the UK's *Sea of Souls*, about a team of university paranormal investigators who begin each episode as sceptics, yet end up proving supernatural phenomena real. This charts the culture shift from *Scooby Doo*, in which the protagonists begin by believing in the ghostly phenomena, only to unmask someone like the local estate agent faking it to drive someone out of the house; but *Sea* also offers a clever tilt at the scientific establishment as the opponents of the supernatural, by 'showing' such phenomena turning up on the computer monitors of characters who 'are' scientists and watching them become convinced that they are real.

The documentaries are increasingly positive, though with the requisite proportion of alternative views. There have been several sympathetic programmes on mediums, a whole series on faith healers and numerous programmes on haunted houses. In one of these, *Haunted Homes*, houses are investigated *Sea of Souls* style, and while the results rarely look as good as the fictitious counterpart, they clearly convince the crew and the psychic investigator that something is there. It is then left to a medium to comfort the frightened family and exorcise the ghost, intriguingly with a Latin rite. The traditional role would have been that of the local priest, but not here. Dr Chris French appears on this show as resident sceptic. He remains resolutely unconvinced, prompting on one occasion the show's presenter to do a piece to camera in which he explains how the whole camera crew had been convinced, that several would now not go into the building, and Dr French was in a minority of one. The presence of French is clearly seen as necessary to maintain balance but the show is entirely geared to the plausibility of the other view.

Another show in which French featured was Britain's *Psychic Challenge*, a gameshow format in which psychics performed tasks under the watchful eye of a studio audience and a panel of sceptics who sought to prevent cheating as well as offer sceptical analysis of the psychic feats apparently completed. Each week the psychic deemed the least effective was voted off the show until one was voted winner. Needless to say, much of this was classic reality TV gameshow entertainment, but I doubt it would have happened 30 years ago or that several thousand psychics would have applied to be on the show. On a similar level was the *Real Witch Project*, which featured a group of women who formed a coven for a month under the guidance of a witch, their experiences forming the content of the show. Regular documentary shows have also done several sympathetic programmes on Paganism.

Such programmes represent only a small slice of the regular viewing, but a generation ago fictional programmes with supernatural themes were primarily seen as children's viewing, and the documentaries, if they had happened at all, would have been geared to expose the folly or fraud of the practitioners rather than give them a sympathetic hearing. Perhaps the ultimate accolade was paid to the New Spiritualities in a couple of programmes by the scientist Richard Dawkins, arch-proponent of secular atheism, which sought to discredit them. Dawkins' attention is traditionally drawn to attacks on conventional religion, but recently he's clearly spotted what I think may be for him the unexpected rise of the New Spiritualities; he views them as an essential target if the goal of establishing a secular atheist society is to be achieved. Dawkins might also have spotted that the majority of programming in this area is now sympathetic, and felt he had to redress the balance. All of this points to a significant move away from the scientific rationalist approach Dawkins advocates.

These observations make sense in a postmodern culture that has shifted from the objective rational understanding of life to a subjective experiential approach. Things that once were viewed as irrational, unscientific and thus untrue are now allowed to re-enter people's world-views. There is what one might call a re-enchantment of western culture.

Charting the spiritual shift

The pattern of shifting belief is complex. In Chapter 2 I showed how belief in God remains high but the understanding of God is moving away from a traditional Christian one. A Populus survey of 2005 gives a snapshot of beliefs, by age, in a number of areas. In some areas beliefs associated with religion are higher among the 18–24 year olds. Amid a fluctuating pattern, this is true of both belief in the soul and belief in an afterlife. (See Figures 12 and 13.)

The *Soul of Britain Survey* shows these two areas of belief rising over time as well, suggesting a generational rather than an age effect. But what understanding of the afterlife is growing? The World Values Survey[2] suggests a generational effect here too, with younger segments of population less likely to believe in heaven. It also shows that where a question on reincarnation was asked in Italy, Sweden and Northern Ireland[3] there is a rise in belief according to age as one looks at progressively younger segments of the population. *Soul of Britain* doesn't record a similar rise but does show that about half of those who believe in an afterlife also believe in reincarnation.

Populus records two other beliefs related to the afterlife: belief in karma and in restless spirits (Figures 14 and 15). Belief in karma is, of course, the traditional eastern counterpart to belief in reincarnation and here shows a distinct generational effect. A growing belief in restless spirits adds to the options

Figure 12 Belief in the soul

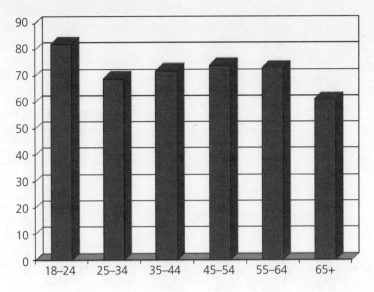

Figure 13 Belief in an afterlife

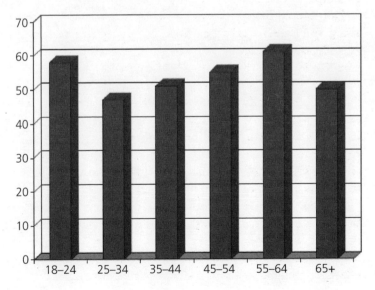

Figure 14 Belief in karma

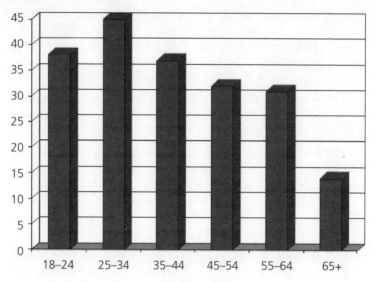

Figure 15 Belief in restless spirits

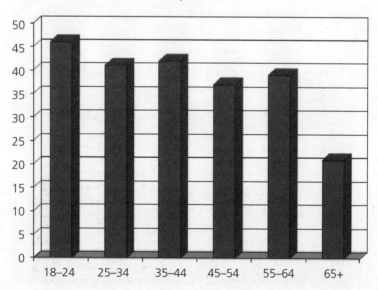

of what happens after death. It also seems likely from this that many people hold several beliefs about what might happen after death.

Another feature of belief in karma and restless spirits is the radical difference between those over 65 and those just under, with over-65s about half as likely to share these beliefs as the 55–64s. A similar pattern can be seen with regard to experience of various fortune-telling methods and belief in contacting the dead. (See Figures 16 and 17.)

In these and the previous two questions we have moved into areas of belief not associated with the Christian faith, so this large gap between the beliefs of those under and those over 65 may be related to the shift in culture during the 1960s, with these more 'alternative' beliefs present in those growing up in the 1960s and after.

With regard to contacting the dead, Populus also asked who had actually done it. Here the difference is nothing like as extreme. Of course, one might expect older people to know

Figure 16 Experience of fortune-telling, tarot, astrology, psychics, palmists

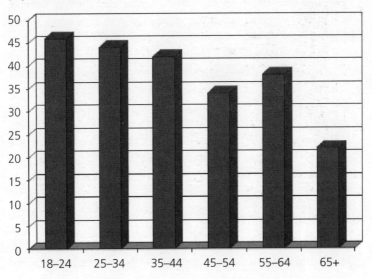

Figure 17 Contacting the dead

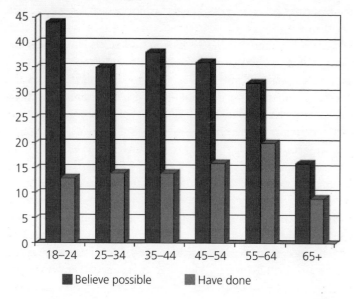

more people who have died and thus have more opportunity to try and make contact with the dead. Whatever the reason for this difference, it shows that the fact that people believe something is possible is not the same as saying they are actually doing it. *Soul of Britain*, without noting age of respondents, asked whether people had tried a range of alternative therapies or fortune-telling methods, and also if these were important to them. On the whole there was a considerable difference between the answers, with on average only a third to a quarter of people who had tried the various alternative practices rating them as important. These sets of figures would imply that while people are becoming increasingly open to New Spiritualities, that doesn't mean they are committed followers.

Generation Y and spirituality

The previous analysis has been used by a number of people, myself included, to argue that while religious affiliation, belief and church attendance are declining, this is being matched by a rise in spirituality. The phrase 'spiritual but not religious' seems to sum much of this up. Some recent reports have questioned whether this is true for those who would count as generation Y: those born in the 1980s and 1990s.

In 2006 *Making Sense of Generation Y*[4] presented analysis from research undertaken among 16–25 year olds at youth groups. This explored how groups of young people expressed their world-view through interaction with the media, using clips and stills from television, film and music. The research offers valuable insights; two ideas in particular are worth noting. First, the authors describe the overall world-view as the 'happy midi-narrative'. It's a midi-narrative because it happens at the level of a group rather than the individual or society. It is also a midi-narrative in the postmodern sense in that it isn't a narrative that explains the big picture of how the world is. The core of this world-view is that the goal of life is to be happy, and that the world is basically a good place in which family and friends help us overcome those things that threaten our happiness. Second, they noted that the types of media that generated the deepest engagement for these young people were those that were ambiguous in their message. These tended to elicit searching questions, whereas clear messages prompted no deep engagement. These insights clearly have valuable implications for evangelism.

What the researchers were surprised not to find was any deep interest in either religion or New Spiritualities. This would not have been predicted from the survey data above. So how can British young people seemingly give such different responses? The title of some research by Phil Rankin, *Buried Spirituality*,[5] gives us a clue. His fieldwork and that of the *Generation Y* researchers are qualitative rather than quantitative, seeking to explore people's approaches to a subject through discussion and observation rather than by conducting a mass polling exercise that provides statistical results. How this relates to the survey data matters, because while it offers only a limited sample size, qualitative research can often expose misunderstandings in survey data about the meaning of questions asked. However, where *Making Sense of Generation Y* used group interaction, seeking to observe the operation of a world-view at a social level, *Buried Spirituality* was focused largely on conversation with individuals or very small groups of friends. At this level Rankin found that young people talked readily of things one might label as spiritual, including supernatural experiences and questions of meaning, the afterlife and similar. However, they did not use the words 'spirituality' or 'spiritual but not religious' to talk of these; spirituality was in fact often viewed as religious, and usually connected to Christianity.

What both sets of authors agree on[6] is that at a group level spirituality is not in evidence; rather it is buried by the happy midi-narrative so that it only surfaces at the individual level. But, if the happy midi-narrative is burying the spiritual dimension of life for young people, why at an individual level should surveys show these beliefs to be more prevalent among young people than older generations? Are these personal beliefs significant for our understanding of the world we are seeking to be missionaries within?

A paper by Sylvia Collins-Mayo and Phil Rankin answers the first question, using research carried out by Paul Heelas and Linda Woodhead across all ages in the town of Kendal in the English Lake District.[7] This suggested that New Age style practices were very much the preserve of the 1960s boomer generation and that the New Age was ageing with them. On the second question they refer to a model developed in *Making Sense of Generation Y* which sought to distinguish between what the authors call 'formative' and 'transformative' spirituality. The members of generation Y interviewed were seen as expressing formative spirituality; yet it is transformative spirituality that the authors consider socially important and that classifies people as 'spiritual seekers'. The implication is that while the boomer generation were actively pursuing a socially significant transformative spirituality, the generations since are not only moving away from Christianity, but are not replacing this with a spirituality that has any real significance. If this is true, the New Spiritualities may have limited cultural significance. However, I think there are a number of reasons why this conclusion is mistaken.

The Kendal thesis of the 'ageing New Age'[8] has recently been criticized by one of the Kendal researchers. Paul Heelas, writing with Benjamin Seel, points out that the predominance of boomers as practitioners of New Age therapies and spirituality should not be confused with the age profile of the consumers of what these practitioners offer, the majority of whom are in their twenties.[9] The boomer practitioners were the founders of the movement in the late 1960s, and until they retire from leading it they will inevitably be its prominent figures. Also, this spirituality does not operate like Christianity; it is a provider-consumer faith, not a congregational one. The evidence points to an expanding client base and one that is predominantly youthful. Further to this, young practitioners are being apprenticed to step into the shoes of the founders.

Heelas and Seel go on to say that for the boomer founders, 'New Age' sprang out of a counter-cultural movement. For those under 45, generations X and Y, it is seen as 'mainstream' spirituality with a place in both the education syllabus and healthcare. While Höllinger[10] is right that elements of counter-culture remain in the New Spiritualities, especially in ecological and holistic lifestyles, spiritualities with roots in the New Age are in many ways natural expressions of consumer religion. Hence the great influence for New Age teaching in business consultancy. The conclusion Heelas and Seel draw is worth noting:

> Whereas until the 60s it was 'natural' for people to turn to Christianity, it is becoming 'natural' for increasing numbers to turn to alternative spiritualities of life. So long as great value is attached to the development, cultivation and exploration of subjective-life, so long as we live in a subjectivized consumer culture propounding expectations of well-being, there is no reason to suppose that the future of New Age spiritualities is anything but promising.[11]

This reinforces the importance of the 1960s; indeed, many of the New Age movement's founders were student protest leaders at that time. As the political dreams failed to materialize, these people shifted from a political to a spiritual revolution. This was also a turn from an outward to an inward approach to life, representing the shift from the modern to the postmodern.

The mistaken assumption that the New Spiritualities would operate like Christianity may also affect the way Savage, Collins-Mayo and Mayo describe the difference between formative and transformative spirituality. For them, formative spirituality

> focuses on an individual's sense of raised awareness of re-lationality (with, for example, self and others, and possibly God, the universe, etc.), which may include mystery sensing (awe, wonder, dread), meaning making and value sensing (delight and despair, right and wrong, existential meaning).[12]

In the paper, Collins-Mayo and Rankin are clear that this is what they find present, but should not be viewed as a return to the spiritual in society. On the other hand,

> Transformative spirituality involves the individual in delib-erate practices (whether overtly 'religious' or not) which aim to foster mindfulness of the [transcendent] Other (howso-ever conceived – e.g. God, Self, Universe) and help maintain a sense of connectedness. This spiritual mindfulness then has significance for the individual in so far as it permeates daily life, guides his or her decisions and provides a continued appreciation of the Other. When people describe themselves as 'spiritual seekers', we understand this to be engaging with transformative spirituality.[13]

Definitions of spirituality are difficult if they are to span such things as atheistic expressions of Buddhism, animistic tradi-tional faiths and monotheistic religions. This is evident when talking of a 'transcendent Other'. Many in the New Spirituali-ties, at both the Pagan and the New Age ends of the spectrum, consciously reject the language of transcendence, seeing this as referring to a God who is remote and unconnected with the planet. Instead they emphasize this world as the place of spiritual meaning. For Pagans the emphasis is on creation and 'mother earth'. At the New Age end spirituality tends also to be about self-improvement and therapy. Some might talk here of a higher self, but it is not clear that such approaches would obviously fall into the definition of transformative spirituality. Most have some concept of connectedness, but when does this stop being the 'raised awareness' used in the definition of formative spirituality and become the 'spiritual mindfulness' of transformative spirituality? In many ways there is no clear divide; we are talking about a sliding scale.

If much of what survey data uncovers can be referred to as formative spirituality, Heelas' observation that New Age practices are normal within consumer culture highlights the way this is the basis from which more active participation grows. The distinction between formative and transformative spirituality at this point asks us to distinguish between passive and active approaches to faith, rightly suggesting that finding out what someone believes in response to a survey question is not the same as finding out if that belief matters to them. The concept of transformative spirituality thus concentrates on deliberate practices. One can see the sense of this with regard to many religious systems, but there are potential problems.

In countries with a Christian heritage, claiming a religious *identity* is the most common religious expression and demonstrates the least commitment to the claimed faith. A smaller, more committed group of people hold religious *beliefs*. Finally the 'truly committed' adopt religious *practices* like regular church attendance or daily prayer or Bible study. However, eastern religion works very differently; indeed Yao draws the picture of Chinese urban spirituality as the complete inverse of Christendom, personal religious practice as the cultural norm, religious belief less common but widely held and religious identity very rare. In such a tradition deliberate practices might not be a mark of a more intentional spirituality.[14]

Figure 18 World Values Survey 2000

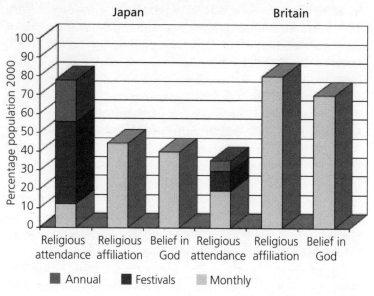

Figure 18 shows the 2000 World Values Survey data for Japan compared with that for Britain and illustrates this 'client-based' approach very clearly; the strength of religious practice over affiliation is the opposite of the British situation.

About 25 per cent of Japanese are members of one of the many new religions:[15] fusions of traditional Buddhism or Shinto with western New Age beliefs that have emerged as Japan has modernized and westernized. Apart from the small communities of non-eastern traditional faiths, most Japanese practise any or every faith; one simply chooses to visit the temple you like for whatever occasion you choose. This is also evident in a 2000 survey by Japan.com in which 45 per cent of young Japanese declared their preference for a Christian wedding. This was nothing to do with Christian marriage beliefs and everything to do with liking the ceremony and its western culture.

In the British survey data above we noted that New Spirituality beliefs were higher among the young, and New Spirituality practices in the area of divination had been tried by 46 per cent of generation Y. Alternative therapies, according to Heelas and Seel,[16] are more popular than these divination practices; indeed, the *Soul of Britain* survey shows about twice as many people experimenting with alternative medicine as those trying tarot or astrology. The numbers of young people trying out the whole range of New Spirituality practices is thus likely to be higher than 46 per cent, perhaps considerably higher. All of this suggests that generation Y spirituality functions very much like eastern client-based religion. As already noted, for many this adoption of New Spirituality practice is not deeply important, but if this is the way religion of many nations functions, not only does it mean we have to change the way we look at expressions of 'religion' in the West, it means we may have to change our assessment of what counts as socially significant in the religious sphere.

The possible exception to the client model of faith is contemporary Paganism. While shamanism often takes a solitary path and some shaman act as practitioners serving clients, Pagan faiths like Wicca, Druidry and Norse/Saxon belief systems have been group-oriented with distinct members as well as further casual followers. This practice often goes hand in hand with a counter-cultural approach to global capitalism; Pagans tend to protest about road building, airport extensions and outside global summits. Ten years ago I would have seen Paganism as quite distinct in this regard from the way the more New Age beliefs have been at home in the capitalist market place. Recently this has been changing, and is evident in events such as Witchfest, run by the Children of Artemis, which are like a Pagan version of the commercial Mind Body Spirit fairs connected to the New Age tradition. As Jo Pearson has noted,[17] this trend is especially present among young people; many who claim to be Wiccans never join a coven, making this a more consumer-friendly faith bought into via the internet and gatherings like Witchfest. Douglas Ezzy[18] sees this as stemming from the kind of 'white witchcraft' inspired by media portrayals of witches. If there is a trend to a more consumer form of Paganism, then it too may become a client-based religion, though for a while at least, I suspect, one with a stronger religious identity than its New Age cousins.

Making Sense of Generation Y deliberately worked with included young adults. This would almost certainly involve many who were at some level clients of New Age practices. However, many Pagans are critical of mainstream society or see themselves as 'different' and thus choose not to be 'included'. This seems true even for those entering into more commercialized forms. For this reason, if the research 'buried' New Age spirituality it probably largely excluded a growing group of young Pagans.

A larger study that combines survey data with personal and group interviews is needed in the UK. Two studies, one conducted in the USA and one in Australia, do provide such data. The USA still has very high rates of Christian affiliation even among young people, so it is hardly a good comparison, though the authors of *Making Sense* rightly note that this report also suggests a 'happy midi-narrative' approach to life. The Australian data, however, come from a society closer to that of the UK, though without the same level of Christendom legacy. This research helpfully combines qualitative with quantitative material and also includes generation X and boomer respondents.

The Australian survey initially split the generation Y population into three groups: those with a religious affiliation; those who were 'eclectic', a group who are active participants in or hold a number of beliefs associated with the New Spiritualities; and a humanist group. However, the 0.2 per cent who described themselves as 'neo Pagans' had been placed in the religious group. Further to this, only 17 per cent of the religious group claimed to be committed or active. A further 5.5 per cent of generation Y Australians, while identifying with a religious tradition, were actually eclectic in their belief and behaviour pattern. If we include those with religious identity but eclectic in behaviour and neo Pagans, we could reasonably say that 23 per cent of generation Y are followers of New Spiritualities. In

Figure 19 Triangle of beliefs

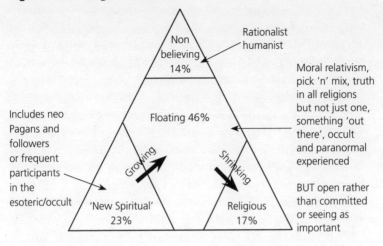

Non believing 14%

Rationalist humanist

Floating 46%

Moral relativism, pick 'n' mix, truth in all religions but not just one, something 'out there', occult and paranormal experienced

Includes neo Pagans and followers or frequent participants in the esoteric/occult

Growing

Shrinking

'New Spiritual' 23%

Religious 17%

BUT open rather than committed or seeing as important

the humanist group 78 per cent believed in God, or a life force or higher being. Over half of this group also believed that there are elements of truth in many religions, with only 14 per cent of generation Y saying that religion is false.

We can plot the generation Y population on a triangle of beliefs (see Figure 19). The largest group, 46 per cent, don't fit any of the three categories; they sit in the middle of the triangle at varying distances to the different poles. With regard to values they are very much like the *Making Sense* description of the happy midi-narrative. The beliefs of this group are similar, regardless of having different religious identifications. All express moral relativism: it's OK to pick and choose beliefs from different sources; there is truth in many religions but not in one only; they hold a belief in either God or a life force; and express some New Spirituality ideas, notably either reincarnation, angels, contacting the dead or astrology. However, these beliefs are not seen as central to their lives. This group thus has far more in common with the New Spiritualities than either the traditional religions or atheist humanism. In 'Christian' countries we are used to viewing those who are not closed to faith as 'our fringe'. If these people are anyone's fringe it is the New Spiritualities who can claim them.

In comparing generation Y with generation X and boomers there is a shift away from Christian identification and away from belief in God. However, this last shift has been more than compensated for by an increase in belief in a life force or higher power, so generation Y are more likely to believe that there is 'something there' but less likely to adhere to more traditional religious beliefs about what that is. With regard to the New Spiritualities the picture is more complex. In many areas beliefs had changed little but in general members of generation Y are more likely to have 'new' beliefs than boomers and on average as likely as generation X. On the whole, generation X and boomers also hold to the 'happy midi-narrative'.

This all fits the UK data quite closely. Generation Y are not less interested in spirituality than generation X or boomers, rather they are less interested in religion. However, while many are open to the New Spiritualities, most are not committed to them. This suggests a picture in which many young people will hold beliefs in alignment with the New Spiritualities and participate loosely in their practices as clients of the 'faith'; and within this large group is a smaller core of committed followers, but one that already makes it the major 'faith' among young Australians. The same is probably also true among young Britons.

Spirituality and daily life

One of the strengths of client-based religion is that it can be practised as part of daily life. It appeals to people who want spirituality at work or at home and have busy schedules that make it hard to fit with a faith centred on a particular time and place. Many Christians struggle with this challenge too and find that meeting on a Sunday morning becomes increasingly difficult. The emerging client-based religions are good at creating rituals and practices that foster informal gatherings and personal devotion. Paul Heibert, writing in the 1980s about the 'excluded middle',[19] argued that western churches understood the transcendent sacred level and the scientific secular world, but not the middle area common to most societies that was the realm of luck, spiritual beings, healing and so on. Arguably the New Spiritualities have filled the middle excluded by the modern church and as such are far more relevant to people's daily lives. I first came across Heibert's ideas in the work of John Wimber and the advocacy of 'power evangelism'. This move and others in the charismatic renewal have certainly opened up the church to the supernatural, but I suspect that they have simply renewed the sacred space, leaving the excluded middle to the New Spiritualities.

In the 1980s a number of charismatic church leaders were prophesying a great revival in Britain. Conferences and prayer meetings attended by people from around the world occurred in anticipation. Beyond some notable spiritual experiences and renewal of faith, people were disappointed when nothing grand came to pass. But what if God was enabling a great spiritual awakening, not in the church but outside it? David Hay records a big rise in spiritual and supernatural experience among non-churchgoers, from 48 per cent of those he surveyed to 76 per cent between 1987 and 2000.[20] It is easy to point to the sociological reasons why people are so much more open to the spiritual, but if people are as they say actually having more spiritual experiences, where are these coming from? If God is at work in the world, might these experiences be of God? In my work I have met people who have encountered forces that I believe were spiritually evil; indeed, Hay records a big rise in such experiences. But they remain much lower than the positive encounters, and among these positive experiences I have come across many Pagans and New Agers who I think are encountering the God I know through Jesus Christ. We are used to people encountering God being among those raised in the Christian faith, using Christian language to describe their experiences. People raised in a culture that has forgotten the Christian language of faith will speak of their encounters with God in a different language; we must listen for what is going on underneath. In doing so we may also learn how to communicate the Christian faith in language those not raised in the church understand.

Religion as a resolution of the problems of postmodernity

Part of the appeal of the New Spiritualities is that they offer answers to the problem raised by postmodernity, of celebrating creation in its diversity while facing the danger that this becomes an expression of Nietzschean original violence.

Our culture at large is waking up to important issues like climate change, responsible farming and livestock care and the protection of natural habitats and wildlife. The New Spiritualities speak in very ecological terms and their adherents are often active campaigners at the forefront of attempts at sustainable living. Our faith is accused of being anti-ecological because its beliefs make God remote from creation, see the world as a possession to be exploited and are focused purely on salvation in the next life. The church has certainly been slower than these new faiths to put ecology on its agenda, and for some Christians God is indeed set against the world seeking to save souls out of it. I have also encountered Christians who argue that God is going to destroy the world on the day of judgement, so Christians should not be concerned about it. Indeed for them the ecology movement is not only unnecessary but a path to lead unwary Christians into 'false New Age belief'. Such approaches to Christianity are indeed anti-ecological. I think we need an alternative to such views that offers a robust Christian ecological framework.

Contemporary Paganism and New Age style beliefs offer different solutions to the postmodern problem of unity and diversity. Paganism looks to the eco-system for a model of interdependent diversity and seeks ways for humanity to play a role in this system. The problem is that reading ethics from nature can justify Nietzschean conflict as much as harmonious living. Pagans can choose to see nature as a celebration of diversity but ultimately they have to fall back on their own discernment of this. If this world is all there is, we have no viewpoint that can preserve us from the logic of postmodern relativism, continuous conflict and the likelihood that the strongest call the shots.

New Agers tend to turn to eastern ideas of cosmic unity, and stress the idea of each finding their own path towards a common goal. Such thought also raises problems; the supposed unity often makes the diversity only a surface accident. We can become mere projections of the 'cosmic one', deluded into thinking we are separate entities. They also tend to share the Romantic modernist view of people as basically good when freed from oppressive creeds. So the many diverse expressions of spirituality are all expressions of one benign reality in which evil doesn't exist. This often sits alongside a belief in some sort of irresistible cosmic force at work in all creation to draw it forwards to a positive yet unknown destiny. This might well be attractive; the question it faces is the same one the Romantic modern liberals had to face: are people actually innately good? If they are not, then there is no real answer here to nihilism, and the problem of diversity leading to conflict is not solved nor the environment saved.

Whatever their strengths and weaknesses, the New Spiritualities challenge the church to offer a viable approach to this crucial issue. Our stress on one God and the uniqueness of Jesus has meant that Christianity is viewed as innately totalitarian and anti-diversity. Can we find a spirituality that enables us to embrace diversity and remain true to Christ?

The modernist tendency has been to suggest that only the material is real and humans are minds with machines attached called bodies. The New Spiritualities reject this dualism in favour of a holistic view. We have been used to addressing the rational and material as superior in our evangelism, suggesting that it is people's minds that come to God and not whole people and that salvation is about what happens in the next life, not this one. We need a holistic Christianity that enables us to love God with all our heart, mind, strength and spirit.

The New Spiritualities have also promoted the feminine in

spirituality. Many have left a Christian faith that is seen as based on a male misogynist God for this reason. How might this be addressed? We certainly cannot adopt the Pagan god and goddess approach and maintain continuity with our tradition, but are there alternatives to entirely male language for God that are consistent with scripture and tradition? What also of the role of women in the church? Too often we have seen these as 'feminist' issues only. We must realize that they are also crucial mission issues for the church today as well. We cannot ignore them and expect to be viewed as a viable religious option, especially when compared to the New Spiritualities.

People are attracted to Jesus

If the rise of the New Spiritualities seems to be at the expense of Christian faith, there is one thing that should give us hope: people are attracted to Jesus. Nietzsche may have viewed him as in many ways the antithesis of his 'superman' but few in our world do not actually find Jesus a figure worthy of admiration. I am always struck by this at places like Mind Body Spirit fairs. Jesus is viewed by many as exactly the kind of spiritual and moral person we should aspire to be like. But if people admire him, they can also fit him into their contemporary systems so he becomes a New Age guru rather than a Jewish rabbi, and one among many incarnations of deity rather than uniquely the Son of God. We must remember that debating the proper understanding of Jesus is not the monopoly of Christians. Can we explore Jesus as an open subject and then approach the disagreements as fellow travellers?

The future of spirituality in a postmodern culture

The rise in spirituality observed since the 1960s seems to be growing as we move from boomers to generation X and into generation Y. For most, this represents a change in beliefs and openness to a range of practices, while a smaller group are committed followers centred on a group of providers in a client-based religious culture. These client-based spiritualities have become natural in a consumer culture and have in many ways ceased to be counter-cultural. This is fuelling their growth from generation to generation, in contrast to the traditional faiths that find themselves not at home in a postmodern global capitalist culture. A Christianity truly incarnate in this world should therefore not only undertake incarnational mission among spiritual seekers, taking them seriously as followers of a major world religion, but also expect to express the Christian faith in terms that emerge from this missionary engagement with the natural spirituality of the culture.

Notes

1 Bristol University, 1996. Steve Hollinghurst, *New Age, Paganism and Christian Mission*, Grove Books, 2003; *Equipping Your Church in a Spiritual Age*, CBTI, 2005; and *Coded Messages*, Grove Books, 2006.

2 For Britain this data comes from 1981, as this statistic isn't present in the 2000 data. That more recent data, however, shows the same age effect in other European countries.

3 The question is recorded only in these countries.

4 Sara Savage, Sylvia Collins-Mayo and Bob Mayo, *Making Sense of Generation Y*, Church House Publishing, 2006.

5 Phil Rankin, *Buried Spirituality*, Sarum College Press, 2005.

6 As laid out in an unpublished conference paper, '*Making Sense of Generation Y* and *Buried Spirituality*', 27 September 2006, presented by Sylvia Collins-Mayo with Phil Rankin.

7 Collins-Mayo and Rankin, '*Making Sense*'; Paul Heelas and Linda Woodhead, *The Spiritual Revolution*, Blackwell, 2005.

8 The term New Age has now fallen out of use among those who practise it, but is still used by some researchers, journalists and others writing about it.

9 Paul Heelas and Benjamin Seel, 'An Ageing New Age?', in Grace Davie, Paul Heelas and Linda Woodhead (eds), *Predicting Religion*, Ashgate, 2003; cf. Daniel Mears and Christopher Ellison, 'Who Buys New Age Materials?', *Sociology of Religion* (2000) 61(3): 289–313.

10 Franz Höllinger, 'Does the counter-cultural character of New Age persist?', *Journal of Contemporary Religion* (2004) 19(3): 289–309.

11 Heelas and Seel, 'An Ageing New Age?', pp. 242–3.

12 Savage, Collins-Mayo and Mayo, *Making Sense*, p. 12.

13 Savage, Collins-Mayo and Mayo, *Making Sense*, pp. 12–13. Their concept of transformative spirituality has much in common with Sandra Schneider's definition of spirituality, discussed in Rankin, *Buried Spirituality*.

14 See for instance Rodney Stark, Eva Hamberg and Alan S. Miller, 'Exploring Spirituality and Unchurched Religions in America, Sweden, and Japan', *Journal of Contemporary Religion* (2005) 20(1): 3–23; Raymond L. M. Lee, 'The Re-enchantment of the Self: Western Spirituality, Asian Materialism', *Journal of Contemporary Religion* (2003) 18(3): 351–67; and Yao Xinzhong, 'Religious Belief and Practice in Urban China 1995–2005', *Journal of Contemporary Religion* (2007) 22(2): 169–86, particularly p. 178.

15 David A. Rausch and Carl Hermann Voss, *World Religions: Our Quest for Meaning*, Trinity Press International, 1993, p. 111.

16 Heelas and Seel, 'An Ageing New Age?'.

17 Jo Pearson, 'Witchcraft Will Not Soon Vanish From This Earth', in *Predicting Religion*, pp. 170–82.

18 Douglas Ezzy, 'White Witches and Black Magic: Ethics and Consumerism in Contemporary Witchcraft', *Journal of Contemporary Religion* (2006) 21(1): 15–31.

19 Paul Heibert, 'The Flaw of the Excluded Middle', *Missiology and International Review* (1982) 10(1), January.

20 David Hay, with Kate Hunt, *Understanding the Spirituality of People Who Don't Go to Church*, Nottingham University, 2000.

5

Is Society Becoming More Secular?

Secularization under attack

For much of the latter half of the twentieth century secularization theory was largely accepted as the explanation for falling religious observance. This process was seen as a product
of the Enlightenment: after the Reformation and the split in
the western Church, and religious wars between Christian
nations, there was pressure to separate public life from personal belief. Society was to be governed by objective human
reason, bolstered by scientific discovery to which over time was
added democratic political progress. In this schema religion
was viewed as purely subjective, a matter of personal opinion and thus something for the private rather than the public
sphere and therefore removed from power in public life. Many
of those who forged such ideas, like Descartes or Kant, were
not seeking to promote atheism or attack all forms of Christian belief, but the experience of religious conflict led them to
seek another source of social unification. Where social unity
had been part of the function of the one Church in medieval
Christendom, now a common human rationality would provide that unity.

The initial effect of the Enlightenment was to remove religion
to the private sphere, but eventually religious belief itself came
under scrutiny. Science over time disenchanted the universe,
beginning with an attack on the supernatural and ultimately
suggesting that God did not exist and the workings of the natural world as uncovered by science offered complete explanations
of life. Archaeological evidence and critical analysis of religious

texts undermined the notion that these were historical records; instead they were mythical expressions of personal belief. The emerging science of psychology added to this picture, suggesting that religious belief was a sign of mental delusion. All of this led to a powerful attack on religion even as a private matter; religious belief could be viewed as a reliance on the idea of a 'god' that was unnecessary. Indeed, if they led to delusional behaviour, denial of scientific truth and worst of all human conflict, such ideas were downright dangerous.

If Enlightenment thought would lead to first the marginalization and then potentially the elimination of religious belief, social factors associated with industrialization and urbanization were seen as having helped the demise of the church as a social institution. For the secularization theorists all this combined to create a process by which the church gradually became marginalized as a political institution throughout the nineteenth and twentieth centuries, while church membership declined, slowly until the 1960s, then more steeply. There are variants on this theme among those supporting some form of secularization thesis,[1] from religion disappearing to those who might see it persisting for some as private belief, or even in the public sphere in a weakened form; but it seemed clear to many that this process would continue until religious belief was largely eradicated save for a tiny pocket of remaining believers marginalized from mainstream society.

However, by the end of the twentieth century the secularization thesis was under attack for a variety of reasons. A number of critiques, like that of Callum Brown mentioned in Chapters 2 and 3, have been levelled at the idea that the move to the city led to falling church attendance. Robin Gill also showed how this was exaggerated by the over-building of urban churches.[2] For others the persistence of religion, especially in the USA, a nation that was constitutionally secular, cast doubt on secularization. Indeed, Grace Davie famously suggested that the decline of religion in Europe made it an 'exceptional case'[3] in a world that on the whole showed little sign of becoming unreligious. Various theories have been put forward to explain such differences. Both Davie and Casanova note the idea that the USA has unusually had a free-market approach to church from its inception, making its churches ideally suited to contemporary free-market culture.[4] However, not all countries with high church attendance in developed nations possess this trait; Casanova points here to Bruce's analysis of Poland and Ireland. This, of course, raises issues of their Catholic nature, but explaining high church attendance as a product of Catholicism seems problematic again when considering the USA. Casanova in the end suggests that we could argue that most countries are exceptions; if so, what of secularization theory?

Secular spirituality

The rise of spirituality in Europe at the end of the twentieth century prompts others, like Chris Partridge, to question secularization theory. In *The Re-Enchantment of the West*, he argues that the New Spiritualities cannot be ignored as 'entertainment' with no real social significance, as the prominent British sociologist Steve Bruce has suggested. However, as we have seen, the New Spiritualities are not a direct replacement for the kind of national religion witnessed under Christendom; their client-based operation means that they impact society in a different way. If in the West, as Heelas argues, this fits consumer culture, observers of religions like Shinto, Daoism and Buddhism in Japan and China would suggest that these are religions at home in traditionally secular societies.[5] Secular societies are nothing new.

Mary Douglas[6] defined societies according to two axes: 'grid', which is about goals, hierarchies and ideologies, and 'group', which is about corporate identity and clearly defined social roles. For Douglas modern society expresses a type found elsewhere, for instance New Guinea, defined by a strong 'grid' and weak 'group'. Such societies praise the 'self-made individual' and tend to a tolerant pluralism. However, they contain an inherent tension in that only the few may rise to the top; thus movements arise that defy accepted social categories enabling those who feel excluded by them to find an alternative. In New Guinea she saw this as expressed by millennial 'cargo cults' and in the West by the student revolts of the late 1960s and early 1970s. As the New Spiritualities came from that 1960s' counter-culture, it is no surprise that the drive for self-empowerment in the New Spiritualities, and postmodernity's desire to celebrate each and every culture without privileging one above another, fits Douglas' theory.[7]

What these examples show is that certain forms of religion can thrive in secular societies. Suggestions that US Christianity has always operated in a free-market manner in a constitutionally secular state may indicate something similar. In contrast to France, which became a secular nation at a similar time but in violent opposition to the church, in the USA leaders desired to permit religious diversity after experiencing religious persecution abroad. Indeed, the very different fortunes of the church in Europe may be due to the European church having its home in a non-secular society and then seeking to fight the process of secularization rather than find a way of operating within it.

Europe: the exceptional case?

Might there be a way of determining the factors that create apparent 'exceptional cases'? Comparisons across Europe, using data from the European Values Survey, allow us to do this. These can then be compared with data from places like Africa and America, from both the comparable World Values Survey and other sources. The information in this section draws on analysis available online.[8] It is worth bearing in mind that this data is survey material and thus almost certainly overestimates statistics such as church attendance figures.

What the data shows is that as countries develop economically religious belief and practice decline, with falling church attendances and changing beliefs, and a move towards New Spirituality ideas and liberal social attitudes. Differences between countries are not due to some following this process and others not, but to the different positions from which they started and to uneven rates of development across Europe. Over the 1980s and 1990s the EVS records the fastest decline in Christianity in the countries that had initially the highest attendance, that is, those in southern Europe, because it was these that went through the greatest development, catching up with northern European nations that had lower rates of church attendance initially but were also more developed.

Further variants are explained first by the predominant Christian expression of each country; Protestant countries record lower regular attendance than Catholic or Orthodox, and Orthodox show a tradition geared to attendance at festivals rather than weekly. Second, former communist countries had, not surprisingly, lower attendances but many are showing a return to faith after communism. Interestingly, in many eastern countries this is expressed in a new Paganism rather than in Christianity, as documented by Shnirelman.[9] In these countries Christianity has been associated with Russian or western colonialism, and Paganism, as well expressing the rise of New Spiritualities, also expresses a strongly nationalistic variant of it.

Between 1999 and 2002 the European average church attendance was 31.8 per cent per month. Attendances in the Protestant countries of north-east Europe[10] and Protestant Scandinavia were all at 15 per cent or lower. Great Britain was a little higher, with 18.8 per cent monthly attendance. Complex countries, like Hungary which is eastern and Catholic but with a significant Protestant community, Albania and Bulgaria, both mixed Orthodox and Muslim, and Russia being northern, eastern and Orthodox, all had around the European average attendance, as do Catholic countries in the east and north.[11] Southern Catholic countries had above average attendance, of around 45 per cent. However, most of these countries are losing young people and show the fastest decline in Christian faith. The countries in this group on the whole also represent those that developed later and remained relatively traditional. With development, most are now rapidly liberalizing. It is this issue that marks out the important difference between two of the highest attending countries, Malta and Ireland.

Ireland saw rapid economic development and growing wealth towards the end of the twentieth century. With it has come a rapid loss of young people from the church. Though nearly 70 per cent of people still attended regularly in 1999, there is a much larger than average variation than elsewhere in Europe between the over-50s with 90 per cent attendance and the under-30s at 47.5 per cent, which indicates a future rapid decline in overall attendance. Social attitudes are liberalizing, too, especially among the young. Ireland is rapidly joining the move away from Christendom. Contrast this with Malta, which with much slower development than mainland Europe society remains traditional. Even here there has been some liberalization of belief, with the young leading the way, but this still only reflects where Ireland was 20 years ago. Malta and Ireland may have high church attendance but they don't represent exceptions. Rather they show that Christendom has held on much longer in Europe's more traditional societies. In Malta it is alive and well for now, but there is nothing to say it would not follow Ireland if it too saw rapid economic growth. The comparison with northern Catholic countries also shows that economic development is the key factor in assessing decline in Christian influence, not Catholicism; this merely changes the point from which decline happens.

If a lack of economic development can maintain Christendom in some countries, political conflict has done so in all but one of the remaining 'exceptional cases'. This is not at all surprising when one remembers that Christendom was a political reality and not just a social and religious one. In Poland, Croatia, Bosnia, Serbia and Northern Ireland, religious identity was closely coupled to ethnic identity in a struggle to assert independence in the case of Poland and in inter-ethnic violence in the other countries. Significantly, all these countries are fairly traditional societies when it comes to values and beliefs. Of them, Northern Ireland looks most vulnerable to change and there is already evidence that peace is leading to lower levels of religious affiliation among the young. Otherwise these countries show little variation between the religious beliefs and practices of older and younger sections of population, suggesting that at present their Christian affiliation will remain high. However, the Polish church is increasingly concerned for young Poles who emigrate to the West looking for work. In Poland faith among the young is strong, but many who live abroad suffer a loss of faith and significantly this continues when they return to Poland.[12] This suggests that Polish Catholicism might also be affected by exposure to secular cultures as it becomes more a part of Europe.

The political role of religion with regards to ethnic conflict raises the question of whether fear of immigration might lead to a return to Christendom for some as part of asserting national identity. There is evidence to suggest that Muslim immigration affected church attendances in West Germany in the period during which the EVS material was gathered (1981–2000). In the UK sections of the press are using the rhetoric of our 'Christian heritage' as part of its critique of Islamic influence. It is interesting to note reports from English ministers in areas with high Muslim populations of a revival in infant baptisms; people seem to want to assert their British identity in the face of a perceived assertion of identity by the Muslim community. We may, however, ask if this kind of approach to Christendom is really something to celebrate.

If individual history can slow the secularization process it can also accelerate it, as evidenced in the rapid collapse of Catholicism in Spain during the 1980s and 1990s, with monthly attendance falling from 54.5 per cent to 36.1 per cent. Beliefs have also liberalized dramatically. The reason for this is almost certainly the linking of the Franco regime with the Catholic Church. Significantly the post-Franco constitution of 1978 separated the church from the state and cut its funding. Similarly the effect of the French Revolution two centuries earlier explains France's exceptionally low attendance. The Czech Republic's low attendance probably reflects its experience of internal Christian conflict following the Reformation, then the imposition of Catholicism under Austro-Hungarian occupation, and finally its voluntary choice to become communist after

World War Two. Prague was the centre of European occultism from the sixteenth to the nineteenth centuries, and this legacy may be reflected in what are probably the highest rates of alternative belief in Europe. In 1999 only 6.5 per cent of people said that they believed in a personal God, whereas 50.2 per cent stated a belief in a spirit or life force. A staggering 72.9 per cent apparently believed in telepathy. In both latter figures these beliefs rise among the younger end of the population.

During the time I was working on this book an article was published by David Voas based on material in the different European Social Survey.[13] His conclusions are that secularization is happening right across Europe and differences relate to different starting points. Differences in affiliation according to age are signs of religious decline, not growing religiosity in later life. What he calls 'fuzzy fidelity', a persistence of some levels of religious belief and identification, are seen as stages of decline in faith. This agrees with my analysis in this and previous chapters, with one notable exception. Voas sees the data on a sliding scale from religious to secular, with fuzzy fidelity, by which he means fuzzy Christianity, as a transitional phase. For Voas the New Spiritualities are part of fuzzy fidelity. My analysis of the Australian material also puts much of this in a rather 'fuzzy' middle area, but I think significantly suggests a more solid reality to the New Spiritualities than Voas seems to allow. I suspect that this is because he is looking at religion and doing so in traditional western terms, thus missing the very different client-based model these beliefs operate under. If I agree with him that various attempts to dismiss traditional secularization theory on grounds of exceptions or a shift to something like 'believing without belonging' are flawed, the re-enchantment idea remains an essential qualification of traditional secularization theses.

In 2002 Massimo Introvigne of the Centre for Studies on New Religions used the experience of Italy in the 1990s to support 'rational choice' theory against advocates of the secularization thesis.[14] This theory proposes a religious economic model in which competition is good for religion and monopoly bad. This is because consumers are in the habit of regularly switching products, and if people have a large choice of Christian options they are more likely to switch from one Christian option to another, as opposed to switching away from Christianity. The same theory lies behind a whole variety of breakfast cereals being made by one manufacturer; when you switch products you are still more likely to be buying one of their brands. Hence US attendance is high because there is considerable Christian pluralism and total freedom of religion, leading to such competition. Conversely Europe with its state churches sees these languishing and declining. A much debated prediction of this theory is that countries in which the church is declining will see a large rise in New Religious Movements; that is, new religious choices. Introvigne thus sought to show that there is far more new religious activity in Europe than secularization theorists had allowed.

The EVS shows that in Italy religious affiliation and church attendance rose in the 1990s, including among the young. With modernization and liberalization in the 1980s and 1990s the Italian church should have shrunk. Even more dramatic was the switch away from New Age beliefs to more traditional Christian spirituality among not only churchgoers but non-churchgoers. The key event seems to have been the political and financial disestablishment of the Roman Church. However, disestablishment alone is not the answer, as Spain shows. In Italy the church's finances, once guaranteed by the state, weren't cut but became dependent on popular vote and thus on the church's successful advertising, both through the media and through public experience of the church. This required the church to discern what would make it relevant to the public. In short, it was compelled to develop a process of double listening and incarnational mission. This process might also change the church's message. Indeed, there is evidence from both the European Values Survey and research by *L'Espresso* magazine in 2007 that shows a liberalization of moral views by the church in Italy at this time.[15] If this is a religious revival it is not a conservative one.

So does rational choice theory offer an answer? How might

this look in other places with high church attendance, like Africa and the USA?

Africa: the new Christendom? The case of Nigeria

Looking at Africa, the persistence of Christendom in some countries in Europe frames the key question, how much are high rates of church attendance linked to an underdeveloped traditional society there too? Might religious conflict and the relationship of religion to ethnic identity also contribute to high church attendance? Further to this, might African churches be vulnerable if these circumstances change? On the other hand, might the vibrant African church be the springboard for a new global mission? Indeed, is Africa the 'New Christendom'?

Unfortunately there is a lack of data for many African countries; the World Values Survey offers some details for Nigeria but only in the 1990 survey, and simple data for a few countries in the 2000 survey. There is also a study of secularism drawing on material from a detailed survey of the Kenyan church from 1997.[16] Combined with these I have drawn on discussion with pastors, mission agencies and researchers in Africa. That these point to what appears to be a coherent analysis is encouraging. Without further study it must be provisional.

The *Worldmark Encyclopedia of Culture and Daily Life* describes the religious situation of Nigeria in the following way:

> Nigerians widely hold to their traditional African religious beliefs in addition to subscribing to various branches of Islam and Christianity . . . Muslims now constitute 45 per cent of the population . . . Currently, Protestants account for 26.35 per cent, Catholics 12.1 per cent, and African Christian 10.6 per cent of the population.[17]

The figures appear accurate when compared to the World Values Survey. The comment about traditional religions is also perceptive. It is difficult to know from the World Values Survey how many sole practitioners of traditional religion there are as the question is not asked, but we are talking fewer than 5 per cent. However, it is clear that many Christians and Muslims also maintain some level of traditional belief and will practise both their faiths. I have often heard African pastors talk of the challenges of educating and discipling their people and Christianity can remain very much a surface faith. Needless to say, this was also true in European Christendom.

The World Values Survey in 1990 showed 24.3 per cent of Nigerians believing in a spirit or life force and 39 per cent in reincarnation, with Christians more likely to share these beliefs than average and Muslims slightly less. Unlike the West, where such beliefs reflect the influence of the New Spiritualities, here they are likely to suggest an understanding of God derived from traditional African beliefs. If this is so the beliefs of 40–65 per cent of Christians are at least partly those of traditional African religion. The Kenyan study suggests that about 63 per cent of the rural population are practitioners of traditional religion, even though this population is 73 per cent Christian.[18]

Many African countries were formed by colonial powers artificially cutting across tribal groupings. These tribal divisions play an important part in religion, as do tensions between Muslim and Christian communities. In Nigeria these led to civil war in the 1960s when the Christian south-east declared itself the independent nation of Biafra, breaking alliance with the more Muslim Hausa north. Sectarian violence is still a potential feature and clashes frequently occur between Muslim and Christian. Indeed, a missionary I spoke to who had been in Nigeria for several years agreed that the situation there was not dissimilar to that in Northern Ireland, where religious identity was closely wedded to ethnic and political conflict. In a classic example, rioting in the Muslim north was sparked in 2002 by plans to hold the Miss World contest in the Nigerian capital Abuja. The riots left churches burned and over 100 dead. Such clashes can easily escalate, with reciprocal rioting and the destruction of mosques in the mainly Christian south. Leaders on both sides have learned to be sensitive with regard to moral and religious issues in order to avoid this type of violence.

Nigeria has very traditional moral values; significantly, even more so among the non-Muslim or Christian population, and views became even more traditional as society increasingly polarized between Muslims and Christians during the 1990s. By comparison South Africa has seen views liberalize over the same decade. Unlike Nigeria those outside religion are more liberal. The pressure on the South African church, like those of Europe, is in the liberalizing direction.

The lesson of Europe was that against the pressure of global cultural change Christendom could survive better if one or several of three factors were in place: a significant Muslim population, a conflict or political struggle in which religious and ethnic factors combined, or a very traditional economically underdeveloped society. In 1990 World Values Survey statistics for Ireland and Malta were almost the same as those for Nigeria. The removal of these factors in Ireland has enabled the cultural changes that have eroded Christendom elsewhere in Europe to reach it, while traditional Malta defies the global cultural stream. Nigeria has all three factors, and in spite of some level of economic development the pressure is towards traditionalism both from society at large and from an increasingly conservative Islam ready to judge the church if it looks too 'western'. If these factors remain then it would be no surprise if church attendances remain high. Questions might be asked about levels of underlying traditional belief among many who also identify as Christians, a situation church leaders are seeking to address, but if this is an issue it may also make Nigeria very much like a new version of medieval European Christendom.

The future of African Christendom: the case of Kenya

Over the past few years, as I have explored how globalization might affect the church beyond Europe, it has occurred to me that economic development might lead to diminishing attendances among the vibrant churches of Africa. If this can be seen happening anywhere it will be in Africa's mushrooming cities where traditional society begins to encounter western culture. I have raised the issue with African pastors and missionaries who have been to Africa. Usually they agree that this is exactly what is happening in their cities. However, some voices have suggested this is a partial view, that churches are growing fast in cities but there is also a shift from traditional to pentecostal churches that makes this uneven.[19]

The same question prompted Shorter and Onyancha[20] to explore secularism in Kenya, as people moved from rural areas to Nairobi. Their material provides both statistics and qualitative analysis. It is only one study but interestingly its main conclusions fit the anecdotal evidence I received; this encourages me to suspect that these conclusions are useful and may have wider application than Kenya. Only further studies can show if this is the case.

Their survey data showed that while 73 per cent of rural dwellers said they were Christians, the figure was 80 per cent for Nairobi. However, when those attending church were counted it was discovered that in rural areas 40 per cent of the population attended weekly while only 12 per cent did so in urban areas, with 20 per cent attending less frequently. This big difference in attendance was hidden by the rapid growth in the urban population of Nairobi. This meant that although churches were growing, the population was growing at a faster rate, so church attendance was falling as a percentage of the urban population. Coupled with this, church building had not kept pace and many were over-full, adding to the impression of church growth.

The picture across Nairobi was also uneven. There was, as my own respondents suggested, a move from the traditional churches to newer pentecostal ones. Church attendance was uneven according to district, with areas of poverty showing lower than average attendance. The issues were partly economic: many people had to work on Sunday. In the poor district of Eastleigh, Sunday church attendance was recorded as 2.5 per cent; however, this still meant the average congregation size was 250.

In the villages, traditional social structures had maintained church attendance from generation to generation, while these had been lost with the move to the city. However, such structures had never stopped many Christians also practising traditional religions; about two-thirds of the 63 per cent who do so are Christians by the judgement of the authors.

> Traditional religion is part of ethnic identity. There is no visible organization other than the ordinary structures of society: the clan, the family, the territory. Prayer and worship take place primarily in the home, and public manifestations of traditional religion, such as territorial rites and offerings on behalf of the community are somewhat rare. Nowadays they are even less frequent than they used to be. Traditional religion is typically integrated with human life and its rhythms.
>
> There is no regular, weekly attendance at public rituals. Such rites as there are take place on specific occasions or at certain seasons. There is little formal, explicit practice, let alone organization.[21]

However, traditional African religions are very much located in a specific place; while some elements such as divination, charms and healing can be practised anywhere there is access to a medicine man or priest, many others have meaning only in the home village. This means that patterns of traditional religion can break down when someone migrates to the city, leading to something similar to the client-based religions we explored earlier.

Economic pressures are compounded by advertising and western media creating the desire for goods and economic prosperity. These work differently in the various communities of the city. The poor are inspired with dreams of a better life and this fuels the pressure to work all hours. The authors feel that the church often adds to this pressure, both through a process of westernization initiated by missionaries and through health and wealth preachers, popular among the poor. Indeed they accuse the church itself of being an instrument of secularism.[22] In more affluent areas these pressures have a different effect, creating westernized intellectual elites often embracing western anti-religious thought. These individuals tend to be lecturers at universities, advisers to government and controllers of the media. This often results in a dismissive attitude in the media and in education to the faith of ordinary 'uneducated' Africans. Westernization is also seen as a challenge to traditional moral values, at both an intellectual level and a popular one, through things like music videos. The authors cite the 'pop-culture' surrounding the decoration and operation of Matatu buses as a good example of this.[23]

Secularization has seen many people becoming non-practising Christians but also often returning to some level of practice of traditional religion, yet in a highly secularized form.[24] Nairobi's secularization is creating client-based religious practice within an increasingly westernized urban culture. The authors of *Secularism in Africa* want to wake the church up to secularism in African cities because they believe the situation can be changed; they advocate a more African approach to churches, a better awareness of the impact of globalization and economic pressures, and concerted dialogue with traditional culture and religion to preserve what is best while the creation of churches that genuinely address the realities of people's lives in cities like Nairobi would be a real alternative to aspects of traditional religion.

The example of Kenya points to the very real possibility of the vibrant churches of Africa following in the footsteps of their European parents. Such churches have formed an African cultural version of Christendom that is potentially just as vulnerable to economic and social development. As in Europe, religious and ethnic conflict can enable Christendom to persist, but this is not encouraging. We all want such conflicts to come to an end. The African church can address these issues but it does not yet seem to have realized that it may have to do so. I think too often the collapse of western churches can be blamed by Africans on a combination of a lack of faith among

Christians and western decadence in the culture in general. Such 'western problems' may become their problems not because they have failed to resist western culture but simply as a consequence of economic development, peace, prosperity and technological advance in African nations. Indeed, although it is distinctly African the secularism of Nairobi, with its low rates of church attendance, Sunday working and client-based religion, looks far closer to that of London or Prague than one might have suspected.

In recent years Africans have become missionaries in Europe, and this is very welcome. They bring with them faith and experience, and perhaps most of all confidence and passion, from the African mission field. They have planted thriving African churches among immigrant communities, boosting overall UK church attendance, although they have failed to plant churches among the rest of the population. Most believe that doing this is part of their calling, and Europeans have generally welcomed them, believing that what they have achieved in Africa can be repeated. The reality is that the African church has no more skill in creating churches in a postmodern global capitalist culture than their shrinking western counterparts, and probably even less experience of the issues faced. We all need to learn how to do this, and I think we will be stronger both in Europe and in Africa if we can do so in partnership. The barriers to such co-operation are, however, all too clear from the tensions that can exist between churches from African culture and those in western culture. We will need to apply cross-cultural sensitivity to each other, not just in our mission. Neither church has the definitive answers to take to the other. Both have experience and gifts to bring to the search. It may also be that in Africa lessons learned too late in Europe can prevent a repeat of the European church experience.

Church in the USA: a marketing success story?

The comparison between Britain and America reveals very different positions for the church in public life. Britain has a state church, worship in schools and bishops in the House of Lords. The USA has an official separation of church and state, worship in schools is illegal and there is no official place for church leaders in politics unless they get elected as ordinary citizens. On the surface one might therefore think Britain was a Christian nation and the USA a secular one. A comparison between recent British Prime Minister Tony Blair and the office of US President, however, highlights something closer to the truth.

The British prime minister is involved in helping fulfil the monarch's role as head of the Church of England. As such the prime minister is expected to be, in appearance at least, an Anglican. This was considered sensitive enough for Tony Blair to wait until he had left office before he announced what people had suspected for years, that his sympathies lay with Catholicism. Yet while outward Anglicanism is seen as constitutionally sensitive, actual Christian faith is an embarrassment best avoided. Press spokesman Alistair Campbell famously said of the Blair government, 'We don't do God', and when it became apparent that Mr Blair actually did 'do God', after he mentioned that he prayed about decisions to do with the Iraq war, this prompted a savage media attack and was viewed as making him unfit for office. A British prime minister, it seems, should officially be an Anglican Christian but actually be a non-practising one without a faith. This rather sums up a nation where most say they are Christian but hardly anyone practises their faith.

The USA is perhaps the opposite of the UK: officially, the state doesn't 'do God' but a candidate who didn't 'do God' would be completely unelectable as president. While church and state are officially separated, most Americans would be horrified if a president didn't pray about important decisions; indeed, regular public prayer meetings have been held in the White House with a mix of prominent politicians and church leaders. Officially the USA has no national religion, yet the percentage of people who say they go to church regularly is almost three times that in officially Christian Britain. How might the US experience compare with that of Europe and

Africa? Does it support rational choice theory as an alternative to secularization?

First, it should be noted that US church attendance varies between states. Survey data from ARDA and David Olson's probably more accurate head count figures show places like Louisiana and North Dakota have similar rates to Poland and Ireland.[25] Yet places like Nevada, Maine and Oregon are around the European average; not all of the USA is far from the European 'exception'. All the highest attending states are in the south or mid-west; the second highest group are their neighbours. The lowest attending states are in the north-west and north-east, with the second lowest being their neighbours in the west and on the east coast. On the whole the divide is between those areas dominated by small rural communities like the mid-west and also the heartlands of the old slave-based agricultural economies of the south on the one hand, and on the other the highly urbanized centres of the global capitalist economy like Seattle, San Francisco and New York. The agricultural areas of the USA are not the equivalents of traditional European agricultural societies, but they are far more traditional in American terms. Like Europe, the US church is strongest in the more traditional areas and weakest in the most developed. This in itself suggests that the market model may be overrated as the cause of US church success.

The Olson material doesn't provide attendance by age, but several recent surveys do. The General Social Values Survey 2004 gives weekly attendance at 43.5 per cent for the over-65s but only 23.5 per cent for the 18–30s. Head count figures would suggest more like 12 per cent of people in their 20s actually attend. There is clearly some level of return to church in the USA when people have children, but the Barna group[26] noted that in 2006 there was a big age divide among those with children who went to church with them. Of parents in their 20s, 33 per cent did, compared to 40 per cent in their 30s and 50 per cent in their 40s. As already noted, Barna showed in 2001 that those who attend church regularly as a child are nearly three times as likely to attend a church today as adults than their peers who didn't go to church during childhood. Those who did not attend themselves as children are also half as likely to take their own children to church. All this suggests that the attendance figures by age are indicators of falling future attendances, as Olson records. The Christendom pattern in which there is fairly constant high childhood attendance, some fall-off in the teens and some level of returning adults, with enough sending their children to maintain the pattern, has broken down, as it did in the UK. ARDA surveys from 1988 to 2002 asked questions about childhood attendance and in 2002 also gave an age breakdown for current attendance. Since this is survey data the figures are not comparable with the UK Church Census, but a similar graph can be plotted (see Figure 20). The situation shown is similar to that in the UK, in which falling childhood attendance leads to lower adult attendance, and a repeat of this cycle, just as the Barna data suggests.

Apart from attendance figures, the rise of alternative beliefs has been an indicator of the move from Christendom. A survey by the Baylor Institute in 2006[27] asked a range of questions, plotted on Figure 21.

Figure 20 US attendance patterns

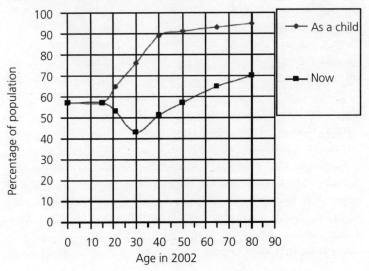

Figure 21 US adults believe in . . .

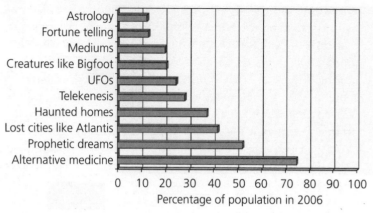

Percentage of population in 2006

All this is perhaps surprising in such a church-going nation but comparison of data from the USA and Britain on telepathy in the 1999 World Values Survey reveals that regular church-goers in the USA are twice as likely to believe in such phenomena as those in the UK.

Baylor also asked people what experience they had of the paranormal; this data is broken down by age, so it can be compared to the UK Populus material (Figures 22–26). The results are very much like those in the UK. The 1960s effect is also clearly present. It might be expected, in a nation where about 40 per cent of people say they go to church regularly, that belief in the paranormal would be lower than in one where the figure is only 15 per cent.[28] That this is not so not only suggests that the USA is likely to have a level of client-based religious activity similar to post-Christendom Europe, but also that many of the 'clients' are regular churchgoers.

In some areas of beliefs, however, the USA is more traditional. An ABC poll in 2004 found that around 60 per cent of Americans believed literally the biblical accounts of the six-day creation, Noah's ark and Moses parting the Red Sea. These US figures are far higher than regular US church attendance, suggesting that such beliefs are held by many who don't go to

Figure 22 Experience of the paranormal: consulted horoscope

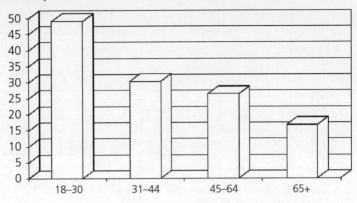

Figure 23 Experience of the paranormal: consulted psychic

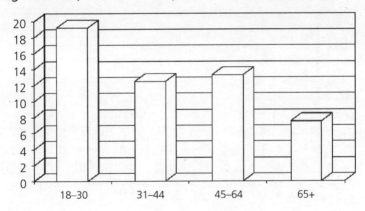

church regularly, who are also those most likely to believe in paranormal phenomena. One would think that this combination was unlikely, but clearly it isn't. Again, this suggests a very pick-and-mix approach to religion.

Between 2001 and 2005 a comprehensive study of US teens and religion was carried out, the survey findings of which are shown in Figure 27.[29] When it came to a range of beliefs to do

Figure 24 Experience of the paranormal: experienced haunted home

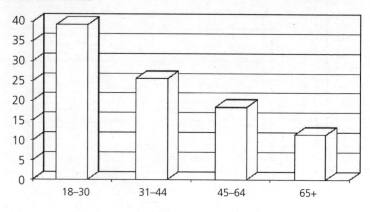

Figure 25 Experience of the paranormal: tried ouija board

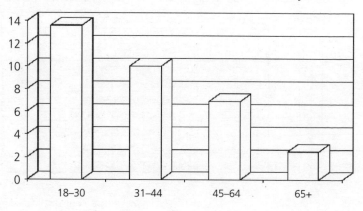

with spiritual or paranormal phenomenon, the research asked the teens if they definitely believed, maybe believed or definitely didn't believe.[30] When asked about traditional Christian beliefs the tendency was to believe. For more New Age beliefs the tendency was to say they might believe. When compared with the Baylor figures this suggests that many of those who have participated in the paranormal would respond that they might

Figure 26 Experience of the paranormal: seen UFO

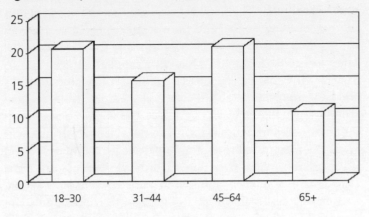

Figure 27 Religion and US teens

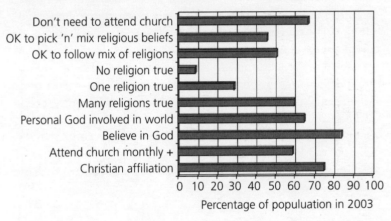

believe it works. The authors also draw attention to the high level of 'maybe' with regard to paranormal phenomena among conservative Protestant youth who might be expected to be certain that these are not true, with just over a quarter saying they may believe in reincarnation and astrology. The non-religious follow the general trend, being more likely to accept Christian beliefs than paranormal ones, but in each category they are the most dismissive of Christian beliefs and the least dismissive of paranormal ones. This suggests strongly that the non-religious are not heading in the direction of atheism but away from Christianity and towards New Spirituality belief. This is the same as we saw in the Australian generation Y survey.

Across the board teens showed a tendency to a pluralist pick-and-mix approach to faith, a view that there was truth in many religions and that it was OK to pick and choose beliefs from different religions without regard to the teachings of that religion.[31] Conservative Protestants and black pentecostals showed little difference here from the majority view. American teens clearly have a very postmodern attitude to religion. Holding such beliefs also makes it plausible to go to church and share traditional Christian beliefs, but also hold alternative beliefs and take part in New Spirituality practices.

Christians said that they were not consciously incorporating practices from other faiths in their own religious practice.[32] I don't think this contradicts the high levels of client-based religious practice among Christian teens reported by Baylor; such practices are seen as tools to relate to the spiritual realm rather than elements of a specific religious tradition. Further to this, US teens, like those in the UK, clearly don't relate to the 'spiritual but not religious' tag.

Overall the report found many teens fairly content with church and happy to call themselves Christian, but with little real understanding of faith, or much commitment to it. The authors comment:

> For many US teens, God is treated as something like a cosmic therapist or counselor, a ready competent helper who responds in times of trouble but who does not particularly ask devotion or obedience . . . (parents) use religion instrumentally to achieve prosocial outcomes for their children, to help their kids be more healthy, safe, and successful in life.[33]

This strongly suggests that Christian teens have adopted a 'New Age' Christianity and have been allowed to do so because their

Christian parents are not interested in Christianity as a belief system but as a social institution.

The authors go on to describe a model of American religion that is almost an 'informal Christendom'. At the top is the American civil religion that is part of national identity with the president expected to be Christian and Christian beliefs and values the norm. This may be what makes people with apparently little religious commitment give very conservative answers on issues like biblical stories; this is simply what good Americans believe. Churchgoing is also expected, and this operates at the next level with organized religion and the large US religious industry. Underneath this, however, is the actual belief system described by the authors as 'an interreligious faith fostering subjective well-being and lubricating interpersonal relationships in the local public sphere'.[34] At the individual level faith is of the pick-and-mix variety we have seen. The real driving force behind this situation is seen to be mass-consumer capitalism.

> The more American people and institutions are redefined by mass-consumer capitalism's moral order, the more American religion is also remade in its image. Religion becomes one product among many others existing to satisfy people's subjectively defined needs, tastes, and wants. Religious adherents thus become spiritual consumers uniquely authorized as autonomous individuals to pick and choose in the religious market whatever products they may find satisfying or fulfilling at the moment.[35]

This probably explains why the difference in belief between regular and irregular churchgoers was so much less in the USA. Many in the USA are attending church for social reasons rather than because of religious conviction. The loss of Christendom means that this is now rare in the UK where once it used to be common. However, it is also true that at the core of American churches there are Christians of sincere faith wanting to lead lives centred on Christ. When I have spoken with those seeking to plant churches and engage in effective mission within the USA they are very aware of the nominal character of much US faith. The US church still has energy and resources and there are encouraging new Christian communities and missionary projects springing up across the denominational profile often under a variety of 'emerging church' labels. It may be true that many of those making up large church attendances are 'cultural Christians' but that leaves many who are not. If the US church could address this, the impact it could have in the world would be enormous.

We began this section looking at rational choice theory and free-market approaches to church as the means of resisting secularism. We have returned there but with some irony. It seems indeed correct to view this as a defining feature of the US church, but at the level of individuals' lives the USA is as much a secular nation as most in Europe with a similar move to client-based religion. The difference is that this has found its home in the church rather then instead of the church. The free-market approach to religion may indeed have kept church attendance high, but it has also made it increasingly irrelevant. This may be why we are starting to see a pattern of falling attendance like that in twentieth-century Europe. With evidence that most Christian teens think that you don't need to go to church to be a good religious person, and the Barna material on the relationship of childhood to adult attendance, this looks set to get worse. In the end the free-market approach to religion may not have been the means by which America has proved an exception by resisting secularism, rather it might have been the means by which the church has been conquered by it.

A revival of conservative religion?

Gilles Kepel in his book *The Revenge of God* argued that contemporary culture was seeing the rise of a very different religious expression from the client-based religions of the New Spiritualities; that is, a rise in conservative religion.[36] This takes us back to Bosch's comments about the very different ways people can act towards paradigm shifts. The adherents of the New Spiritualities are enthusiastic adopters of the new, who, as Bosch suggests, feel as if the 'scales have fallen from their eyes'; this lies behind the whole concept of the New Age. Others, however, both religious and non-religious, do not welcome the new paradigm. Writing in 1991 primarily as a scholar of Islam, Kepel was charting a global rise in fundamentalist Islam as a counter-culture opposing initially the westernization of the Ottoman Empire, but evolving to oppose the growth of global capitalism and its effects on Islamic nations. Ten years later this understanding is evident in 9/11 and Al Qaeda. Importantly this represents not only a strain of Islam that is opposed to western global capitalist culture but also an internal debate within Islam about how it should properly engage with these.

If the rise of religious conservatism was a purely Islamic phenomenon we could argue that its impact beyond Islam was a consequence of a 'clash of cultures' between Islam and the West. However, similar debates are opening up within many religions and cultures in societies across the globe, which therefore can be viewed as part of the tension Bosch describes at a time of paradigm shift in what is increasingly a global culture. So we see the rise of conservative Hinduism in India and conservative Buddhism in southeast Asia, together with a rise of conservative Christianity within Protestant, Catholic and Orthodox churches across the globe. The culture clash is, I believe, between the emerging postmodern world and those who seek to resist it.

Of course, the beliefs of conservatives in these different religions reflect the differences between those faiths; indeed, conservatives often reflect faith distinctions more strongly. However, in relating to global culture they often find common cause, supporting traditional approaches to marriage and the roles of women and men, opposing liberal attitudes to sex and sexuality, challenging the presence of sex, violence, swearing and certain portrayals of religion in the media, opposing abortion and certain forms of medical research. Strong views on such subjects are usually supported with reference to revealed scriptures or divinely inspired teachings seen as representing something like objective truth; thus religious conservatives of all faiths are often understandably wary of the tendency towards relativism and subjectivity they see within postmodernity.

If I am right about this, and the rise of conservatism is indeed, as Kepel argued, a reaction against an emerging global culture that is increasingly postmodern, then this has important implications for how we view many of the current debates within Christianity. Such debates are not just about theological differences; they are cross-cultural mission discussions about faithfulness to the Christian tradition at a time when cultural change forces us into new territory.

British conservative churches, especially if they are also charismatic, are not in such a decline as others, and indeed some are growing. It would be easy to claim therefore that these churches are those most successfully proclaiming the gospel in our culture. What they might actually be doing is providing a refuge for those seeking to reject our culture, both concerned Christians leaving other churches and non-Christians seeking a solution to their own cultural discomfort. There are some indicators that might point this way. Recently published data by Richter and Francis shows that many people who left church for reasons of belief did so because they rejected conservative theology, while others left because they rejected liberal theology.[37] However, there was on the whole a clear age divide; it was largely older people who wanted conservative churches and younger people who were leaving them. As we have seen elsewhere, there is an obvious difference between older and younger people with regard to many cultural indicators, and this seems to be the case with regard to conservative Christianity.

Similarly the 2005 Church Census showed that the largest group leaving church was women between 15 and 44 years of age, but this was not a uniform movement away; they were more than twice as likely to leave charismatic or conservative evangelical churches. Needless to say, there are young men and women joining conservative churches too, and people not in church who are threatened by cultural change, but the vast majority of non-Christians are heading the other way. We need to find how Christianity might speak to them effectively while also remaining faithful to the Christian tradition. Of course, Christianity should seek to connect with those who are threatened by cultural change as much as those who embrace it. For such people conservative faith will be attractive and these churches are needed. But there is a real danger of the church unwittingly becoming the refuge of a minority seeking to reject cultural change and in doing so further undermining its ability to effectively evangelize within the majority cultures.

The impact of the rise of conservative religion on secularization may well be different from country to country and religion to religion. In the UK recent surveys have shown a general decline in religious adherence among the young; the exception is Islam, where increasingly the young, especially men, are showing much greater commitment than their parents and grandparents, and this is coupled with a rise in more conservative approaches to faith and culture. The effect is small with regard to the place of the traditional faiths in British culture as a whole, but it is having a significant impact on Islam in Britain. This trend seems to be part of a phenomenon among young Muslims in many parts of the world, and thus will have some impact on global culture. In a number of areas of the world Islam and Christianity divide a nation's population, and in an uneasy balance between the two the rise of conservatism in one is often mirrored in the other. In this way parts of Africa and Southern Asia may prove more resistant to a global postmodern secular culture.

The end of secularism?

Shorter and Onyancha compared the process they saw in Africa of economic development and urbanization leading to secularism to that classically put forward for secularism in Europe.[38] Returning to Callum Brown's thesis, I note that his point is not that there was no decline prior to the 1960s but that radical decline began then and therefore was not the product of industrialization. What I think the European figures show is a two-stage process: a modernist secularization based on economic and social modernization and urbanization, and a postmodern one based on pluralism, globalization and the rejection of the divide between objective and subjective. In Europe the first was slow and its likely end was a secular atheism; the second has been much more rapid and is likely to lead to a secular religiosity with the rise of client-based religions. Countries now entering secularism in a global culture will find that they are accelerated into the final phase. Just as much of Africa looks set to never have a landline system as they go straight from no phones to satellite-receiving mobiles, so traditional societies are likely to progress from premodernity to postmodernity sooner or later depending on local factors. How they express this global culture will, of course, be locally unique; a postmodern Africa will not be identical to a postmodern Europe, and indeed without a preceding modernity it is debatable if it can really be called postmodern at all. However, issues now perhaps seen as 'western' may well be part of such a local cultural expression. The question will be, for traditional societies like those in Africa or the Islamic world, can they both develop while maintaining traditional values?

The public sphere now contains a whole variety of religious and spiritual belief systems, all viewed as potentially valid, and none seen as uniquely true. There is currently no way back to the position of privilege that Christianity has known in Europe, and any attempt to operate as if it still holds this place may lead the church to be marginalized from the new toleration of the religious and the spiritual: what Nick Spencer refers to as 'totalitolerance'.[39] All beliefs are tolerated except those that won't tolerate all. Indeed, while claims to the Christian heritage of western nations may well be able to draw on positive contributions often underacknowledged, they may do more to raise the memory of religious war and persecution. The call of the church to 'remember we are a Christian country' can thus sound like 'Can we go back to the Middle Ages, please, so we can oppress you some more?'.

Is Society Becoming More Secular?

In many nations new forms of religion are finding a place within a postmodern global culture, but there is also a rise of conservative religion, reflecting the desire of some to resist the onslaught of this culture. It is likely that the rise of conservative religion, especially in the global south, may create places that are resistant to the global spread of postmodern culture, and that this might be a long-term situation. The evidence from the USA and Africa, however, suggests that here too there is a switch from Christianity to client-based religion, initially showing itself in a mixed religious practice. It seems likely that the kinds of problems facing the European church will have locally expressed but similar counterparts in countries that for now have much higher church attendance.

Our reason for exploring the impact of secularism as a global phenomenon is because some have looked to African and American churches as examples of how to resist secularism and build churches that are effective in such a culture. If that exploration leads me to conclude that this is not so, and further that underlying high levels of church attendance in both places is largely nominal Christianity, this is no reason for Europeans to decide that they can safely ignore these churches or feel better about their own shortcomings. Faced with the options of either having lost the social Christians and more nominal believers, as most of us have in Europe, or still having them and thus the potential to change the situation, perhaps helping these people to become committed mature Christians, which would I choose? I think I would want the opportunities of the churches in Africa and America. The global church has in them a great potential resource. Equally I hope that a realization of the pressures of secularism in Africa and America may help churches there to understand that they have an affinity with the European experience. The state of Christianity in Europe may be their future if things carry on as they are now. We all need to wake up to the cultural changes around us so that churches around the world seek to help each other face the challenges they bring. My prayer is that this will indeed happen, and Africans, Americans and Europeans, with others from developed and less developed nations, can together travel to a place as yet unknown to discover a global missionary vision to meet the diverse expressions of postmodern global capitalism.

Notes

1 See Chris Partridge, *The Re-Enchantment of the West*, T&T Clark, 2004, p. 8 for a useful summary of different approaches.

2 Robin Gill, *The Myth of the Empty Church*, SPCK, 1993.

3 Grace Davie, *Europe: The Exceptional Case*, Darton, Longman and Todd, 2002.

4 Grace Davie, 'From Obligation to Consumption', in *The Future of the Parish System*, Church House Publishing, 2007, pp. 33–46; José Casanova, 'Beyond European and American Exceptionalisms', in *Predicting Religion*, pp. 17–29.

5 For example, Casanova, 'Beyond', Yao, 'Religious Belief', and Stark, Hamberg and Miller, 'Exploring Spirituality'.

6 Mary Douglas, *Natural Symbols*, Penguin, 1973.

7 Douglas' work, published in 1973, was unlikely to consider these ideas.

8 See further material and updates at www.sheffieldcentre.org.uk, on the 'Evangelism to Post-Christian Culture' pages.

9 Victor A. Shnirelman, '"Christians! Go home": A Revival of Neo-Paganism between the Baltic Sea and Transcaucasia (An Overview)', *Journal of Contemporary Religion* (2002) 17(2): 197–211.

10 Former East Germany, Estonia, Finland and Latvia.

11 Belgium, Lithuania, Luxembourg, and to lesser extent the Netherlands, which is 50 per cent Catholic.

12 As reported in interviews for *The EasyJet Priests*, Radio 4, 30 July 2007.

13 David Voas, 'The Rise and Fall of Fuzzy Fidelity in Europe', *European Sociological Review* (2009) 25(2): 155–68.

14 See Massimo Introvigne, *Praise God and Pay the Tax: Italian Religious Economy*, online at www.cesnur.org/2002/mi_italianrel.htm.

15 'Italian church attendance not as high as thought', *Telegraph*, 23 February 2007.

16 Aylward Shorter and Edwin Onyancha, *Secularism in Africa*, Nairobi, Paulines Publications Africa, 1997.

17 Timothy L. Gall (ed.), *Worldmark Encyclopedia of Culture and Daily Life: Vol. 1 – Africa*, Cleveland, OH: Eastword Publications Development, 1998, p. 330.

18 Shorter and Onyancha, *Secularism in Africa*, pp. 126–7.

19 I am indebted to Andrew Kirk, formerly Director of the Centre for Mission and World Christianity at Selly Oak, Todd Johnson of the Centre for the Study of Global Christianity, Chris Neal of CMS and the Rt Revd Zac Niringiye, Bishop of Kampala, who all responded by email to my request for information on this.

20 Shorter and Onyancha, *Secularism in Africa*.

21 Shorter and Onyancha, *Secularism in Africa*, pp. 126–7.

22 Shorter and Onyancha, *Secularism in Africa*, p. 25.

23 Shorter and Onyancha, *Secularism in Africa*, pp. 86–99.

24 Shorter and Onyancha, *Secularism in Africa*, pp. 26–7.

25 American Religious Data Archive, available at www.arda.com; David Olson, American Church Research Project, www.theamerican church.org.

26 *Most Twentysomethings Put Christianity on the Shelf*, Barna, 2006 (online at www.barna.org).

27 *American Piety in the 21st Century*, Baylor Institute for Studies of Religion, 2006.

28 Research Matters, poll for Tear Fund, 2006.

29 The National Study of Youth and Religion, published in Christian Smith and Melinda Denton, *Soul Searching*, New York, Oxford University Press, 2005.

30 Smith and Denton, *Soul Searching*, pp. 43–4.

31 Smith and Denton, *Soul Searching*, pp. 74–6.

32 Smith and Denton, *Soul Searching*, pp. 78–83.

33 Smith and Denton, *Soul Searching*, p. 148.

34 Smith and Denton, *Soul Searching*, p. 169.

35 Smith and Denton, *Soul Searching*, pp. 176–7.

36 Gilles Kepel, *The Revenge of God: The Resurgence of Islam, Christianity and Judaism in the Modern World*, Polity, 1994.

37 Leslie Francis and Philip Richter, *Gone for Good?*, Epworth, 2007. The material used here came from discussion with the authors as part of a research meeting just prior to publication.

38 Shorter and Onyancha, *Secularism in Africa*, p. 39.

39 Nick Spencer, *Beyond Belief*, LICC booklet, 2003.

PART TWO

Listening to God in the Christian Tradition

6

The Mission of God in the Ancient Pagan World

We may not expect to find lessons for Christian mission in the Old Testament, but with the *missio Dei* beginning in creation we can expect to see God at work in cross-cultural mission prior to Christ. Indeed, the New Testament authors often see the themes of salvation through Christ as present in Old Testament accounts, such as the story of Noah and the flood, the sacrifice of Isaac, the parting of the Red Sea, and Jonah and the whale. If these are pointers to the death and resurrection of Christ, and not of themselves ultimate acts of God's saving grace, they still show us God's character in mission.

The need for missionary people to be distinctive

Ancient Judaism did not seek to convert Pagans, yet it did seek to influence them, and was interested in how they related to God. It must also be remembered that Judaism emerges from near-eastern Paganism and then exists alongside it. How ancient Judaism and ancient Paganism interact is thus a crucial issue and one that develops over time. The idea of different races and cultures comes from the story of the Tower of Babel in Genesis 11. God creates cultural division in order to prevent people working together to achieve their aim of building a tower to reach God. This adds a further division to the post-Eden situation. The new creation may also thus entail reconciliation between different people groups. Against this backdrop Abraham is called to start a new people who will demonstrate

God's image in humanity distinctly (Genesis 12). This raises the important question of how the Jews were to be distinctive yet also points towards God's ultimate vision, which was not that one people alone should be his but all creation restored. Distinctiveness is needed for there to be a mission. Just as the Jews would not have been a sign among the nations if they had not been distinct, so Christian missionaries who are no different from those they seek to witness among will not be a sign of the coming of God's kingdom. The debate that ensued later, in the early church, was about discerning what of Jewish distinctiveness was to be preserved by Christians and what was not essential. The outcome of this debate seems to suggest that some of the distinctions were ethical and to be preserved, but some were purely cultural, and while they had served a purpose in marking the Jews out from the nations, they were not essential for the people of God.

Discerning Yahweh in the stories about the Pagan gods

The later chapters of Genesis suggest that Abraham and his family came to understand over time that Yahweh was the only God. For instance, in Genesis 35 we find Jacob, Abraham's grandson, for the first time deciding that they must get rid of the Pagan idols representing their family's ancestral gods. Yet we still see Jacob pouring out drink offerings on stones erected in Canaanite fashion. The standard assumption would be that while a particular deity might be connected to a family, and might bring good fortune, that deity would be one of many. So Yahweh is initially seen as Abraham's God and one among many. It was a gradual process for his descendants to realize that following Yahweh was not compatible with worshipping other gods. Similarly the early worship of Yahweh described in Genesis arises out of Pagan practice. This evolution is largely a peaceful one; surrounding nations are condemned not for their religion but for immorality. So even after the move from pantheism to monotheism the descendants of Abraham on the whole live peacefully with their neighbours and intermarry with Pagan families.

Abraham's approach to Paganism is illustrated by the story of Melchizedek in Genesis 14. Melchizedek is not Jewish; we are told that he is a priest of God Most High, but that is an English translation of El Elyon, a title of El the Canaanite deity. Melchizedek's blessing of Abraham shows that the Pagan priest attributes Abraham's victory earlier in this chapter to El Elyon's action. Abraham doesn't dispute this but when he addresses the king of Sodom in verse 22 he adapts Melchizedek's formula, saying that he has made a promise to Yahweh El Elyon, putting the name of his deity in front of the salutation to El, suggesting El is in fact Yahweh. This pattern is repeated throughout the Old Testament, where the names and stories associated with Canaanite deities are taken and applied instead to Yahweh. Yahweh fights Baal's battle with the sea and the chaos monster that dwells there. He takes on Baal's role as God of thunder and rain, and even his mountain-top throne at Zaphon.[1] Yahweh, not Ashtoreth, provides grain and gives children to the barren. He is depicted as El, with white beard and seated on a heavenly throne. The deities of the Canaanite pantheon are viewed as aspects of Yahweh, so to some extent they are genuine revelations. What is rejected, however, is the polytheistic system within which they operate, and so while the language and imagery of Paganism can be seen as speaking of Yahweh, these gods cannot be added to Yahweh in worship. Neither therefore can Yahweh be accommodated as a new god in the pantheon. So the family idols must go and the worship of Canaanite deities must cease in the promised land.[2]

Discerning what must be rejected in ancient Paganism

The idea that the gods are actually revelations in part of Yahweh yet also in part rivals for Yahweh in the people's practice also helps explain the ambiguity surrounding the treatment of idols. They are both mocked as being nothing but blocks of wood, used to supply the language of the Bible for Yahweh, and yet also viewed as demonic. These views are not contradictory. The gods are not real for the very reason that there is only one God and what people have seen as other gods are in fact all partial revelations of Yahweh. However, since this is true, Yahweh alone should be worshipped and therefore the continued worship of idols is to turn away from God. Further, while some aspects of the Canaanite deities are applied to God, not all are. We may see Yahweh as Baal, Ashtoreth or El but we don't see Yahweh as Moloch, who delighted in child sacrifice.[3] There may be an inculturation of Yahweh in the appropriation of Pagan imagery but there is also the counter-cultural rejection of other aspects of ancient Paganism.

Is Yahweh just a tribal deity or God of the nations?

The language used for God in the Old Testament is partly a clue to the process of its development. Belief in Yahweh grows out of the experience of his words and actions among those who were originally near-eastern Pagans. Their inherited religious language is that of Paganism, yet they discover as they follow the new God that actually those things they attributed to the old Pagan deities are the acts of Yahweh, that he isn't just a new god but the God of all creation. This leads to a tension in the Old Testament with regard to the other nations. Is Yahweh their God also, or just the God of Israel? At times we find the other nations viewed as Yahweh's enemies and the Israelites feeling that faithfulness to God requires the slaughter of non-Jewish life and the refusal of contact with non-Jews. Yet at other times the prophets admonish their hearers for poorly treating the non-Jews in their midst and prophesy that all nations will come to worship Yahweh who is in truth their God also, not Israel's tribal deity. The natural assumption of an ancient near-eastern population would be that their God is a tribal deity and war between peoples was also a battle between their gods. This is evident, for instance, in the speech of the Assyrian leader before the attack on Jerusalem.[4] In the prophets we see this attitude challenged by the implications of the growing realization that Yahweh is not a tribal deity but in fact the God of all nations.

The exile is an important experience that helps expand the Jewish view of Yahweh. The people have been taken captive to Babylon. This is a double blow. The conquest invited the interpretation that the gods of Babylon were stronger than Yahweh. As God of Israel it would also be feared that Yahweh would not be present in Babylonia. In spite of this the Jews are told to be a blessing to the people among whom they are in exile. The story of Daniel illustrates the desire to serve the Pagan society yet also maintain Jewish integrity. So Daniel serves a Pagan monarch as an adviser along with the royal astrologers, but he will not worship a Pagan idol. In a sense cross-cultural mission is like this; we are called to be a blessing to those we are among yet discern the points at which we cannot embrace their culture.

Through the experience of exile the Jews would discover that Yahweh was actually working through the Babylonians and was present in Babylonia. Indeed, he would eventually use Cyrus to bring the people back to the promised land and help restore the temple. Cyrus and Melchizedek are not the only people Yahweh uses. Even the more ambiguous figure of the prophet Balaam, hired to curse the Israelites, is used to speak for God. If God is partly revealed in Pagan religion he can also work through Pagan kings, priests and prophets. We too may find God at work in those of other faiths and cultures.

Notes

1 This is obscured by the translation of Zaphon as 'north'; see Psalm 48 as an example.

2 For more on this see Tikva Frymer-Kensky, *In the Wake of the Goddess*, Free Press, 1992, pp. 162–7; and Foster McCurley, *Ancient Myths and Biblical Faith*, Fortress Press, 1983, pp. 73–124.

3 Indeed, this may be part of the lesson Abraham learns with the potential sacrifice of Isaac. Abraham had once been part of a faith that in its pantheon contained deities who demanded child sacrifice.

4 2 Chronicles 32.9–19.

7

Jesus the Evangelist

Evangelism can be seen as starting with the followers of Jesus. However, people like the Old Testament prophets, John the Baptist and Jesus are preachers of the kingdom of God, which is the goal of the mission of God. Jesus describes his followers as sent by God as he is sent, and Paul would speak of the Church as Christ's body. The call to evangelism is not just to speak about Jesus but to embody Jesus and to witness as he witnessed. This is inherent in the way Jesus trained his followers, modelling mission for them, then sending them out to do the same and to report back to him, before the final commissioning of them as his witnesses after the resurrection.[1]

Proclaiming the kingdom in word and deed

Jesus' mission is characterized by the proclamation that the kingdom of God is at hand both as a spoken message and also in healings and deliverance.[2] The message is that Jesus fulfils God's mission to restore humanity to God, each other and creation, breaking the power of sin, death and the devil. This is demonstrated in forgiveness, healing and deliverance. Luke 8.22–55, for instance, shows Jesus as conquering the devil in the calming of the storm, alluding to the Old Testament battle of God and Leviathan[3] and in the exorcism of the Gadarene demoniac. His triumph over sin and death is shown in the raising of Jairus' daughter and the healing and restoration to the community of the woman made both sick and unclean through her continuous bleeding. The Twelve and seventy-two are told do the same when they are sent out.

God's mission seeks to be radically inclusive

The kingdom seeks to welcome those that people like the Pharisees believed should be excluded.[4] The Jewish system of ritual cleanliness embodied the avoidance of the power of sin, death and the devil. Dead bodies couldn't be touched without passing on impurity. The same was true of the chronically sick, like lepers, who would be outcasts from society, as were the possessed. In a similar manner those seen as sinners would be shunned by people who sought to keep themselves holy. Jesus, in his ministering to a Gentile centurion and the Samaritan and Syro-Phoenician women, points to the reconciliation of all peoples to God. By accepting intimacy from sinful women and touching the dead body of a widow's son he shows his difference from those who, for the sake of their desire for holiness, shunned such people.[5] Following on from the story of the sinful woman, Luke tells us of the female disciples travelling with Jesus, which was unheard of for a rabbi. Jesus sees himself as called out of his way to break these taboos and include excluded people. This demonstrates not just his ability to reconcile these people to God but his intention to reconcile them to each other. The kingdom of God seeks to welcome rather than exclude.

The radical inclusivity of the kingdom is also shown in the call to love one's enemies, and refusing to judge others.[6] It is not that there will be no judgement; Jesus often speaks of such a day, but we are not called to judge ahead of that time. The very different value system of the kingdom is essential for a ministry that seeks to reconcile people in Christ. The evangelist is called to be one who loves, accepts and forgives even those who would harm them.

Making disciples to become Christ's witnesses

Jesus' followers are to do what he has been doing and live as he lived; a change of belief or a profession of faith is not enough.[7] In the classic mission parable of the sower, the seed is recklessly and generously offered regardless of the apparent goodness of the soil; the evangelist is called to sow generously.[8] Response to the gospel is seen through long-term fruitfulness, not short-term acceptance. Indeed, it is rather like the classic evangelistic rally where many come forward but few are active Christians a couple of years later. The evangelist is not to count converts but create disciples.

Jesus' explanation of the use of parables is that it makes his teaching enigmatic and difficult to grasp. Only those who are being discipled get to understand them. Others must rely on the grace of God, not intellectual understanding. After the mission of the Twelve, the theme 'Who is Jesus?' becomes prominent. Jesus is a living parable. He doesn't make sense and can't be fathomed by human reason; only the divine inspiration of the Spirit can enable Peter to see Jesus for who he is. The truth of the gospel is too big to understand and can only be grasped by faith inspired by the Spirit. The same will be true for the evangelist; people don't come to faith because of the evangelist's persuasion but because of the inspiration of the Spirit. Indeed, the enigmatic nature of the message points towards the need for faith before understanding can come and as such is not a barrier to faith but an aid to it.

If the disciples are being called to sow, they are themselves the fruit of Jesus' earlier sowing. At the core there are the twelve apostles, but a much wider group is often present, such as the seventy-two[9] sent out like the Twelve. The numbers carry meaning. The twelve apostles parallel the twelve tribes of Israel. In the Greek Old Testament, 72 is the number of nations in the world in Genesis 10.[10] If the Twelve are a new Israel, the seventy-two are a new humanity. However, the task of both is not to replace Israel or the peoples of the earth, but to witness to them, for them to be seeds sown that bear fruit in the soil of each tribe and each nation. This fits with Paul's description of Peter as apostle to the Jews while he is apostle to the Gentiles.[11] In Jesus' sending out of the Twelve and the seventy-two there is a prophetic image of the mission to the Jews and Gentiles in Acts.

The description of the Twelve as apostles is not straightforward. The use of the verb *apostello*, to send, is common and can refer to a group of people, as the ones sent out. The New Testament use of the word as a title is not the same and there are few parallels in Greek. Indeed, in Acts where we see Luke use the term only of the Twelve, they are the ones *not* sent out in the missionary journeys he writes about. There are parallels in later Jewish use of the Hebrew equivalent, *saliah*, meaning someone who is a representative. This seems likely to be the meaning of apostle as a title in the New Testament. In the later Hebrew usage a *saliah* was given the authority to speak and act as if they were the one who appointed them. The Twelve are called apostles because they will act for Jesus in this way once he has gone. This lies behind the description of them as the foundation of the Church in Ephesians 2. There they are paralleled with the prophets who were also sent as God's representatives. In a sense the role of an apostle is to pass on the mantle of Jesus and bear that mantle in each generation, ensuring that the Church is Christ-like and the mission of God in Jesus entrusted to the Twelve is carried on in each generation. The uniqueness of the Twelve is that they are the ones who received their apostleship direct from the earthly Jesus who is rightly described as the Apostle and High Priest of our faith in Hebrews. That is, Jesus represented God to the world as Apostle and the world to God as High Priest, thus highlighting the incarnational nature of apostolic ministry. Its missionary character is also not just about going in mission but about incarnating Christ; it is therefore about being and doing as much as about speaking. Finally, it is also right to speak of the Church as apostolic; to do so is to say that it is the Body of Christ in mission.

The kingdom is counter-cultural

The kingdom of God is supposed to embrace the world but is not of this world, and so it will be opposed.[12] Herod and the crowd may not have been sure who Jesus was, but the recognition of who Jesus is in the days of the early church means that they refuse to worship Caesar. If Jesus is Lord, no other is; a call to loyalty that will lead to persecution. Indeed, Jesus warns the disciples of this and tells them that the call to follow him means bearing your own cross.[13] Further to this, Jesus' values as presented in the Sermon on the Mount and his desire to include the excluded are deeply counter-cultural.

The kingdom's power lies in weakness

The kingdom doesn't come by conquest or power, but in weakness and humility working to transform society from within, like leaven in dough or the plant from a mustard seed.[14] This is demonstrated by Jesus when he rides triumphantly as Messiah into Jerusalem not on a horse but on a donkey, and also in the very centre of his victory over sin, death and the devil, which is achieved through the apparent defeat of his death.

In Luke 9.1–6, when Jesus sends out the Twelve they are to go as poor and needing hospitality. They are to stay wherever they are welcomed. The cross-cultural missionary is the guest of those they are among; this requires the kind of behaviour one would expect of someone receiving hospitality. This fits well with the teaching on love, generosity and not judging others. Again the theme of Christ as victorious through the apparent defeat of death points the way for the evangelist also; it is in accepting weakness that God's power is shown. We too are drawn to follow Jesus in the missionary call to die and rise with him so that we bear much fruit.

Notes

1 See for instance Luke 6—10.

2 Matthew 4.23; 9.35; 10.7; Mark 1.15; John 5; 8.31–38; 11.1–44; 16.9–11.

3 This also is a sign of Jesus' divinity, therefore.

4 Matthew 9.10–11; 21.31; Mark 2.15–17; John 4.1–42; 8.1–11.

5 Luke 7.1—8.3 covers this account and that of the sinful woman and the women who followed Jesus.

6 Matthew 5.43–46; 7.1–5; 19.19; Mark 12.30–33; John 12.44–50; Luke 6.27–42.

7 Matthew 7.15–27; 25.31–46; Mark 10.17–31; John 8.31–38.

8 Luke 8.4–15.

9 Or seventy, as in other manuscripts. Either fits the passage but the loss of the word 'two' in copying is more likely than its addition; so seventy two seems more likely.

10 The Hebrew has 70 nations not 72, possibly adding to the confusion about the correct number in Luke 10.

11 Galatians 2.7–8.

12 Matthew 5.13–17; 13.24–50; 24.9–14; Mark 13.9–13; John 3.16–21; 7.6–7; 14.30–31; 15.18–19.

13 Luke 6.20–26.

14 Matthew 5.19–20; 13.31–33; 18.1–4; Mark 4.26–32; 10.13–17; John 3.1–10.

8

From Jerusalem to the Ends of the Earth

Sent out in Jesus' place

The evangelists each give a commissioning account, sending the disciples out in mission. Matthew's centres on the authority Jesus passes on to them by which they are sent out to make 'disciples of all nations'.[1] They are disciples, not converts, so they are to live out Jesus' teaching in their lives. The word for nations here in Greek is *ethnos*, implying cultures rather than geographic nations. The emphasis is on establishing the church in each culture with the aim of discipling entire people groups.

Mark's commissioning story belongs to the disputed longer ending.[2] It reads more like a summary of Acts than a genuine commissioning account, but is still instructive. The disciples are to go into all the world and proclaim the gospel to all creation. Mark emphasizes Jesus' rising on the first day of the week as the first day of a new creation. Later in 2 Corinthians Paul declares that there is a new creation; the old has passed away and all is made new.[3] Paul depicts the world being reconciled to God through Christ. The Greek grammar of this passage suggests that the focus is not Christological, as some have translated 'God was in Christ'; rather it is about Christ as the means by which God and the world are reconciled. A translation consistent with the grammar would be 'the world was in Christ being reconciled to God',[4] the old order dies with Christ and the new rises to life with him. This gospel focus is not aimed just at individuals but at the whole of creation.

Whereas the emphasis on baptism in Matthew seems corporate, in Mark it is the one who believes and is baptized who will be saved. Both emphases are needed. As Roland Allen observed, one of the problems with foreign mission was that after people groups became Christians there was too little effort to disciple all the individuals concerned.[5] However, we must also be careful of a western individualism; the point is not that it is wrong for people groups to become Christian en masse, but that all need to be discipled.

John has a short commissioning that builds on the pre-crucifixion teaching about the Spirit.[6] The disciples are sent by Jesus as Jesus was sent by the Father. The gift of the Spirit is breathed onto them as part of this and they are granted the authority to forgive sin. John's model is very much that the Spirit will be with them as Jesus was so they can be Jesus to the world.

Luke puts his commissioning into the book of Acts.[7] Like John, this includes the promise of the Holy Spirit who will enable them to be Jesus' witnesses in Jerusalem, Judea, Samaria and to the ends of the earth. A global mission is again in view, but the territory described records an expansion plan. The mission of the disciples begins in Jerusalem, then heads into the Jewish fringe to Judea and Samaria and then out beyond Jewish territory.

Another to go with the apostles in mission

The Twelve were called apostles because Jesus had appointed them to go in his place; yet they would not go alone. As the upper room discussion in John 13—17 shows, Jesus would send another to be with them: the Spirit of truth, called another, *paraclete* in the Greek. The meaning of this word is much debated.[8] The concept is closely related to that of a legal counsel, but here with a very wide brief. So we see the Spirit testifying on Jesus' behalf and supporting the testimony of the disciples when under opposition from the world, but also enabling the disciples to remember Jesus' teaching and convicting the world about Jesus' power over sin and the devil so that Jesus is glorified.[9]

John uses the Greek word for 'another that is similar' to speak of the Spirit.[10] Jesus has been the disciples' *paraclete*; now the Spirit will come to take over this role after Jesus is gone. The Twelve, having once travelled on mission with Jesus, will now do so with the Spirit. What the disciples were able to do they can still do because God remains with them, both Father and Son, through the presence of the Spirit. This is why it is the coming of the Spirit at Pentecost that relaunches the disciples' mission after the Ascension. The Spirit is essential to evangelism; without him the evangelist cannot witness properly in word or deed, and without him no one can discover the true nature of Jesus and become his followers. Mission requires us to find out what the Spirit is doing and join in.

Crossing cultures from Jerusalem to Judea, Samaria and beyond

Essential to our learning from the mission in Acts is realizing that mission in Jerusalem is between Jews raised in the same faith and is therefore like mission in Christendom. The move from mission in Jerusalem to mission among Gentiles in Acts is today like the move from mission among people with a strong Christian background to those with no such background. At Pentecost Peter preaches to those raised in the same faith. Yet in addition to this the Spirit enables the praise of the disciples to be heard in the different languages of the Jews present from many nations. The parallel with the tower of Babel story is intended. The Spirit enables communication across languages but doesn't end the linguistic distinctions. The Spirit draws the divided peoples together but doesn't create one people with one language, as existed before Babel. The Christian culture does not come to replace all cultures with a new humanity; rather people are to become new beings in Christ while remaining in their culture. Like the leaven in the dough, change comes from within, transforming cultures rather than replacing them.

Escaping Jerusalem captivity

We see from Acts 2 and 3 that the Jerusalem church maintained Jewish temple worship and Acts 10 suggests that Peter
has never broken Jewish dietary law and has kept ritually pure
by avoiding contact with Gentiles. At this point we have a
Jewish group who met to break bread and discuss Jesus' teaching but who saw themselves as Jewish followers of the one they
believed to be the Jewish Messiah. Even with the commissioning to go into all the world there was a large Jewish community
spread across the Roman empire to whom news of the Messiah
could be taken, and some, especially the Hellenists, were used
to seeking proselyte converts to Judaism from Gentiles. As a
new messianic Jewish group a mission to Jews that also created proselytes looked likely. How things actually worked out
forged new understandings that profoundly shaped a Christian
approach to cross-cultural mission.

An essential part of Jewish faith were the purity and dietary
laws that made Jews distinct. To surrender these was unthinkable; many had died rather than do this.[11] For the early followers
of Jesus, the idea of abandoning these laws would be deeply
offensive to the Jews they wanted to convince of Jesus' messiah-
ship. In hindsight the Gospel writers saw in Jesus' teaching the
justification of abandoning these Jewish practices, but the texts
of Acts and Galatians show that they had not realized this at the
time. In many ways the expectation that they were to found a
Jewish messianic movement was a Jerusalem captivity that had
to be escaped if the commission to make disciples of all peoples
was to be fulfilled. Two significant events broke this captivity
and neither were the result of the initiative of the Twelve.

The first arose from tensions between Hellenist and Hebrew
Jewish Christians. The Hellenists were asked by the Twelve to
choose seven from their number to act as administrators to
make sure that food was received by their widows. These men
seem to have had gifts beyond food distribution. A number of Hellenist
Jewish teachers, most notably Philo of Alexandria, had already

engaged with Greek philosophy and culture to create cross-cultural apologetics for Judaism aimed at a Gentile audience. There had also been a strong missionary movement among Hellenists that was mainly responsible for the recruitment of proselytes; one of the seven, Nicholaus, was in fact a proselyte from Antioch. They also had contacts in major cities and regions of the empire. Bearing all this in mind it is perhaps no surprise that the mission beyond Jerusalem and Judea was spearheaded by Hellenist Christians; they were ideally suited to cross-cultural evangelism in a way that Hebrew Christians were not.

The first-mentioned Hellenist is Stephen, perhaps the recognized group leader. His public witness gets him accused, as was Jesus, of threatening to destroy the temple. This charge actually had a grain of truth in it. Stephen clearly taught the destruction of the temple and saw this as God's will. That his approach comes from Jewish apocalyptic literature is suggested by his belief that the temple was no longer the seat of God and his description of it as being 'built with hands': an earthly copy of the true Temple in heaven.[12] The apocalyptic writers believed that Jerusalem temple practice had become heretical and God would replace the earthly temple with the true Temple, 'not built with hands', coming out of heaven, the image we see in the Christian Apocalypse of John. Such thinking put Stephen deeply at odds with the Jewish authorities in a way that had not been so true of the temple-attending Twelve.

Our first introduction to the person who becomes the key character of the book of Acts happens as Stephen is martyred; he watches over the coats of those stoning Stephen. Ironically he is to receive Stephen's 'mantle'. The persecution that follows drives the Hellenists from Jerusalem while the Twelve remain. So it is Philip the Hellenist we next see witnessing in Samaria as the persecution enables the gospel to move from the Jewish centre to the Jewish fringe and out to the once-Jewish Samaritans.

The Gentile mission, however, begins not with the Hellenists or Paul but with Peter, through his encounter with the first person to become a Christian who was not a Jew or proselyte, the Roman centurion Cornelius.[13] He is described as a devout God-fearer but he is not a proselyte, otherwise Peter would not have had to break Jewish purity law to enter his house. Some Gentiles were inspired by Judaism but didn't go through circumcision or adopt Jewish purity law, and so become proselytes; these were often called God-fearers.

Cornelius has a visit from an angel and is told to seek out Peter in Joppa. As Cornelius' men approach Joppa the next day Peter is on the roof looking forward to his lunch. At this point he has a vision of a sheet coming down from heaven full of animals that he both can and cannot eat as part of the Jewish purity law. Yet God tells him to 'get up, kill and eat'. Peter protests that he has never eaten anything unclean. It is difficult to understand just how shocking this is for Peter the Jew, though imagining a Christian who feels it wrong to drink alcohol having a vision of a bar and being told by God to go in and have a few drinks might give some idea. The purity laws marked the Jews out as God's people, the clean from the unclean. So God's reply, 'what God has made clean, you must not call unclean', is deeply unexpected. Peter does not yet have a context for this vision, but will realize that the vision is not just about food purity, it is about the separation of Jews and Gentiles.[14] The mixed animals are understood by Peter to be a vision of a mixed humanity. Hence when entering Cornelius' house he says, 'God has shown me that I should not call *any-one* profane or unclean.'[15] I wonder also if he is thinking back to the foot-washing in John 13 where Jesus tells him that he is clean, so doesn't need a bath, only a foot-washing.[16] Peter has come to realize that God has declared Cornelius and his household clean, as he has been declared clean, and has done so even before Peter has preached to him about Jesus.

When Peter arrives at Cornelius' house not only are his household present but a lot of his friends and neighbours. When he has heard Cornelius tell of his account he says, 'I truly understand that God shows no partiality, but in every nation anyone who fears him and does what is right is acceptable to him'.[17] The word translated nation is *ethnos*, like the commissioning of the disciples in Matthew 28; it is not just the Jewish people who are acceptable to God but all people groups. It is this point that Paul pushes home in insisting that Gentiles do not have to become Jewish in order to be Christian.

If God has declared Cornelius clean, and Peter has acknowledged him as a God-fearer who does what is right, there is nothing to prevent him being invited to be a follower of Christ, so Peter goes on to tell him about Jesus. The understanding here is similar to that in Paul's letter to the Romans where he argues that both Jew and Gentile are judged by God according to the same standard: that of doing what the law requires, not simply having the law.[18] Yet Paul will conclude that all, Jew and Gentile, need to be set free of the power of sin by Christ.[19] Peter never finishes his message; God interrupts him by pouring out the Holy Spirit, as on the day of Pentecost, not just on Cornelius but upon the entire Gentile audience. No wonder the circumcised believers who had come with Peter are amazed! We might be too: no invitation has been issued, and Cornelius has not been led in any response. God acts miraculously to overcome the barriers to Cornelius' acceptance by Peter and makes it obvious that he should be baptized by giving the Spirit first. The problem God had been dealing with was not that there were barriers to welcoming a Gentile in to the church, or indeed that he had any difficulty communicating with this non-Jew, a person not of the faith who was having visions of angels. God's problem was getting through to Peter that he should accept Cornelius, and he knew this was going to be difficult.

As I write this I am reminded of a friend I met through Mind Body Spirit fairs who would not call herself a Christian; she encounters and receives messages from angels, and she paints them. I suspect that God might find it as difficult to persuade some Christians today to welcome her as he did getting Peter to welcome Cornelius. Like Peter, I want her to discover the way I believe Christ fulfils her own spiritual journey but this begins with my respect for her spirituality, believing that God is already at work in her life. Cross-cultural evangelism will challenge our conceptions, as it did Peter's, of whom God wants us to welcome in his name, and our understandings of the way the Spirit works in mission ahead of us.

If God had trouble convincing Peter that Gentiles could become Christians, the Jerusalem church was no different. In Acts 11 they are appalled to hear that Peter has been associating with uncircumcised men and eating with them. For now he manages to win them over by recounting his experience, though they're clearly still rather in shock as they say 'then God has given even to the Gentiles the repentance that leads to life'.[20] This does not resolve the issue. Acts 15 and Galatians 2 record a further disagreement when men from the Jerusalem church tell Gentile Christians that they cannot be saved unless they are circumcised. Paul tells us that even Peter stops eating with the Gentile Christians. The issue is clearly only partially settled at the council in Jerusalem recorded in Acts 15, which agrees that Gentiles don't need to be circumcised to become Christians. There are Jewish Christians in Galatia still trying to persuade the Gentiles to be circumcised when Paul later writes his letter to them.

Cross-cultural mission to the Gentiles

Cornelius' story is a one-off, not a targeted mission to Gentiles. The Gentile mission begins in Acts 11 when Hellenist believers from Cyprus and Cyrene preach to the Greeks[21] when they get to Antioch. The result is that Antioch becomes the first mixed Gentile and Jewish church with a mission to both communities. This marks it out as something other than a Jewish sect; hence this is the first place the disciples are called Christians. The Jerusalem church is again concerned about Gentile believers, and sends Barnabas to find out what is happening. Barnabas, pleased with what he sees, sends for the recently converted Paul. Barnabas fulfils a crucial role legitimizing the new expression of church, vouching for its genuine character to the existing church and giving affirmation to the new church.

By Acts 13 Antioch has replaced Jerusalem as the missionary

centre of the church. Jerusalem would still have a special role, so in Acts 15 the council takes place there; and later Paul calls for support for the Jerusalem church, acknowledging its special status. The centre, however, has shifted to Antioch, as it would later shift to Rome. The nature of the mission shapes the church and does so in strategic places; Antioch is the empire's third city, making it an ideal mission base. Paul similarly plants churches in the major cities of a region, using them as local mission bases.

From synagogue to market place

During the first missionary journey, in each place Paul and Barnabas preach at the synagogue. After Lystra, where they end up preaching by accident to Greeks, we note a new strategy in Athens.[22] Paul not only goes to the synagogue, he also preaches in the market place and debates with Epicurean and Stoic philosophers. This is the first attempt to target Gentiles directly, separate from the Jewish community. This move is not without difficulty: among those familiar with Judaism he could quote the psalms and speak of the Messiah, but being understood by Greek philosophers was another thing entirely.

We have no record of Paul's discussion with the philosophers in the market place, but Acts records them being quite rude about Paul, calling him a *spermalogos*, someone who picks up bits of knowledge but doesn't really know what he is talking about.[23] They also clearly struggle to understand him, taking him to the Areopagus as someone speaking about foreign gods or spirits called 'Jesus' and 'Anastasis', the Greek for resurrection. The Areopagus message, however, suggests that Paul has been doing some 'double listening' and has learned from these encounters.

In Ephesus in Acts 19, Paul preaches in the synagogue for three months, but after opposition repeats the pattern from Athens; here going to the lecture hall of Tyrannus. The Greek calls this a school: a place where young men could learn the arts of philosophy and rhetoric. Famous examples were the schools of the Sophists, Socrates, Plato and Aristotle. Luke tells us that he debated there daily for over two years, enabling many people to listen to him and discuss with him. As in Athens, this moves Paul very much from the Jewish to the secular and Pagan context.

Preaching shaped by context

Peter's message on the day of Pentecost was preached to an entirely Jewish audience. It made sense, therefore, to quote the prophets and seek to show Jesus as the Messiah, drawing on what they knew. Much of Peter's address relates these scriptures to current events, especially questions raised about the disciples' actions. His intention is to get people to change their view of who Jesus is, and he clearly succeeds, as we are told of about 3,000 converts. We find a similar approach by Peter in Acts 3. However, Peter's sermon to a Gentile audience in Acts 10 doesn't contain such Old Testament quotes or proofs that Jesus is the Messiah; he just relates an account of recent events the disciples have witnessed in Jerusalem and that Jesus has been appointed judge of all people.

A good example of Paul's message to Jews is Acts 13.16–41. This passage begins with the call of the people of Israel and a brief history leading to David, presenting Jesus as his heir and Messiah. The death and resurrection of Jesus is then spoken of in relation to prophecy centred on David and now seen as fulfilled in Jesus. Jesus changes the situation of the listeners enabling forgiveness wider than that offered by the Law of Moses, extending it both to sins that the law excluded and to non-Jews.[24]

In each place that he visits, Paul's preaching is among the Jewish community at the synagogue.[25] Greeks do come to faith but this happens at or in the vicinity of the synagogue. It is worth noting phrases like 'the devout Greeks' or 'converts to Judaism' as descriptions of these people.[26] The Greeks then seem to spread the word, so for instance in Antioch in Pisidia in Acts 13 we see that most of the town goes to the synagogue the next sabbath after the word has been spread by proselytes among the Gentile community. What is crucial to note in these examples is that Paul preaches a Jewish message to a Jewish audience. However, there are also proselytes and God-fearers present, people who are Greek but who know the Jewish faith so they can understand Paul's Jewish message. If, as in Acts 13, others are attracted to listen to Paul it is because they have been spoken to by Greeks versed in Judaism.

At Lystra the healing of a crippled man leads local Gentiles to decide that Barnabas and Paul must be Zeus and Hermes in human form and they have trouble persuading the priest of Zeus not to sacrifice a bull to them.[27] These Greeks are not familiar with Judaism, so Paul takes a different approach. He tells them that the good news they bring is that they

> should turn from these worthless things to the living God, who made the heaven and the earth and the sea and all that is in them. In past generations he allowed all the nations to follow their own ways; yet he has not left himself without a witness in doing good – giving you rains from heaven and fruitful seasons, and filling you with food and your hearts with joy.[28]

It is clear that Paul wants them to turn from Paganism to Christ, but his attitude to Paganism reflects that of the Old Testament. The Pagan deities are related to the experience of nature, and Paul appeals to this as a witness to the goodness of the living God who is not only the creator of all but is seen in nature. In effect the Pagan deities are partial revelations of God in the Greek pantheon, just as they were in the Canaanite. What has been attributed to the different deities is now shown to be the deeds of the one God.

In Athens Paul enters into a more deliberate engagement with Greek religion.[29] This begins with him noticing the idols that fill the city. This was no cursory glance; he had studied the statues enough to note one dedicated to an unknown god. We know from history that there were several of these in Athens; a desire to honour all religions led to the repair of old altars even if the deity it was dedicated to was no longer known. The altar would be rededicated 'To an unknown god'. Also we have an account by Diogenes that in about 600 BC the Cretan philosopher Epimenides appeased the gods when a plague threatened Athens by releasing sheep to roam the area and, when each lay down, sacrificing it to 'the unknown god' of that spot.[30] Diogenes records altars erected at these sites still standing in the third century AD. Paul quotes Epimenides in his address, so it may well be that the story Diogenes recorded was known in the Athens of Paul's day.

As in Lystra, Paul turns to nature and Pagan religion as witnesses to the one true God of all creation. Such a God can't be represented by an idol in a temple. This Old Testament[31] idea was also present in a Greek philosophical critique of pantheism by writers like Euripides and Plato. Paul quotes two pieces of Greek Pagan poetry from this tradition to emphasize the nearness of God to humanity. The first is from Epimenides, the possible builder of the altar to the unknown god. The full quatrain is written as an attack on his fellow Cretans for building a tomb to Zeus on Crete.

> They fashioned a tomb for thee, o holy and high one –
> The Cretans, always liars, evil beasts, idle bellies! –
> But thou art not dead; thou livest and abidest for ever,
> For in thee we live and move and have our being[32]

Paul quotes the second line at Titus 1.12, which suggests that he did indeed know this piece. The second quotation is from Aratus' *Phainomena*, and is also about Zeus. The last line, from which the quote comes, is 'In every way we have all to do with Zeus, for we are truly his offspring'.[33] Paul's audience would be familiar with both of these, which praise Zeus not as a member of a pantheon who could die but as a supreme and immortal deity. Applying language used of Zeus to Yahweh is completely consistent with the Old Testament approach and enables Paul to speak of God in ways his audience will understand.

If the following of idols in the past was excused because of human ignorance, Paul warns them that a time for judgement is coming, so it is now time to repent, and turn away from idols to God. The appointed judge is a man attested to by being raised from the dead. Jesus' name is not mentioned in Luke's account here, though we know he was preaching about Jesus and the resurrection in the market place earlier. The idea of someone being raised from the dead is clearly too foolish for some, and Paul may well have left this key part of his message until last for this reason. However, others want to explore this further, and some, including a member of the Areopagus, come to faith. The impact is clearly not as great as had been the case among those connected to the synagogue, but Paul is reaching a new audience while leaving believers within their culture.

Some have argued that following the 'failure' of the Athens sermon Paul abandoned this cross-cultural approach in Corinth, citing 1 Corinthians 2.2 where he says, 'I decided to know nothing among you except Jesus Christ, and him cruci-fied.' However, in all the accounts of Paul's preaching in Acts, Jesus' death occupies only a small proportion of his message as part of an explanation to Jewish audiences about how this ful-fils the scriptures about the Messiah.[34] Indeed there is often no mention of Jesus' death, the main emphasis being on the mes-siahship of Jesus and the resurrection rather than the cross.[35] This is as true of Acts sermons after Athens as it is before. Of course, Paul has much to say about the cross in his letters, and it certainly forms much of his teaching to Christians about the work of God in Christ. However, he cannot be seen as advocat-ing a gospel message reduced to a core of the cross when this is clearly not how he himself explains the Christian message to others. In fact his approach is strongly geared to his audience, in keeping with his statement in 1 Corinthians 9.19–23 in which he speaks of becoming like a Jew to win Jews and a Greek to win Greeks. Paul's approach builds from the position of his listeners to a need to respond to Jesus as Lord and Saviour and thus his message changes according to his context.

Signs of the kingdom

Throughout Acts we see a continuation of the healings and miracles that were part of Jesus' ministry. These often lead to successful evangelistic outcomes. Yet in Ephesus in Acts 19, despite miracles of healing and deliverance happening caused just by cloth Paul had touched, they seem to have had little impact. It is only later, in verse 18, that we read of many believing; and it is only after this that the makers of artefacts for use in the worship of Artemis, the main deity in Ephesus, begin to be worried that the number of people becoming Christian will harm their trade. The fact that Artemis is the local deity and the description in verse 18 of many magicians coming to faith is perhaps the clue to this lack of impact. Artemis, Diana in the Roman usage or Isis in the Egyptian, was a deity strongly associated with magic. Ephesus would have been full of magicians, among whom Paul would have seemed to be just another. This may be why the strange story of the sons of Sceva is the turning point. This group of travelling Jewish exorcists, impressed by Paul's own deliverance ministry, decide to employ his approach, trying to cast out a demon in the name of Paul and Jesus who he preaches. Their attempt is a failure. I suspect they assume that Paul is using a spell to cast out demons and are attempting to copy his formula. Their failure proves that it was not a spell at all, and therefore Paul isn't a magician. This makes the magicians take notice of him, which is why so many of them are among the first converts.

The situation Paul faced here is not unlike that of the church in our day. People are very open to healing through Christian prayer, but also to healing from all sorts of practices. Without the miraculous it is hard to get a hearing for a Christian faith deemed 'unspiritual'. However, it takes something other than the miraculous to suggest that there is more to the Christian message.

Christianity and Paganism

We have seen how in his preaching to Greeks Paul drew on Pagan imagery and poetry to speak about God, in the same way as the Old Testament writers did. The Acts 19 account of his ministry at Ephesus tells us more about his approach to Paganism. The temple of Artemis at Ephesus was one of the seven wonders of the ancient world, dominating the city. Any threat to the temple would be a major issue. It is on these grounds that Demetrius the metalsmith incites a riot, accusing Paul of preaching against the temple and its deity. Yet in verse 37 the town clerk says that Paul and his followers have clearly done no such thing. Neither the message in Lystra nor that in Athens could be described as an attack on Greek religion either. Indeed, the Athenians are complimented on their religiosity and their beliefs used to speak of God. It is clear from Acts and the epistles that Paul believed that God could not be worshipped properly through idols, and as Paul pointed out in Athens, many Pagans also thought that. This is why he tells the Corinthians not to participate in ritual feasts in Pagan temples, but is happy for them under other circumstances to eat food sacrificed to idols in people's houses or after it was sold in the market place.[36] For Paul, Paganism could perhaps be seen to point to Jesus and Pagan ideas incorporated into Christianity, but Jesus could not become another idol in a Pagan temple. So while Paul didn't attack Pagan religion, he certainly expected Christianity to replace it. In this perhaps Demetrius did have something to fear, even if his accusation against Paul was false.

Paul's explanation of his missionary method, becoming all things to all people, comes in the context of discussing religious freedom and participation in ritual Pagan feasts in 1 Corinthians 9. So Paul freely enters Pagan temples, reads Pagan writings and quotes them as pointing to Christ. He debates with philosophers and Pagans on their own territory and will join in the lecture programme alongside the philosophy and religion curriculum. He is free to become like a Pagan religious teacher, so that Pagans can hear about Jesus in their own culture. Like-wise when he goes to the synagogue he will observe the Jewish customs he was raised in, and debate in the manner of a rabbi for the same motive: that Jews might discover who Jesus is in their culture.

The motive of all coming to faith in Christ also means choosing not to do things that may hinder that end. So later he says that while God can be thanked for all food, if a Pagan host points out that the food about to be eaten has been sacrificed to an idol, Christian guests shouldn't eat it, to prevent them being wrongly understood as idol worshippers by the Pagan host.[37] The main principle is contained in verses 32 and 33: 'Give no offence to Jews or to Greeks or to the church of God, just as I try to please everyone in everything I do, not seeking my own advantage, but that of many so that they may be saved.' This meant that Paul would not attack the worship of Artemis, but could not be seen as advocating it either; he must always be an advocate of the worship of Christ even when arguing for that from Paganism.

Paul has no place for a Christian polytheism. This differs from the Pagan approach of the day, which assumed that foreign gods were really the same as the local ones and parallels were sought and dual dedications created to form a new pantheon of harmonized foreign and local deities. A classic example would be the shrine of Sulis-Minerva at Bath in England. Minerva was a river goddess associated with springs and sacred wells in the Roman pantheon. Sulis was a Celtic deity worshipped at a sacred well in British pre-Roman Bath. The Roman baths built around the Celtic sacred site from which the city is named were thus dedicated to Sulis-Minerva, a harmonization of both deities.

Sometimes parallels are drawn between Jesus and ancient Pagan deities. So Jesus is seen as being like Osiris, who dies and rises from the dead, or the sacrificed Mithras. Mary has simi-larly been compared to Isis, Osiris' mother. The similarities are indeed there, but how are these to be understood? Some have tried to argue that the story of Jesus is simply another version of that of Osiris, for instance, indeed that all these stories are different local expressions of a universal set of stories that are essentially all the same; this is the way the Pagans of Paul's day thought. The result of such an approach might be a temple of Jesus-Osiris alongside one of Mary-Isis in first-century Alexandria. This is what Paul's approach doesn't allow for. Instead, following Paul, the Coptic mission to Alexandria used the myth of Osiris as a prophecy of Christ, and turned the temples of Osiris and Isis into Christian churches. However, it would *not* be consistent with Paul's approach to send a mission to Alexandria that denounced the worship of Osiris, told people to surrender anything that was associated with it, and then destroy the temple and build a church on another site to break all association with the Pagan past. Such an approach would be to reject all that Paul fought for in insisting that Gentiles did not have to become Jews to be Christians.

Creating Christian communities

The early chapters of Acts are marked by the impressive community life of the Jewish believers who held their goods in common, cared for one another and were filled with joy. Meeting for worship and teaching formed a part of this too. The text tells us that this witness led daily to people being added to their number.

We note that on each of Paul's journeys he leaves a Christian community and appoints elders to oversee them. The next two missionary journeys contain a pattern of return visits and he stays much longer in each place teaching the church, continuing that connection through his epistles. It is quite apparent from these that the local leaders are in charge and may well decide a course of action different from that advised by Paul. Roland Allen contrasted this with the tendency of colonial churches to run their foreign mission churches from home and send out leaders to run them rather than use indigenous leadership.[38] He also commented on Paul's trust in the Spirit as guide to local Christians, though it seems to me from the epistles that he wasn't always sure they had heard the Spirit correctly! The point is that local expressions of church should develop, though I note that there is no evidence he planted two churches, one for Jews and another for Gentiles. If the gospel was different to each community, its message of reconciliation was meant to draw them into one body.

Notes

1 Matthew 28.16–20.

2 Mark 16.14–20.

3 2 Corinthians 5.14–21.

4 This translation not only fits the grammar, it also fits the theology of early church fathers like Irenaeus and other passages in Ephesians and Colossians. The other option is the softer 'the world was being reconciled to God in Christ'; but in both cases the world is reconciled to God, and the means of that is Christ.

5 Roland Allen, *St Paul's Missionary Methods or Ours?* Original 1912; this edition in D. Paton and C. H. Long (eds), *The Compulsion of the Spirit: A Roland Allen Reader*, Eerdmans, 1983.

6 John 20.21–23.

7 Acts 1.6–8.

8 For a good discussion see Leon Morris, *NICNT: John*, Eerdmans, 1971, pp. 662–6.

9 See John 15.18—16.4; 14.25–26; 16.4–15.

10 There is an alternative word for 'another that is different'.

11 One of the best examples was the refusal to abandon Jewish purity laws during the reign of the Greek monarch Antiochus. The story of this is recorded in the books of Maccabees.

12 Acts 7.48.

13 See Acts 10.

14 Though Peter's experience clearly does have implications for food purity, leading to statements in the Gospels; written of course much later than Peter's experience, where the Gospel writer understands Jesus to have declared all foods clean to eat, for instance Mark 7.19. It is clear from Peter's reaction here that this was not how the disciples understood Jesus at the time but they came to realize the implications of Jesus' words later.

15 Acts 10.28.

16 John 13.10.

17 Acts 10.34–35.

18 Romans 2.6–16.

19 Romans 3.9–26.

20 Acts 11.18.

21 Some manuscripts have Hellenists at this point but that version makes no sense. The point here is to contrast preaching to Jews with the innovation of preaching to Greeks. Since Hellenists were Jews and preaching to Hellenists was clearly already well established, there is no reason to point that out here. Further, unless the issue is that Greeks have joined the church at Antioch the sending of Barnabas by the Jerusalem church to check what is happening makes little sense. Nor does the needed defence of a Gentile mission based in Antioch by Paul and Barnabas in Acts 15.

22 Acts 14.

23 Verse 18.

24 The long sentence in 13.38–39 is not straightforward, and it uses twice a key word in Paul's epistles, the Greek *dikaioo*, meaning to justify. It contains a contrast between what Jesus does and what the Law of Moses could not do, relating to being justified. This approach has sometimes been misinterpreted as suggesting that Paul believed forgiveness was a new thing not offered by the Jewish Law which was based on 'works righteousness'. This contrast has now been largely rejected for one in which it is accepted that the Jewish law clearly offered forgiveness through the sacrificial system, but the scope of that forgiveness did not cover all sins or those who were not Jews.

25 There appears not to have been one in Philippi (Acts 16.11–13), but it is clear that the place of prayer they went to functioned on the sabbath, suggesting it was the nearest equivalent to the synagogue there.

26 Acts 17.4; 13.43.

27 Acts 14.8–18.

28 Acts 14.15–17.

29 Acts 17.16–33.

30 Diogenes, *Lives of the Philosophers*, 1.110.

31 For instance Isaiah 66.1–2.

32 This version is from M. D. Gibson, *Horae Semiticae*, X, Cambridge, 1913, p. 40.

33 The NRSV rendition of the quote in Acts 17.28 misses the special *gar kai* combination in the Greek, 'for and' in English, which should be rendered 'for truly' as per the quotation cited from Aratus. NRSV thus mistakenly translates Paul as saying 'for we are also' when it should be 'for we are truly'.

34 Acts 13.16–41; 17.22–31; 22.3–21; 26.2–23. All contain long

From Jerusalem to the Ends of the Earth

addresses by Paul: the first a message to Jews, the second to Greeks, and the last two being centred on his personal testimony and defences of it. Acts 17.3 tells us that Paul explained that the Messiah had to suffer and rise from the dead, which is similar to the full sermon of Acts 13 and also appears in the Acts 26 sermon before Herod. Acts 18.5 tells us that Paul proclaimed to the Jews that Jesus was the Messiah. Acts 17.18 tells us Paul had been proclaiming the good news of Jesus and his resurrection from the dead. The resurrection theme is mentioned again in Acts 23.6 and appears in the Acts 13, Acts 17 and Acts 26 sermons and in Paul's defence of his actions in the temple in Acts 24.15. In Acts 20.21, Paul says that he preached repentance to God and faith towards Jesus to both Jews and Greeks, a theme present in more depth in the Acts 17 and Acts 26 sermons, the last of which mentions forgiveness too. In other places references are made to him proclaiming the kingdom of God (Acts 19.8; 20.25; 28.23, 31). On numerous occasions we are told that he proclaimed the good news or simply the word of the Lord, but are given no indication of the content.

35 The same is true of Peter's Acts sermons; although his epistles make salvation through the cross a clear part of his belief, it is not part of his evangelistic message.

36 1 Corinthians 10.14—11.1.

37 1 Corinthians 10.23—11.1.

38 Allen, *St Paul's Missionary Methods or Ours?*

9

The Post-Apostolic Age and
the Birth of Christendom

The separation of Jews and Christians

Paul's mission began in the synagogue and then moved to
the market place, leading to mixed Jewish/Greek churches.
Growing tensions between Christianity and rabbinic Judaism
made this process increasingly difficult; even Jewish Christians
found it hard to go to the synagogue. Judaism was recognized
as different from the Pagan religions of the empire and Jews
were allowed special religious privileges. In AD 49 Christians
were ordered from Rome by Claudius, as part of the expulsion of Jews.[1] Suetonius suggests that the cause was internal
arguments in the Jewish community between Christians and
Jews, suggesting that at this time Christians were still viewed,
in Rome at least, as a Jewish sect.[2] That in AD 64 Christians
were targeted in Nero's persecution shows that they were then
viewed as separate.

Much early Christian apologetic was aimed at showing
Christianity's Jewish heritage. This was not only missionary
but defensive, arguing that Christians should share Jewish privileges. Justin in his *Apology* developed this, seeing the Jewish
inheritance not as having been widened to include the Gentiles
but as being replaced by a very Gentile Christianity. His writings did not yet show the enmity for Jews that would develop
later; in his *Dialogue with Trypho the Jew*, this Jew was a
friend to be respected, but his faith was seen as superseded.
As relations between Christians and Jews later deteriorated,

such apologetics increasingly argued for God's abandonment of the Jews in favour of Christians. History was cited in support of this: first the destruction of the temple and then after Constantine the good fortune of the faith in the empire. In 361, however, the new emperor Julian rejected Christianity and sought to re-establish Paganism. Part of his plan was to destroy the Christian appeal to history by rebuilding the temple and removing imperial patronage. Julian made little progress in his short reign; he died 18 months later. However, he may have caused a hardening of the church's attitude towards Pagans and Jews. So John Chrysostom attacked both Julian in his *Demonstration to Jews and Greeks that Christ is God*, and Judaizers and Jews in his *Homilies*, with abusive rhetoric that would set the tone for an increasing anti-Semitism during the medieval period.[3]

With some periods of repression, Jews had received tolerance from the emperor. The church increasingly opposed such tolerance. During the reign of Theodosius, a North African Christian mob incited by the local bishop looted and destroyed a Jewish synagogue at Callinicum. The emperor felt that this was criminal activity and ordered the church to pay reparations to the Jewish community. Bishop Ambrose of Milan insisted that the church would do no such thing and threatened to excommunicate the emperor if he pressed his case. The emperor backed down.

Jerome, at the start of the fifth century, reported that orthodox but thoroughly Jewish Christian churches still existed in Palestine. While distinguishing them from the heretical Ebionites he condemns them for being neither Christian nor Jew, and writes against Augustine's affirmation of distinct Jewish Christian practice.[4] However, these churches seem to have disappeared by the end of the century, caught between Jewish and church rejection. Though the edict of Justinian in 529 exempted Jews alone from becoming Christians,[5] it was not unknown for them to be forcibly baptized anyway, a practice that would become more prevalent over time. A once persecuted Jewish sect had become a Greek faith that persecuted Jews.

The gospel in Greek culture, incarnation and heresy

The fact that Christianity became an increasingly Gentile faith meant that its missionary activity become focused on Greco-Roman culture. The early apologists, like Justin, showed their connection to Judaism by borrowing Philo's approach in advocating Judaism to Greeks. Links between Moses and the Greek philosophers were demonstrated, but Moses was argued to be older and superior and even the source of the philosophers' ideas. Christian apologists then argued that Jesus fulfilled the Mosaic revelation, and that Christians were the true heirs of Jewish faith and Greek philosophy. In this tradition Justin developed Plato's idea of the Logos found in the Gospel of John, arguing that Jesus was the Logos that inspired the prophets and the philosophers, Greek philosophers being 'schoolmasters for Christ'. Others would continue this tradition, ensuring the legacy of Plato and Aristotle as the basis for much Christian theology.

Not all shared this approach. Tertullian argues:

> What has Jerusalem to do with Athens, the Church with the academy, the Christian with the heretic? Our principles come from the Porch of Solomon, who had himself taught that the Lord is to be sought in simplicity of heart. I have no use for a Stoic, or a Platonic or a Dialectic Christianity. After Jesus Christ we have no need of speculation, after the gospel no need of research.[6]

Tertullian was versed in classical philosophy and used its methods in debate, but believed that God was not revealed in human thought or culture. Indeed, the gospel was 'irrational', being not open to human understanding but only grasped by the inspiration of the Holy Spirit. This approach would form the pattern of a recurring debate down the centuries between those who believed that God could speak through non-Christian faiths and cultures and those who saw an exclusive revealed faith standing against the false wisdom of human culture and belief.

While philosophers like the Stoics sought to found more noble moral standards, Greek and Roman religion had a pantheon of largely immoral gods. In contrast, Jewish moral teaching had drawn Roman admiration and led to their special status. Christians could lay claim to this moral code in contrast to their Pagan neighbours. In his attempt to re-Paganize the empire, Julian complained that the reputation Christians had for charity and good deeds made them far more attractive than their Pagan neighbours. He exhorted them to match these good works if the empire were ever to become Pagan again. Not all aspects of Paganism were seen as pointing to Christ.

The use of Greek language and philosophy in mission also determined the church's own language in defining orthodoxy in the creeds. Heresies were influenced by the Greek philosophical view that humans were spirits imprisoned in bodies and needed to escape from the corruption of matter. So the Greek for salvation, *soteria*, was used in most literature to express freedom from the trials of the physical body, both its appetites and its sufferings, ultimately expressing a desire to be disembodied. This was very different from the Hebrew use of *yasha* which expressed being free from political oppression or slavery.

To a Greek, the phrase 'Jesus saves' might suggest that he rids us of the physical body so we could be disembodied spirits. The idea that Jesus would have a real human body, allow that body to be crucified and for God to raise that body after death was unthinkable. Hence the Docetic heresy, which argued that Jesus only appeared to have a physical body; he was not crucified and thus not raised, but simply ascended. Gnosticism later combined this with the idea that the world was created by the devil. Paul's Corinthian epistles suggest that he might have been refuting Docetism. The late first-century epistle of Clement to the Corinthians and several early second-century epistles of Ignatius clearly do so. If incarnational mission meant that Greek religion, philosophy and language were used in evangelism and church life, it also meant guarding against elements of Greek thought and culture that might threaten the essence of the Christian faith.

While the church fathers saw and rejected these Hellenizations with regard to the understanding of Jesus, in other areas they may have allowed them to seep in. Paul distinguished between the body as the temple of the Holy Spirit, and the flesh as the fallen nature, but from the post-apostolic period the church has had a tendency to view the physical body as innately bad and the source of sin, in line with Greek ideas otherwise seen as heretical. Sex especially was viewed as leading to sin, and with Augustine's formulation of original sin as sexually transmitted, an emphasis developed on celibacy as the only holy way to live. In Aristotle the procession of the Spirit of the divine placed women lower than men and only just higher than animals. Gnosticism viewed women as especially sinful, referencing the role of Eve as corrupter of Adam in Genesis. Such approaches can be seen in much Christian writing, hampering the realization of Paul's vision in Galatians 3 of a restored relationship of male and female, reversing the division of Genesis 3. Similarly the focus of salvation shifted towards entry into heaven after death rather than the coming of the kingdom of God on earth. In all these areas Greek thought had a negative impact on the church.

The formation of Christendom

Christians were sporadically persecuted from AD 64 until they were granted toleration by the edict of Milan in 313. Persecution seems to have pushed much church activity underground, including mission. However, we know that Christianity had reached Britain, the farthest outpost of the empire, by some time in the third century. A large convergence of Roman Christian remains in the south-east of England and around Hadrian's Wall suggests that some beliefs at least accompanied the movement of Roman legions. Christianity was developing a reputation through its martyrs for bravery and a costly faithfulness, both appealing attributes to soldiers. If this was happening at one end of the social spectrum, the increasing sophistication of

Christian scholars, especially those associated with the Alexandrian Christian academy like Clement and Origen, was winning followers among the elites. In spite of persecution Christianity was proving resilient and spreading across the empire and through all areas of society. This perhaps made it the perfect choice for a new emperor forced to fight for control of the empire and seeking to unite it.

To what extent Constantine actually became a Christian is a matter of dispute. He was not baptized until he was near death; Stuart Murray is not the first to suggest that this was so he could carry on behaving in a way that might lose his salvation if he had been baptized earlier.[7] He did, however, take an interest in theology, presiding as a non-baptized emperor over the council of Nicaea. His aim seems to have been to ensure unity rather than any personal opinion. In this his likely lack of deep Christian conviction may have oddly been helpful.

If Constantine made Christianity the imperial religion he did not stamp out Paganism. This too was tolerated by the state, but Christian privilege certainly helped draw people to the church in large numbers. Doubts about people's motives for becoming Christian meant that the initiation period of teaching became very important, but also much harder to administer with large numbers seeking baptism. After Constantine's death in 337, with the exception of Julian's brief rule the emperors were Christian and gave patronage to the church. In 391 and 392 Theodosius issued edicts banning Pagan sacrifices and began closing Pagan temples. In 416 employment in the civil service and the army was restricted to Christians. In 438 the Theodosian Code advocated enforced church attendance on Pagans who wanted their children to be educated and enforced the baptism of those children. Finally, Justinian's edict in 529 made conversion to Christianity mandatory for all but Jews. Worship of the emperor had been the imperial cult everyone had to follow or be condemned as a traitor; now it was Christianity, but with an important difference. While sacrifice to the emperor was compulsory, people could also practise any number of tolerated faiths; now only Judaism was tolerated, and barely. People had no choice but to be Christian if they were citizens of the empire and its colonies.

The Church and Paganism, from incarnation to conflict

The church fathers continued Paul's use of parallels in Pagan stories that could be applied to Christian imagery. Orpheus, who had been to the realm of death and returned, was depicted as a shepherd bearing a lamb. Statues of Orpheus became statues of Jesus the Good Shepherd. Early Copts in Egypt altered pictures of Isis holding Osiris to become what we now know as the classic image of Mary seated with the infant Jesus.[8] This tradition also enabled Constantine to continue the imperial cult of *Sol Invictus* (the Unconquered Sun). Its worship was centred on Sunday, by then established by Christians as the Lord's day in commemoration of the resurrection. Constantine declared Sunday a public holiday. Similarly he set the date of Christmas at 25 December, the festival of *Sol Invictus* when the days begin to lengthen after the solstice, which became the festival of the one called the Light of the World.[9]

As the fourth century progressed and Christianity emerged as the faith of an empire, a distinct shift began to emerge. If many early Christian apologetics were pleas to Rome for religious tolerance, now it was Pagans seeking tolerance from the emperor. A notable example was Symmachus' appeal for toleration. This was strongly opposed by Ambrose, just as he had opposed support for the Jews. This was justified by the argument that 'error has no rights', stating that only the champions of truth could be persecuted; what happens to those in error is simply their just penalty. On such logic only Christians could be the victims of persecution, Jews and Pagans could not be. The persecuted church was becoming the persecutor.

If it could be said of Paul in Ephesus that he neither blasphemed Pagan deities nor attacked their temples, the same could not be said of Martin of Tours.[10] In the fourth century Martin, with Hilary of Poitiers, founded the first western monastery. He remained there after becoming Bishop of Tours, making it the base for a mission to convert the Franks. An essential part of this was the destruction of Pagan shrines, idols and sacred groves as a demonstration of the powerlessness of the Pagan deities in the face of the true Christian God. The method was effective, but it was distinctly not in the same tradition as Paul or Justin. Perhaps then the great irony is that among the Germanic peoples, St Martin's Day became a way of continuing the autumn festival of Wotan in the increasingly common practice of reattributing the cult of the Saxon, Norse and Celtic deities to famous saints.[11] Martin's conquest approach to mission would be an increasing trend as the church adjusted to the new situation of power in the empire.

With the code of Justinian the linkage of conquest and mission would be inevitable; all subjects of the empire had to be Christian by law. This certainly created Christian nations, but were people really converted? Whereas the approach of those who sought to show how Christianity fulfilled Pagan religion risked syncretism, at least the Christian faith was positively embraced by converts. Martin may have set people free from fear of Pagan Deities but he may also have simply scared people into Christian faith, allowing their superstitions to be transferred from the old faith to the new.

Notes

1 See from Acts 18.2.

2 Suetonius, *Life of Claudius*, 45.4.

3 Avery Dulles, *A History of Apologetics*, Ignatius Press, 2005, pp. 69–70.

4 Jerome, *Letters*, 112.13–14.

5 *Code of Justinian*, 1.11.10.

6 Tertullian, *Prescription of Heretics No.7:36*, English translation Samuel L. Greenslade, LCC. As quoted in Dulles, *A History*, p. 52.

7 Stuart Murray, *Post-Christendom: Church and Mission in a Strange New World*, Paternoster Press, 2004, p. 31.

8 For further information see Anton Wessels, *Europe: Was it Ever Really Christian?*, SCM Press, 1994, pp. 29–54; Michelle Brown, *How*

Christianity Came to Britain and Ireland, Lion, 2006, pp. 27–47; Dulles, *A History*, pp. 27–87; and Bosch, *Transforming Mission*, pp. 190–213.

9 Wessels, *Europe*, p. 42.

10 Martin was an early fourth-century Roman soldier who famously divided his cloak for a beggar only to find that he had clothed Christ; he then became a monk.

11 Wessels, *Europe*, pp. 121–2.

10

Mission in Christendom and the Medieval World

The marriage of church and state – the genius and failure of Christendom?

A key figure in the theology of Christendom was Augustine of Hippo. When the church had been persecuted by the state, joining it was a risky action; now it was a state religion and everyone was assumed to be a member, raising questions for some about the commitment of the newly Christian population. The Donatists believed that the church and political power should not mix; the world was sinful and the church ought to be set apart from it.[1] In their eyes the new, state-approved church was becoming deeply corrupt, sinful and worldly. Augustine opposed them, applying the parable of the wheat and the tares[2] to the church as a place one should expect to find sinners. He also championed Cyprian's doctrine that becoming part of the church through baptism saved you regardless of whether you fell into sin again. For Augustine the schism of the Donatists threatened the unity of the church. For the Roman authorities it threatened the unity of the empire.

The Donatists wouldn't yield, leading Augustine to decide, following Luke 14.23, that they should be 'compelled to come in' again to the church they had been permanently baptized into. He considered physical coercion acceptable to do this and the state willingly applied it. Others would later apply this logic to mission by conquest. One possible consequence of Augustine's action was the eventual collapse of North African Christianity.

The Donatist controversy turned the regions' churches against themselves, contributing to them being ill-equipped to survive the coming of Islam. As Nthamburi argues, 'When Saint Augustine co-operated with the civil authorities to suppress the Donatist Church he did not realize that he was sounding the death knell of his own church.'[3]

In the early fifth century the British theologian Pelagius also condemned the moral laxity of the Roman church. Augustine's doctrine of original sin taught that people couldn't resist sin even after conversion, but were saved by the irresistible grace received at baptism regardless of how they lived. Pelagius argued instead that through a process of transformation by the Spirit, people could live holy lives but the free will and discipline of the believer inspired by Jesus' example was essential for this. One might wish a third party had offered a middle way, stressing both the need for God's grace and the aim of Christ-like living for Christians. As both Bosch and Murray point out, Pelagius represented the orthodox approach and Augustine was viewed as an innovator.[4] If Augustine eventually won the argument he did so only after the emperor intervened to persuade the pope to change sides. Even then, the final condemnation of Pelagianism at the Council of Ephesus in 431 didn't condemn Pelagius but only his follower Celestius. Much support for Pelagius continued, especially in the Celtic church. As late as 807 Pelagian influence was still in evidence in the *Commentary on the Book of Armagh*.

Murray suggests that Augustine's position was prompted by the reality that in declaring all citizens members of the church, for most faith would be purely nominal. For Bosch, Augustine's teaching effectively turned the call to follow Christ into one to join the church and be assured of your soul's place in heaven, though he is positive about Augustine's rejection of the Donatists' call to withdraw from the world.[5]

The work that formulated the pattern of medieval Christendom was Augustine's *City of God*, written after the shock of the sack of Rome by the Visigoths in 410. Augustine imagined two cities, the earthly and the heavenly. The heavenly, represented through the church, was to be master of the earthly in good society. This didn't make the boundary of state and church identical, but certainly made them intimately linked. It also enabled the church to become the true authority and bearer of culture and good order for society amid a crumbling Roman empire.

Augustine's work also contained a partly realized eschatology. If ultimately we had to wait until Christ's second coming for the kingdom, the thousand-year rule spoken of in the book of Revelation had begun in the Christian empire. The church ruled on God's behalf until Christ returned. With Augustine also emphasizing that salvation came through membership of the church, which was nearly the same as citizenship of the state, deviance from the teachings of the church became an act of treason, and rebellion against the state an act of heresy. Therefore civic and religious penalty could and did follow either.

Could the church fathers have handled the situation differently? Murray, writing within the Anabaptist tradition, offers a number of alternatives. Bosch, however, agrees with Newbigin that the church had to embrace political responsibility at a time of social decay and, while critical of Augustine, feels that he made the only choices sensible at the time.[6]

While agreeing with Augustine's insistence on engagement with society, I am not convinced his approach was the only option. If the church's agenda was to transform the empire into the kingdom of God, the emperor's was to bolster the unity of the empire by making Christianity its religion. In the gradual blurring of the boundaries between church and state, these agendas seem to have become confused. In the terms of Jesus' parable, if the kingdom is like leaven that works through the dough to transform all of it, the Donatists wanted to take the leaven out, whereas Augustine declared the dough already finished regardless of how people lived. Had Augustine seen the empire as an unleavened batch of dough and the church as the leaven within it, he could have argued for the church's role as state religion but also insisted that church and state could not be the same thing, as the church's calling was not to baptize society but transform it. Such an approach would have challenged the Roman concept of state religion in which all citizens were expected to be members as a sign of loyalty and commitment to the empire. However, if the emperor had chosen to favour Christianity because the other religious options were failing him, the church may have had considerable leverage. Perhaps a civic religion with an annual compulsory service but not compulsory membership might have been possible?

The early Christian emperors, while making Christianity their official religion, allowed a toleration of other faiths. If the church had not opposed this it might have enabled church membership to remain a calling rather than a birthright. Ironically it may have been the insistence of people like Ambrose against the toleration of other faiths that led to the corruption of his own. Pelagius' call to work for Christian lifestyle and not just church membership should also have been heeded. Augustine, while he had the vision for the empire to become the kingdom, sadly chose to emphasize the unity and salvation of all the baptized and the place of the soul in the next life rather than the call to holiness in this one. In doing so he probably ensured the victory of the worldly city over the heavenly one. Just as in the pre-Constantinian period, incarnation into Greek culture led to issues in which accommodation was unhelpful, so the same was true in Christendom.

The rise of monasticism and its missionary consequences

As Christian morality in the empire came under question, early monasticism emerged as a counter-cultural movement within the imperial church that would become central to its mission. Bosch notes an affinity between the Assyrian and Celtic churches and the desert fathers. All had a strong asceticism and operated as travelling preachers and healers in the style of Acts, as opposed to the increasingly civic-based church in the empire. The desert fathers sought solitary withdrawal to live a holy life, as Hunter and Bosch point out, whereas the early

Catholic and Celtic monastics formed communities that were inherently missionary: places of learning, healing and agricultural development, transforming the lives of those around them.[7] Within the empire this would affect the lives of local Christians, especially the poor. Beyond the empire, however, it was a far more evangelistic engagement and one that became consciously organized as such.

Mission beyond the empire and indigenous Christianities

Not all the church was within the empire, and thus after Constantine there was a church beyond Christendom. In the East, churches that were largely affiliated to the Assyrian Catholic church had spread prior to the fourth century as far as India and China via wandering healer/missionary bands. It seems that wandering monks carried on missionary activity until the colonial period, when Catholic colonial powers went into India and China and replaced Assyrian-linked patriarchs with Roman Catholic bishops and sought to introduce Latin mass to the indigenous but Syriac-speaking churches. Reports from those who encountered these communities, traditionally associated with the apostle Thomas, suggest that many grew out of Syriac-speaking Jewish communities, pointing to a synagogue-based mission like that of Paul.

After the withdrawal of Roman troops in the fifth century, the British church found itself potentially isolated. Though trade with the empire via Gaul and the Mediterranean continued for several centuries, Roman civic organization began to crumble. Whereas in Gaul the bishops were ideally based to take over the positions of governance in the cities, in Britain the Roman cities were gradually abandoned and communities returned to rural areas. This led to a rural church often based around former Roman villas. These show evidence of adapting Pagan religion to Christian use, with *nymphaeum*, that is, ritual pools often originally British Pagan sacred wells, turned into baptismal pools; they were incised with Chi-Ro symbols and decorated with mosaics and frescoes using Pagan imagery to depict Christian themes. This is very much in line with the approach of the pre-imperial period on the continent.

Soon Pagan Saxons and Angles from the north of the empire began invasion and settlement from the south and east, pushing the Christian Romano-British community to the western fringes of Britain, cutting them off from the continent. Western sea routes remained but this relative isolation enabled the British church to develop differently. Unlike their Roman counterparts, Celtic monastic communities often included non-monastic residents, some becoming small towns of several thousand inhabitants.[8] Many were co-monasteries with male and female houses, possibly including married members. Whereas on the continent the bishop was clear head of the local church, in Britain the bishop was often a member of the monastic community and subordinate to the abbot or abbess who were the key church leaders.

If Germanic tribes hedged in the Romano-Celtic kingdoms of Britain to the east, to the north and west were Celtic countries not conquered by Rome. These were primarily Pagan, though clearly not entirely so, as there was a sufficient Irish church before St Patrick to warrant Pope Celestine sending Palladius as their bishop in 431. In Patrick, however, the British and Irish churches would be drawn together. Patrick was a British Christian, captured and sold into slavery in Ireland; he escaped, dedicated his life to God and then later returned as a missionary among his former captors some time in the fifth century.[9]

Accounts of Patrick's mission have been embellished and may include the stories of other saints, but they offer a picture of the Celtic church's approach to mission. Patrick challenged the Druids by performing miracles that undermined their spiritual power, but also adopted their practices. A classic example is the account of Patrick extinguishing the Beltane fire, lit on May Day and maintained throughout the year by the Druids, and then relighting it from the Easter candle. Similar is the story of Col, a representation of the Celtic sun god.[10] Col seeks to kill Patrick but is instead converted and becomes a Christian saint. Many Celtic gods were transformed into Christian saints by having their legends and religious festivals applied to the saint. It is worth noting that Patrick 'defeats' Col not by killing or banishing him but by converting him. The story is a parable of the way Pagan religion itself became Christianized by the Celtic missionary monks. This set it apart from the Roman tradition of Martin, who destroyed the shrines he encountered.

The Celtic church was a fusion of Celtic Pagan practice with Roman-British Christianity. It contained the asceticism of the desert fathers and mothers, the learning of Roman monasticism and the awareness of the divine presence in nature of the Pagan Celts, along with the preservation of Celtic festivals and devotions paid to saints in the place of Pagan deities. Patrick's mission changed the British church as much as it Christianized Ireland just as the mission to the Gentiles had changed the Jewish church in the first few centuries. This powerful new expression of Christianity would send missionaries from Ireland into Pictish Scotland, where the British Ninian had already established a foothold, then on into Northumberland and the continent under Columba, Aidan and Columbanus.

If the Celtic church evangelized Celtic Pagans, the mission to their enemies the Saxons was undertaken by the continental church through Augustine of Canterbury. Augustine was sent by Pope Gregory to Kent to meet its Saxon king Ethelbert, whose wife was a practising Gaulish Christian, in 597, the year Columba died on Iona. He arrived with 40 monks, seeking the king's protection for a mission to the English. Ethelbert, like Constantine, saw the promotion of the new faith as a chance to forge alliances and extend his own power among the Saxon English and supported Augustine. Their missionary method was the conversion of local rulers who then encouraged the baptism of their subjects. Sometimes these baptisms were enforced; other rulers, like Edwin of Northumbria, called assemblies to involve the people in the decision over their kingdom's faith. For a while faith remained dependent on the ruler, and areas initially converted to Christianity reverted to Paganism several times under future rulers before settling as Christian areas. The political issues involved are demonstrated by the fate of the devoutly Christian king of East Anglia and monk, Sigeburt. He demonstrated that the pacifist tradition of the early church was alive and well in the seventh century when he refused to fight the Pagan Mercians attacking his kingdom. He was forcibly dragged onto the battlefield by his people, who felt they needed their king at their head, but he refused to take up a weapon and fight, and died in the battle. The royal advisers decided that Paganism was much healthier for their kingdom's welfare.

Gregory had instructed Augustine to use the religion he found among the Saxons as a basis to introduce the Christian faith. Holy places were stripped of idols but reused rather than destroyed; customs and festivals were Christianized, enabling a synthesis of Roman faith and Saxon expression to develop. In this at least the Christianization of Saxon England was not radically different from that of Celtic Britain. The key issue for the Saxon church was the teaching of people who had in many cases become Christian by royal edict, and monastic founda- tions were set up for this purpose.

Augustine was far less accommodating to the Celtic church. On the continent Columbanus was in dispute with Pope Gregory over issues such as the dating of Easter, highlighting a Celtic disregard for Roman practice. Augustine was charged with drawing the Celts in to the Roman fold. This got off to a bad start. When Augustine came to meet the Celtic church leaders he was backed by Ethelbert's army and would not rise to greet the British, who thus dismissed him as a proud ungodly politi- cian. The presence of Ethelbert did not help either, reminding them that submission to Rome was in effect submission to their Saxon enemies. They refused to accept Augustine's authority and instead argued for the rightness of their own position. Augustine warned that this would precipitate war with the Saxons instead of peace as fellow Christians. The Celts heard this as a threat, a fear realized in 615 when the Catholic king Ethelfrith slaughtered 1,200 unarmed Irish monks praying for a British victory at the Battle of Chester.

Increasing Saxon military pressure and the fear of isolation led the Celtic church to yield to the Roman church at the Synod

of Whitby in 664. The arguments at Whitby about the date
of Easter and the nature of monastic head-shaving can appear
trivial. However, the pope had changed the date of Easter and
the Celtic church saw itself as guarding the true tradition.
The Celtic tonsure was druidic in origin;[11] the monks took
the appearance of Druids for the sake of mission, whereas the
Roman monks adopted a standard appearance regardless of
local culture.[12] Gildas tells us that the Roman church saw the
Celtic tonsure as a sign of witchcraft, suggesting that they no
longer saw Pagan religion as a preparation for Christian faith
but as demonic superstition to be fought. This may explain
why the later seventh-century lives of Patrick by Tírechán and
Muirchu both portray the saint in almost military terms fighting the Druids, in contrast to the more gentle tone of Patrick's
own surviving letters and the few earlier pieces we have.[13] The
Synod of Whitby may be a turning away not only from local
expressions of faith in favour of those dictated from Rome, but
also from the early church's incarnational approach to cross-
cultural mission towards an increasingly martial and colonial
approach.

Mission as imperial expansion and the homogenization of the Church

The spread of Roman Christianity increasingly followed the
Saxon model, with kings and monks working together. This
became tied to the conquests of the Franks after the conversion of Clovis who established the Frankish kingdom. Like
Ethelbert, Clovis was married to a Catholic Christian prin-
cess.[14] Belief that the Christian God had given him victory
over the Pagan Alemanns convinced Clovis to adopt Catholic
Christianity in 496. Declaring this to be the faith of his people
he was baptized in Rheims, with 3,000 others, by the missionary Remigius. Clovis saw mission as both political and religious
expansion; monastic missionaries would destroy Pagan shrines
while Catholic rulers conquered Pagan tribes, demonstrating
the superior power of the Christian God. Frankish kings like

Charles Martel in the eighth century were significant sponsors of missionaries such as Willibrord and Boniface. The letters of the English monk Boniface sent back from the continent to his bishop, Daniel of Winchester, show how the military and political power of Charles was essential in defending missionaries and in the destruction of Pagan shrines.

The final identification of church and state came under Charles' grandson, Charlemagne. After becoming ruler of the Franks in 771 he expanded the kingdom into an empire that stretched from Britain to eastern Europe. Charlemagne viewed all his subjects as Christians and his enemies as enemies of the faith. This vision proved useful to the papacy in Rome where on Christmas Day 800 he was crowned Holy Roman Emperor.

Charlemagne shared with the papacy a concern to standardize and centralize Christian practice across the new empire. In some areas this led to Roman practice being introduced but in many ways it led to Germanic culture shaping the rest of the church, Christianizing Pagan German customs as well as destroying Pagan temples. A classic story tells how in 724 Boniface cut down an oak sacred to the Pagan deity Donar before thousands of locals, who expected their god to strike Boniface down. Boniface's hagiography records that as he cut the oak it was split by a mighty wind, falling to the ground in the shape of a cross. A church was built from the timbers and from the stump grew a pine that was the first Christmas tree.[15] Pagan tradition in the shape of the Christmas tree became part of Christian practice, while at the same time its shrines were destroyed. Other Germanizations include the naming of Easter, after the Saxon deity Oestre, and moving All Saints' Day from Pentecost to 1 November to fit with the Germanic/Celtic new year celebration from which the Christian All Hallows Eve comes. This festival preserves the veneration of the ancestors in All Saints and All Souls, but portrays the ousted Pagans as witches and their deities as demonic forces.

The western church also produced apologetic in Germanic style in works like the *Heiland*, an epic poem. This retells the Gospels as a Saxon saga with Jesus and his followers depicted as German heroes. Depicting Christ as a warrior in Saxon culture was not dissimilar to the *Pantokrator* iconography of the all-powerful ascended Christ in the post-Constantinian church; it reflects a church with political power that equates military expansion with mission. This was evident throughout the conquest of Scandinavia through the tenth to twelfth centuries where conquered rulers converted at sword-point then enforced baptism on their own subjects. This pattern was still evident in the early colonial expansion of Spain and Portugal towards the end of the medieval period. Mission was only deemed necessary in such colonial situations; Christian monarchs viewed their subjects as fully evangelized, only needing pastoral care through the parish system. The legacy of this identification of church and state would be a European culture based on Christian learning and morality, but also one in which diversity was not tolerated, Christian faith was enforced and religious persecution normal. In our postmodern, post-Christendom age this legacy of religious violence is one of the major barriers to Christian mission.

Notes

1 The Donatists formed in opposition to the consecration as Bishop of Carthage of Caecilian. They said he had recanted his faith under the persecution of Diocletian and believed that no one who did this could be a priest.

2 Matthew 13.24–30.

3 Zablon Nthamburi, 'The Donatist Controversy as a Paradigm for Church and State', *Africa Theological Journal* (1988) 17(3): 204.

4 Bosch, *Transforming Mission*, p. 216; Murray, *Post-Christendom*, pp. 100–1.

5 Murray, *Post-Christendom*, pp. 101–2; Bosch, *Transforming Mission*, pp. 216–18.

6 Murray, *Post-Christendom*, pp. 102–8; Bosch, *Transforming Mission*, p. 222.

7 George G. Hunter III, *The Celtic Way of Evangelism*, Abingdon, 2000, p. 28; Bosch, *Transforming Mission*, pp. 231–3.

8 Hunter, *Celtic Way*, pp. 28–30.

Mission-Shaped Evangelism

9 Traditionally the date is 432, a year after Palladius; see Hunter, *Celtic Way*, p. 15. Brown, *How Christianity Came*, thinks later dates more likely.

10 The name Col means 'one-eyed', referring to the great eye of the sun.

11 See Lewis Spence, *History and Origins of Druidism*, Kessinger Publishing, 2003, p. 53, which cites Gildas' discussion of the Celtic tonsure. The Romans said that it came from Simon Magus, but Gildas knew that it came from the Druids in Ireland. See also Tadhg MacCrossan, 'Druidic Vestments', in *Llewellyn Encyclopedia*, www. llewellynencyclopedia.com/article/194 (accessed 1 September 2008); and J. A. MacCulloch, 'The Druids', in *The Religion of the Ancient Celts* (1911), Forgotten Books, 2007. These latter two authors link the druidic practice to Roman accounts by Strabo and Pliny that spoke of them as *Mael*, translated 'bald' on account of the tonsure giving the effect of a very receded hairline.

12 See Hunter, *Celtic Way*, p. 41.

13 See Liam de Paor, *Saint Patrick's World: The Christian Culture of Ireland's Apostolic Age*, Four Courts Press, Dublin, 1993, pp. 154–97.

14 Most Germanic Christians had been Arian.

15 Wessels, *Europe*, p. 10.

152

I I

Mission after the Renaissance

The Renaissance as background to the Reformation

The beginnings of the Renaissance date back to the rediscovery of Classical thought from the Muslim world in the thirteenth and fourteenth centuries. The first evidence of this would be on Christian theology, most notably in the influence of Aristotle on Thomas Aquinas. By the fifteenth century it had led to a Classical revival in art, literature and the birth of what would become modern science. This was marked by a turn from the divine to the human as the centre of the universe and from the heavenly to the earthly as the centre of interest and exploration. This is demonstrated clearly in the art of Raphael, Michelangelo and Leonardo da Vinci. Gone are the ethereal forms of the medieval artist and the false perspective of the icon painter, in which painting was a window onto another, heavenly dimension. The new artists were painters of reality and creation, with flesh and blood human subjects taking central place. Yet this reality is highly idealized, especially in its muscular and voluptuous portrayals of men and women in classical form.

The Renaissance turn to the human is not yet a turn from religion, though in my view the atheist humanism of the eighteenth century is the clear descendant of the Christian humanism of the fifteenth. The subjects are often still Christian, yet in a very different form. A famous example is Michelangelo's Sistine Chapel. God creating Adam is its centrepiece, yet both are given the muscular naked torsos of Greek or Roman gods. The glory of the perfect human form is at least as much the artist's intent as the glory of God. If biblical themes would be reinterpreted, art until the mid-nineteenth century would also be dominated by scenes from classical Pagan literature and epic poetry.

The patrons of this art were also significant. The Medici family in Italy, for instance, were Catholics, several being popes, but they also represented a growing group among the nobility and the emerging middle class across Europe whose wealth came from trade and who sought new political and economic structures at the start of the colonial period. They were patrons of scientific enquiry as well as the new art; both represented human reason as the measure of all things. Following in this tradition, theologians like Savonarola and Erasmus called for church reform and advocated the relationship of the individual to God.[1] In this they were forerunners of the Reformation and witnesses to the growing dissatisfaction with the medieval world-view amid the changing world order.

For Luther and the reformers, people related to God through the work of Christ independent of the church, and God spoke to individuals through scripture alone and not church pronouncement. However, neither the Lutheran nor Calvinist traditions would abandon the notion of the Christian nation. Equally neither advocated total religious tolerance; both assumed the pursuit of right doctrine and saw this as a state issue. Christendom continued in Protestantism but lost the universal form it had achieved with one pope and the Holy Roman Empire. Indeed, this was much of Protestantism's appeal to European princes; they wanted release from the power of the emperor and pope, without danger of being excommunicated. Similarly it offered a faith suited to an age where human independent thought was coming to the fore. As such, this was a reformation of Christendom, and one suited ideally to the emerging modern world after the Renaissance.

Protestant mission after the Reformation

Mainstream Protestantism didn't challenge the notion that the evangelization of Europe had been completed. Protestant mission was only conceivable in new territories ruled over by a Protestant monarch, as indeed happened in Swedish-controlled Lapland. A few Protestants went further, believing the Great Commission to be complete and any nation not Christian to be either not elect of God or to have rejected the faith and deserving of its fate. This lack of missionary vision was compounded by the rejection of the monastic life by all streams of Protestantism at that time getting rid of the main missionary force of the medieval period.[2]

The exception was the Anabaptists, who earned their name from insisting that the church had become apostate and its sacraments invalid, hence the need to baptize people again; and this baptism was only for adults who had made a personal profession of faith. Unlike Luther and Calvin, Anabaptists saw Europe not as Christian but in need of conversion. Also unlike most of the reformers, they rejected paid priesthood and parish boundaries. For the Lutherans and Calvinists the call was to reform the local church through the ministry of duly appointed ministers; for the Anabaptists it was to travel the country preaching to all and seeking their conversion. None of this made the Anabaptists popular and they were persecuted by Protestant and Catholic alike, but they were in effect the forerunners of the modern Protestant missionary tradition.

Catholic mission after the Reformation

In the early modern period, while the Anabaptists were re-evangelizing within their own culture, the Catholic Church was engaging afresh with cross-cultural mission through the colonial expansion of Portugal and Spain. This began in the established Christendom manner with the imposition of European culture on conquered foreign subjects as part of mission, but this approach was challenged by the new Jesuit order after the Counter-Reformation. The Jesuits' approach to mission was pioneered by Francis Xavier in the early sixteenth century in India and then Japan, followed by Matteo Ricci in China later in the sixteenth century and Robert De Nobili in

India in the early seventeenth. All adopted local dress and custom, and looked for contact points in local faith and culture. Between them they converted hundreds of thousands of people and established churches with their own local expression of Christian faith.

The work of the Jesuits was supported by the Roman *Congregation for the Propagation of the Faith* of 1659, which instructed missionaries not to force cultural change on foreign converts. However, this attitude had changed by 1704 when the papal envoy attacked the indigenized practice of the churches in India and China. The pope agreed and a papal bull of 1744 forbade any but minor accommodations to local custom. This was not rescinded till 1938. The Jesuits themselves were proscribed in 1773 and their missionaries withdrawn. Though they were reinstated in the nineteenth century it was not until the latter half of the twentieth century that local leadership and expressions of faith would begin to become normal in former Catholic colonies. The difficulties Donovan had in defending indigenous expressions of church among the Masai later in that century show that in many ways Catholicism still sees Roman practice as normative and struggles with the concept of inculturation.[3]

Colonization and mission in Protestantism

At the start of the eighteenth century, as opposition to the Jesuit Catholic missions was beginning, new Protestant mission agencies like the SPCK and SPG were forming in England and sending missionaries to the British colonies. These societies saw colonialism as in itself missionary and westernization as part of Christianization. In the first centuries after the Reformation only the church itself was seen as a legitimate agent of God's work; the monastic orders had been abolished on such grounds and similarly wandering evangelists of the Anabaptist type were frowned on. Increasingly, however, the principle that the individual was the interpreter of scripture led to an ever-increasing fragmentation of Protestantism as new churches formed around differing interpretations. In this sense Bosch is right to say that the formation of mission societies was little different from the formation of new churches, both were in effect Christian voluntary agencies formed by like-minded Christians.[4] If this is so it might also be argued that the voluntary nature of such societies has had a negative impact on the concept of the church being itself an agent of God's mission; mission was becoming something that a few enthusiasts did rather than something the whole Body of Christ was called to.

One of the important dimensions of mission in the eighteenth and nineteenth centuries was the impact of the evangelical revivals in Britain and America. In America at the time of the new constitution, although the nation was seen as Christian, church membership was only about 5 per cent of the population.[5] The first Great Awakening under Jonathan Edwards stemmed from a belief that people needed evangelizing, as the Anabaptists had in post-Reformation Europe. He had a vision for mission in other cultures, at home among Native Americans and abroad in the European colonies. Edwards also envisioned America as the global centre of the coming of the kingdom of God around the globe. This sense of America's global missionary destiny would inspire America above all other nations to form missionary societies in the following centuries, spreading both the Christian faith and American culture, making foreign mission, coupled with business expansion, America's alternative to European colonialism.

In Britain similar events were connected to the revival led by the Wesleys and George Whitefield. The Wesleys had encountered Moravian inheritors of the Anabaptist tradition while travelling as missionaries with the SPG to the American colony of Georgia. This had a significant impact on the revival of their faith and on their subsequent calling to mission across Britain. John Wesley, when challenged not to preach outside his own Anglican parish, declared that 'the whole world is my parish'. He challenged the Protestant assumption that all that was needed was the pastoral care of Christian England. As in America, an offshoot of the evangelical revival was not only a new belief that Europeans needed evangelizing, but also a new calling to foreign mission. William Carey, himself a convert of the evangelical revival in 1779, formed the Baptist Missionary Society and travelled to India. There he pioneered much of what has become modern practice in foreign mission: the translation of scripture into local languages, a programme of education, the introduction of western medicine and the founding of local industry to provide work for the indigenous population. Smaller evangelical revivals also spawned new mission agencies in Switzerland, Holland and Germany.

Initially British colonies were military trading posts and their sole aim was financial gain for the home country. The local population was seen entirely as slave labour for economic advantage in the colonies. The early missionaries challenged this assumption and often found themselves in conflict with the colonial trading companies who did not welcome their presence. This changed in the nineteenth century as colonial rule sought to extend British 'civilization' and missionaries became agents of the civilizing process. Christianity and western culture were seen as linked and superior to all others. Missionaries rarely questioned this, and so cross-cultural mission of the kind undertaken by the Jesuits was highly unlikely, even if officially in mission society protocols churches were supposed to reflect their locality.

Mission as a reflection of modernity

While the mission societies expanded their work and became part of the colonial system, secularism was increasingly challenging Christianity in the sending nations. For the first time Christianity was not trying to demonstrate its worth against other religions but having to defend the very notion that God existed, leading to a shift in apologetics. Medieval apologetics often pointed to the triumph of Christendom and its superior wealth and culture as proof of Christianity's divine favour, and this continued in the colonies. At home, apologetics shifted to meet the need set by a post-Renaissance world to justify belief by reason. Conversion came to be seen as a rational decision, having been convinced of the truth of Christianity. This generated a debate about the need to educate the 'natives' in the colonies in order for them to have the intellectual capacity to accept the Christian faith.

Through the nineteenth and twentieth centuries three main responses to secularism based on human reason developed. The liberal approach supported human reason as the source of truth and morality, but believed this to be God-given and thus also revealing Christian truth and morality. This tended to equate scientific progress and western civilization with Christianity. The beliefs of the past reflected primitive understanding, and modern faith was called to jettison those that no longer seemed plausible. This was especially true in the demythologizing associated with theologians like Rudolf Bultmann, in which biblical miracles became allegorical tales not based on real events, or alternatively the false impressions of primitive believers for which there were now better explanations. The gospel message in this tradition tended to be about Jesus as moral example and the vision was for the kingdom of God to come through God's work in human progress. This led to a view of mission as social transformation inspired by God rather than personal evangelism. Apologetics in this tradition pointed to the moral benefit of Christianity, and the human psychological need for God.

An alternative approach came from the evangelical tradition of Edwards, Wesley and Whitefield. These went back to Luther's instance that scripture alone is authoritative. The debate within this tradition was about the relationship of science and reason to scripture. At one end of the spectrum a tradition of biblical scholarship developed in which reason and scientific discovery were seen as enabling better understanding of scripture, while rational apologetics enabled its teachings to be argued as reasonable. This approach argued for the historical accuracy of scripture and the reasonableness of the miraculous in central areas like the resurrection. In other areas it argued that scriptural truth was not necessarily scientifically true, so Genesis did not propose an alternative to evolutionary theory but declared God as the source of creation in what was a poetic text.

Other evangelicals would defend the Bible from rationalism by insisting that scripture was inerrant and scientifically accurate. The faithful Christian was to trust in the truth of scripture and reject the falsity of other views. This tended to be accompanied by an anti-apologetic approach in which faith was not something one chose after reasoned thought but something that took hold of one through preaching or divine inspiration. It was still, however, seen as rational and revealed by God in the plain meaning of the scriptures.

The early evangelicals were prominent campaigners for social justice. Later evangelicals increasingly saw social action as a liberal agenda and concentrated on the primacy of personal evangelism. Mission became the activity of winning souls for heaven. This had implications in the colonies; where once evangelical missionaries had opposed the practices of colonial traders, such issues were no longer seen as part of their calling. This gospel was put forward in a very individualistic and modernist way, appealing to the individual human conscience and feelings of guilt and shame. If reason was the guide to truth, then the conscience was the guide to morality. A guilty conscience was a sign of the presence of sin, the need for repentance and God's forgiveness. The gospel message became an explanation of the cross as God's answer. This was an effective response to the problem of the guilty conscience. It relied, of course, on people having guilty consciences. That most of the population until the later part of the twentieth century in Europe were nominal Christians may well have helped ensure that people tended to feel some guilt at their personal failings and falling short of what they had been raised to believe was their Christian duty.

In line with a tendency to reductionism in later modernity, preaching the gospel came to mean almost exclusively preaching the cross as the solution to humanity's problems and inviting a response to this message. In the consumer world of the twentieth century this reductionism led to a 'formula-selling' approach to evangelism in which a set presentation of the product is followed by a request for a set 'buying' response. One approach to mission could be to learn simple presentations of the cross and ways of showing the need for salvation and how to respond, and then merely repeat them door to door. Booklets on the four spiritual laws such as *Journey into Life* were created similar to the pamphlets used by a travelling salesperson. These would spell out the 'client's' need and show how the cross answered it. With the benefits of becoming a Christian now 'sold' you had to make sure the potential convert counted the cost of becoming a Christian, and then you led them in the 'sinner's prayer', the means by which they 'bought' the gospel 'product'.

In many ways this was inculturation, and worked for large numbers in a modernist Christendom context. It could be so simple in part because people had already been brought up knowing the message. However, it has very little in common with the evangelism in Acts or throughout the history of cross-cultural mission. Neither does it work with the post-Christendom non-churched; it doesn't allow them enough space to explore and fails to answer their questions or speak into their context. In this today's Alpha course is a move in the right direction, but it still bears too many traits of the formula approach. Further to this in a postmodern culture increasingly cynical about sales techniques and spin, the preacher can become another dodgy salesperson almost certainly out to con you.

The third major approach to modern rationalism was a Catholic one, both within the Roman church and within Anglicanism following the birth of the Anglo-Catholic movement in the late nineteenth century. Authority is placed in the church in a similar way to the authority of scripture for evangelicals. It is perhaps then no surprise that as some evangelicals were declaring scripture infallible as an alternative to scientific authority at the end of the nineteenth century, Roman Catholics were declaring the pope infallible. Both were attempts to support truth claims that contradicted science. Important to this Catholic approach was the appeal to an unbroken church leadership going back to Jesus himself. One could look back at the history of the church and see it as solid and dependable, a place of God's continuous favour. In a sense such an approach enabled the Catholic Church in particular to carry on as if Christendom was firmly in place until Vatican II in the 1960s.[6]

Conservative evangelical and Catholic approaches may have allowed some Christians to feel confident in their rejection of modernism, but they also led to an increasing sense that, for these Christians at least, the modern world was an enemy to be opposed. Yet at the same time the modernist insistence on rational human thought was dictating the terms of their refutation of modern theories just as much as it was guiding liberal Christians to embrace them as Christian. Traditional Catholicism and conservative evangelicalism might have based their authority on appeals to the origins of the church, but the very way they did this made these appeals expressions of a modernist version of Christianity just as much as liberalism. In the end neither conservative nor liberal approaches provided much ground for an apologetic that might both engage with modernity and offer Christianity as something distinct from a religious modernist humanism. As Dulles puts it:

> Until the enlightenment the churches were on the whole quite secure in their position. The apologist, speaking from the stable platform of official Christianity, whether Protestant or Catholic, had only to refute their adversaries . . . By the beginning of the twentieth century . . . the thoughtful apologist is likely to be situated in a no-man's land between conservative Christians and radical unbelievers.[7]

Alternative voices to the rationalist missionary paradigm

Against the norm, some voices rejected the use of reason as the basis of faith. Blaise Pascal, writing in the seventeenth century, suggests that experience of the Christian life enables faith, not rational proof. Indeed for Pascal, rather than belief leading to joining the church and living a Christian life, we are invited to join the church and try out what it is to be a Christian in the confidence that this experience will lead us to believe.

At the end of the nineteenth century, French philosopher Maurice Blondel dismissed attempts to argue that Christianity was factual in accordance with science.[8] Doing so confused two different approaches to reality; Christianity was simply unprovable by scientific standards. Indeed, even if it could be proved, why should that make it any more relevant than any other proven facts? Likewise, attempts to prove Christianity by appeal to its moral benefit were likely to end up demonstrating that it was just a good form of humanism. For Blondel, faith could be discovered only through experience. Equally the end of faith was not, as the rationalists supposed, right belief but right living.

Søren Kierkegaard, writing earlier in the nineteenth century, also attacked rationalist apologetics, arguing that any expression of faith that could be explained by rational argument must be a human construct and not in fact the true Christian faith, which was beyond comprehension and explanation. In many ways these voices anticipated the postmodern turn from truth as facts demonstrated by reason to truth as experience.

New approaches from the foreign mission field

In the foreign mission field of the twentieth century, voices would begin to be raised against the mission paradigm in which westernization was as much a part of mission as evangelism. I have referred earlier to the work in this area of Allen, and later Bosch and Donovan. As Bosch points out, this would take until the 1970s and 1980s to work its way into mainstream mission thinking in both Protestant and Catholic churches with the development of an inculturation approach to foreign mission, declaring that the 'universal word only speaks dialect'.[9]

As Allen suggested, this should be seen as a recovery of the approach to cross-cultural mission that was consistently followed in the mission of the church until early Christendom. If this has not been the primary approach for a thousand years, this is because Christendom created a false notion of a Christian nation with a Christian culture. As we enter into a mission beyond Christendom it is time for us to abandon our Christendom approaches to evangelism. There is now only foreign mission, a global phenomenon requiring in each culture churches born anew arising from a gospel spoken only in local dialect.

Notes

1 Dulles describes Savonarola as surprisingly modern in this regard. (*History of Apologetics*, p. 142).

2 Anglicanism was to reintroduce it several centuries later, and in recent times new monastic orders have also started to develop in other Protestant traditions, but these are all recent developments in what has generally been a non-monastic church tradition.

3 Donovan, *Christianity Rediscovered*.

4 Bosch, *Transforming Mission*, p. 329.

5 Bosch, *Transforming Mission*, p. 279.

6 Bosch, *Transforming Mission*, p. 262.

7 Dulles, *History of Apologetics*, p. 271.

8 This was, first, in the closing section of *L'Action* (Paris, 1893) and then in response to a discussion of that paper in *Annales de philosophie Chrétienne* (1895) in 'A Letter on Apologetics' (1896) published in the same journal.

9 Bosch, *Transforming Mission*, pp. 452–3, quoting P. Casaldáliga.

PART THREE

Mission-Shaped Evangelism in the Twenty-First Century

12

Reviving Cross-Cultural Evangelism after Christendom

How is the gospel affected by culture?

One of John Hull's criticisms of the *Mission-shaped Church* report is that it doesn't explore the incarnation of the gospel in other cultures. It is easy for us to assume that we 'know what the gospel is' and thus miss the implications of the question, 'What is the gospel in this place?' What scripture and early church tradition show is that while the gospel is eternal in that it is about the mission of God from creation to new-creation with the work of Christ at its heart, the gospel message is expressed differently in each cultural context. How Christian belief is expressed has already changed many times during its journey across different countries and through time to where we are now. Indeed, the belief in a universal expression of church and culture is not in keeping with the tradition of God's mission but instead formed by concepts of imperial religion.

The way culture affects faith cannot be seen as something we 'add' to the gospel message either, and therefore it is not something we can strip away to reveal a pure core of faith at its centre. This idea reflects the reductionism of modernity and is like understanding the incarnation as Jesus wearing a human outer garment while inside remaining God. The church councils were keen to stress that all of Jesus was both fully God and fully man, and so no part of the encounter with God in Christ is not mediated through his humanity and his humanity as a first-century Galilean Jew. If the gospel is the story of the mission of God, the 'Jesus event'[1] is central to this, but not the full story. Much evangelism has even stripped away most of this, making the gospel an explanation of Jesus' death only. We need to realize that focusing the gospel entirely on the atonement is itself a result of modernist syncretism inconsistent with what we saw in the mission tradition stemming from Acts.

Cross-cultural evangelism is not about changing the cultural clothing of an explanation of Jesus' death, but finding which parts of the whole story are 'good news' within each culture and starting from these to explore the rest. To use the seed-planting analogy, the gospel is not a single seed that we plant in foreign soil; it is a whole packet of different seeds that together make a harmonious garden. Certain seeds in the packet will take root better in certain soils, others will need a lot of soil cultivation before planting, and others will be best planted much later when the rest of the garden is established. The art of the skilful missionary is to read the unknown soil and understand the seeds in the gospel packet well enough to know which ones to plant first, to discern when they have taken root in a healthy way, and know when it is time to plant the seeds that will be harder to nurture.

Ultimately the whole packet needs planting for faith to be fully realized. Therefore the gospel message is not something we deliver once in a short presentation, but something unveiled piece by piece over a long period of time. For some a response may come early in this process, for others it may come later, and it could come as a response to any one of the many facets of the salvation story. Finally we do not stop introducing new elements when someone comes to faith; we keep going until the whole story has unfolded. Evangelism flows directly into discipleship. John Stackhouse makes a similar point, stressing that conversion may be a change of direction but the new path then needs to be travelled so that the 'change of mind' at conversion carries on into a 'perfection of mind' as the believer is transformed in Christ.[2] Evangelism should be understood as discipling not-yet Christians.

We also need to move away from a modernist approach that converts minds towards a holistic mission that converts whole people, societies and cultures so that the kingdom of God comes on earth as in heaven. This transformation should be witnessed in the lives of Christians who proclaim the gospel in deeds and not just words. We also need to take on board the importance of spiritual experience for people in today's emerging culture and the need for that to connect with Heibert's 'excluded middle'.

The *Mission-shaped Church* report rightly emphasizes the role of the church in mission. One could describe the church as a series of planted gardens going back to the original seed packet. A healthy garden will bear the seeds we take out to plant through our evangelism. Indeed, from Genesis 2 and 3 we might describe the failed role of humanity in God's mission as the cultivation and spread of the Garden of Eden so that all creation became like it. From Jewish Apocalyptic to the Revelation of John and from Paul in Romans 8 to much Orthodox liturgy, salvation and the coming of the kingdom of God have been pictured as the fulfilment of this transformation of all creation. In this, of course, the 'gospel garden' becomes rightly much bigger than the church; it becomes the kingdom of God in heaven coming to flower on earth as the seeds are spread and flourish.

Another important lesson in 'planting the gospel' is that the soil alters the way the plants grow. An illustration of this might be Burgundy wine. You can use only one grape variety to qualify the wine as Burgundy: pinot noir for red and chardonnay for white. Yet wine from different vineyards doesn't taste the same. This is due to factors such as whether the vines face the sun, or the mineral content of the soil. In the same way the seeds of the gospel adapt to the cultural soil and environment to produce a plant that is not exactly like the plants that have grown elsewhere.

Finally, there is a subtle delusion that we can stand outside culture and think in a 'purely Christian' way, devoid of cultural interpretation. Instead the faith we express is itself an expression from within our culture. If I remain outside another culture and criticize it, there is no way for me to discern if the issues I raise are due to a counter-cultural stand necessitated by faithfulness to Christianity or simply the bias of my culture as it affects my expression of faith.

Does God speak through culture?

Double listening assumes that God speaks through culture. However, others, following Tertullian, still challenge this. Karl Barth saw the idea that God was working through culture as the reason few Christians had opposed Nazism. For Barth, proclamation came with the power to create belief in its hearers, so save for issues of linguistic comprehension there was no need to inculturate the gospel which instead diluted the revealed truth.[3] Barth allows for some 'implicit' apologetics to show error from revealed truth, but denied that God's word was speaking in creation or through human religion or philosophy.[4] This 'exclusivist' approach is often accompanied by a strong doctrine of election. This tends to create a tautology; if one believes that the Spirit ensures that those chosen respond to a proclamation of the gospel regardless of culture, then there is no need to be concerned about why some don't respond. However, if God's revelation is perceived outside of culture in some 'pure' form guaranteed by the work of the Spirit, it is suspicious that in recent experience those who respond to this approach are predominantly those who have had a church upbringing.[5] This doesn't look like the approach we saw in the mission of Paul and the early church either.

The opposite would be an 'inclusivist' approach that viewed all human culture as expressing God because it stems from humanity made in God's image. God is thus revealed through science, progress and the best of human values. Christianity then offers a relationship with God that enables a deeper fulfilment of our divinely inspired human aspirations. This approach has resonances with that of Friedrich Schleiermacher and more recently Teilhard de Chardin and Matthew Fox.

Fox promotes inclusivist theologies of original blessing as a rejection of exclusivist theologies of original sin.[6] However, we do not have to choose one or the other. The image at the end of Genesis 3 of men and women in conflict with each other, creation and God, and ultimately their true selves, clearly fits human experience down the ages. Paul talked of people as slaves of sin, even if they desired not to be.[7] Sin seems to be something that cannot be overcome through enlightenment or progress. However, the divine image also persists. So Genesis 5 speaks again of the making of 'Adam' male and female in God's image, and then of the line of descent through the third son Seth who was in Adam's image. This line produces for us the 'heroes of faith', as the writer of the letter to the Hebrews would later call them: people who bear God's image and yet also remain in slavery to sin.[8] A number of characters who do not belong to the line of Abraham, like Melchizedek, Balaam and Cyrus, clearly reveal God in some way. Similarly Paul saw God speaking in poetry about Zeus. The scriptures affirm the idea that God also speaks through humanity and nature.[9] Yet they also clearly state that all people and all creation are marred by sin and so speak of God imperfectly. In the end this means that neither the exclusivist nor the inclusivist approaches seem consistent with the Christian tradition. This is not to decide if nature and human culture, or scripture and Christian tradition reveal God more clearly, purely that both do.

Looking for a 'point of contact'

The apologetic tradition has claimed that there is an overlap between God's revelation in scripture and tradition, and God's revelation in the world. This has been referred to as a 'point of contact'.[10] The evangelist uses this as the starting point for his or her message, shows that this makes Christianity 'reasonable', and works from there to explain the necessity of coming to faith in Christ. Alister McGrath justifies such a point of contact, on the grounds that God's presence is in the world in both creation and redemption, and because God's revelation comes to us in human language, enabling a common dialogue between Christian and non-Christian.[11] He suggests a number of points of contact based on creation and the human condition. The ordering of creation and the presence of human rationality suggest a rational creator God, whereas unsatisfied longings, a sense that 'there must be more than this', 'existential angst', a feeling of lostness and lack of purpose, an awareness of mortality and finitude which points to something 'bigger than us', are all seen as felt consequences of sin. Theologically these make sense as expressions of the human condition.

However, a number of criticisms can be levelled at McGrath's approach. It is one thing to show how theology explains the problems of the human condition, it is quite another to assume that people must be experiencing them. Unless we pay attention to the culture in which we seek to share our faith, we tend to work from our theology only and construct a view of what human experience 'must' be like. We then present the gospel as the answer to questions people simply aren't asking. The other danger is that we see apologetics as a way of finding out how to get people to feel what we think they 'ought' to feel. If Christianity bears the story of salvation for all creation, then it will have 'good news' to offer in every situation. This challenges us to find points of contact with the questions people are raising, whatever they are. We need to engage with their questions, rather than try to force them to ask ours. This should not be the limit of our discussion; as Stackhouse wisely comments, we need to keep in mind both the questions people are asking and also the questions the gospel asks of them, but the gospel does not ask us questions in a cultural vacuum.[12]

Dietrich Bonhoeffer, in *Letters and Papers from Prison*, has some useful observations about how we present the Christian faith to others as an answer to what we see as their need for God.

It always seems to me that we are trying anxiously in this way to reserve some space for God; I should like to speak of God not on the boundaries but at the centre, not in weaknesses but in strength; and therefore not in death and guilt but in man's life and goodness.[13]

He goes on to describe 'the "clerical" sniffing-around-after-people's-sins in order to catch them out'.[14] It is as if we have conceived of the gospel as something only applicable to people who feel weak and guilty and have to induce this in those who do not in order to make Christianity relevant. The point is not that people aren't in need of the transforming power of God to break free of the power of sin, rather that not everyone feels this need. We cannot assume that this is the place that the gospel makes contact with all people.

We can represent this in terms of transactional analysis. Our apologetic models have a tendency to be 'parent-to-child' in approach; Bonhoeffer challenges us to develop 'adult-to-adult' alternatives. The 'parent–child' approach not only limits the gospel to those who feel needy and dependent, it also breeds Christians unable to leave dependency on their ministers. An adult-to-adult apologetic may involve issues of 'death and guilt',[15] or McGrath's existential angst, unsatisfied longings, and awareness of mortality. We may, however, discover from listening to people as adults, and not as children in need of our correction, that other issues, perhaps even where we want to affirm them, are the right points of contact for the gospel. Returning to the seed packet analogy, because all people need to be released from the power of sin and death, there are seeds in the packet that address these issues. In time these seeds will be sown in everyone's faith journey; they are essential to maturity in Christ. However, this doesn't mean that this is where all people should start their faith journey. So while McGrath is right in his theological identification of the reality of the human condition, he is mistaken to assume it automatically provides a point of contact for apologetics. Any points of contact need to emerge from our listening to the culture and not from our theology. While we cannot enter this process 'theologically empty-handed', we need to apply theology to what we have heard in a genuine process of double listening.

Apologetics and postmodernity

McGrath's points of contact assume a universal objective rationality; in an increasingly postmodern world, however, truth is seen as purely subjective. The 'that may be true for you but it isn't for me' approach makes rational apologetics increasingly redundant. Further, modernist apologetic has seen conversion as coming from a rational decision to change belief. The trouble is, as Kevin Kinghorn points out, there is a growing consensus among philosophers that we actually can't choose our beliefs.[16] They are dictated by our upbringing and experience and change only in response to circumstances beyond our control. This may explain why unexpected or miraculous events aid Christian witness. However, Kinghorn argues that while we cannot decide to believe something is true, we can want to believe it's true. People sometimes say, 'I wish I could believe what you do.' They think they need to believe it's true in order to come to faith. The reality, as in Pascal's apologetics, is that you don't have to be convinced it is true; if you find it attractive, that can be enough and belief follows experience later. The evangelist's task is not convincing people that the gospel is true, rather it is showing them why it is attractive. This could be about what the person gains from it, but do we want Christians only interested in personal gain? For Jesus it's about offering the vision of the kingdom; painting a picture of the world the gospel seeks to usher in. In a world in which a consumer-oriented approach may well end in syncretism, it seems to me that the vision of the kingdom is the key to a cross-cultural evangelism that can also be counter-cultural.

When I was a minister in an inner urban parish I went to see a man who had asked for information on the Christian faith following some leafleting the church had done connected to a big sporting event. He was certainly not from the postmodern generation, but had travelled a lot and explored many belief systems. As we talked it became apparent that he knew quite a bit about Christianity and a number of other religions, but in each case he was left with too many unanswered questions and things he wasn't sure he could believe. I offered my best answers to his questions, but it became increasingly clear that he wasn't going to be convinced and some other approach was needed. I suggested that when trying to make sense of something as vast as God we would never have all the answers, but we could experience something and find out if it worked, even if we didn't fully understand why. I invited him to come along to our church, to bring his doubts and questions, and see how he found it. Ten years later he is a very active member of that church and a committed Christian. I suspect he still has many questions, but the experience of faith and not rational belief was in the end the key issue. We live in a world where this will increasingly be the route to Christianity. As John Stackhouse points out, rational argument has always been only one apologetic approach; the appeal to subjective experience is just as valid in helping people come to faith, particularly when one remembers that God converts, not evangelists. However, Stackhouse wisely rejects the idea that such experience-based apologetics is somehow impervious to reason or hard questions. We will need both reason and experience.[17]

Pluralist approaches in a multifaith world

A famous illustration of religious pluralism is the story of the blind men and the elephant. A version of this story can be found in ancient China about 2,000 years ago but in the West it seems to have come into currency in the nineteenth century. The blind men each touch one part of the elephant; one concludes from the trunk that it is a type of snake, another feels the tail, concluding it is a rope, one feels a tusk and assumes it is a type of spear, the next feels the side and concludes it's like a wall, and finally one feels the leg and decides it to be like a tree. The men then fall to arguing, each insisting their interpretation is correct. The Chinese version ends by making the point that one should not presume to pronounce on the nature of the whole until one knows the sum of all the parts. The later version by John Saxe specifically applies the parable to theological argument; different understandings result from seeing only part of the whole.[18] It has come in popular usage to mean that different religions are like the different perspectives of the blind men; each is true but only partially. All religions then lead to God, but none has all the answers. If all do lead to God, then the idea of seeking to convert someone from one religion to another makes no sense. Instead one enters into dialogue with other religions in order to learn more about the reality that all religions are seeking to express.

Raimon Panikkar expresses a pluralist view in his call to leave Christianity as a distinct religion defined by adherence to historic creeds, for a Christianness that is the part we play from our tradition in a new world consciousness formed by the coming together of all the faiths.[19] God is in all religions; though Panikkar, in an eastern approach, depersonalizes God in favour of non-theistic terms such as infinitude, in order to 'liberate the divine from the burden of being God'.[20] This understandably appeals to many in a society where tolerance is one of the highest virtues. If one accepts such a position, then, as Hall and Panikkar argue, evangelizing those of other faiths is a misplaced proselytism from a colonialist age.

Many pluralists also point to what the faiths have in common; indeed, Panikkar speaks of each as the expression of the others in a different topological form.[21] But what about the apparent differences between faiths? These tend to either be synthesized or abandoned as part of a 'wrong understanding' that reflects cultural bias. In the end the assumption is that there is actually only one true faith, just as there is only one whole elephant; each expression is partly wrong as well as partly right. In many ways this approach to religious pluralism is another version of the modernist concept of a universal true human rationality.

Comments made by John Hick in *The Myth of Christian Uniqueness* are revealing.[22] He suggests that any notion of Christian uniqueness can be rejected by comparing its moral contribution to that of other faiths. All faiths, he argues, share the 'golden rule' of treating others as we would wish to be treated, but all have contributed negatively as well as positively to the good of the world. Good people live in all faith traditions and Christianity cannot claim a moral high ground. Significantly he makes these judgements according to western liberal moral standards which, he argues, are not products of the dominance of the Christian tradition in the West, but the Enlightenment rediscovery of Greek thought. This led to the benefits of science and of human rights initially being opposed by Christians. In effect, Hick believes that all faiths can be judged from the superior position of western liberalism.

Because Christianity is not unique in Hick's judgement, he rejects the doctrine of the incarnation as God uniquely becoming human in Jesus as a creation of the early church alien to Jesus' own understanding. Instead he offers an 'inspirational' understanding of incarnation in which God can be incarnate in any person through inspiring them to good. He notes that such ideas will be opposed by those he refers to as 'creedal fundamentalists'.[23] However, by elevating western liberalism to an objective position from which the world's faiths are judged and then replacing their traditional beliefs with reinterpretations that enable each to fit his position, all Hick does is remake Jesus in his own likeness.

In a similar way Tom Driver argues that each religion can be judged by their work for the liberation of the poor and oppressed; the basis of his 'super-religion'.[24] Those like Hick and Driver take the part of the unnamed narrator who can see the whole elephant and thus know that the blind men are feeling only bits of it. So the claim to affirm every religion masks the reality that some true 'super-religion' is assumed to exist by which all other religions can be judged; the parts of these that conform are absorbed, the parts that conflict are rejected. Panikkar seems aware of this, arguing that there is no objective place to judge religions; they must be recognized to occupy their own segregated worlds of understanding. We must, he argues, not seek a unified position but one in which the faiths travel together in confidence.[25] My question is, confidence in what? I can only assume that he means here the God seen as mystery and infinitude. Panikkar's position is not quite that of the other contributors to *The Myth of Christian Uniqueness*.[26] However, his approach too replaces the salvation story of any one tradition with a new story that can accommodate them all.

In truth, modernist pluralism is probably the ultimate expression of the belief in western colonial superiority, and its advocacy a hidden form of proselytism in spite of its claim to be the opposite. Indeed, what is interesting is that it is so often a belief of western people. It is not just the more traditional Christians who reject this kind of approach; Muslims, Orthodox Jews and even contemporary Pagans reject the assumption that 'all faiths are really the same'. Pagans have a strong sense of the connected nature of life, but they are also very aware that they are not Christians, Jews, Hindus, Muslims or for that matter New Agers. It is at this point that Panikkar is more nuanced, arguing that each faith should advocate what it believes to be true and explain to others where they feel they are wrong.[27] Alongside this he speaks of truth itself as pluralistic. As such he seems to be moving towards a postmodern pluralism.

In postmodern thought there can be no objective place from which to make judgements, only the view from each specific place. There is no chance of seeing the elephant, if indeed there is one. One ceases, therefore, to seek to harmonize religion because the differences between religions don't raise the question, 'Which is true?' All are 'true' even when they make apparently conflicting truth claims. However, while this allows a genuine affirmation of religious diversity, it potentially creates another problem. For many, the motivation to find a pluralist approach is a desire to end religious conflict and promote a working together for the good of creation. At best the postmodern allows a toleration of the faiths of others, but at worst, after Nietzsche, it offers no reason why the different faiths shouldn't simply 'fight it out', with no basis for a common good to work together for. To proceed with confidence in such a situation, as Panikkar encourages, will require us either to believe that Nietzsche is wrong and in fact humans are innately good, or that our confidence is being placed in something or someone at work in the process to transform them. If, as Christianity affirms, human behaviour conforms both to a modernist notion of essential goodness and to a postmodern notion of essential violence, trusting in human nature offers little reason to be confident.

Neither modern nor postmodern approaches to religious pluralism enable all religions to be affirmed as they are and at the same time journey together, learning from each other and benefiting all creation. Such a place can be reached only if we have confidence in some power that saves us and transforms us. It is this very issue on which the faiths do not agree. Is Jesus uniquely God incarnate, and does he transform lives so that the power of sin, Nietzsche's original violence, is overcome? If not, I do not think we can put much hope in a tolerant pluralism that is ultimately based on a notion of some kind of innate human goodness that will naturally emerge and solve our problems. We would need to find another path to follow that truly transforms us, or simply accept that the best we can hope for is a heroic, but ultimately doomed, stand against the inevitability of violence and conflict. Indeed, this is what Jesus' death becomes if it is not a saving act of God. If, however, Jesus is the key to human transformation, we can indeed then go forward in confidence that God is at work, and invite others to travel with us.

Christian mission and inter-faith dialogue

The cross-cultural mission tradition, from ancient Judaism, through Paul, the Celtic monks and the Jesuits, expected to find God present in other religions. This is not to claim that all religions are the same but that God will be found speaking within them. We should also not be surprised when followers of other religions demonstrate that they too are bearers of God's image and show fruit of the Spirit's work in their lives. However, If we need to be set free from all that mars the image of God within us, and if Jesus is who Christianity claims and not one of many gurus demonstrating an 'inspirational incarnation', people can only truly become who they are meant to be because of what God does through Jesus. Christ therefore fulfils the quest of all religions that seek truth, beauty and goodness. In talking about this I often use the analogy of the spectrum of colours coming together in white light; for me, each religion is a colour, including Christianity, in that we do not perfectly represent Jesus, and all come together in the white light of Christ. People of other faiths may not agree, but they usually understand and realize that this affirms their belief as well as my belief in Christ's uniqueness. This is not the same as claiming that all religious people are really anonymous Christians, or that all religions are really some form of Christianity. This is not only untrue, it is insulting to the very sincerely held beliefs and experiences of those following other religions with conviction and integrity. We must take religious differences seriously and look for how God will challenge Christians too, through those of other faiths and cultures.

When looking at the moral case for Christian uniqueness, Hick not surprisingly cites the figure of Gandhi. Undoubtedly Gandhi deserves a reputation as a good and inspiring man, a practising Hindu who also drew on other faiths. The right approach in apologetics will not seek to claim Gandhi as some sort of 'secret Christian' or to 'sniff out his sins' in order to prove he wasn't so good after all. Instead it will affirm that God was at work in him. Does this, however, necessitate the end of Christian mission to Hindus? Let me put that another way. Do you think that Gandhi thought he had reached perfection? Like most holy people he was probably deeply aware of his own failings and sought ways to overcome them. I also doubt that he would be closed to exploring what other faith traditions had to offer; indeed, he seems to have drawn on them and spoke positively of the example of Jesus. Therefore, for a Christian to share in conversation with Gandhi insights from the Christian story that might offer the key to things he was searching for can hardly be seen as unnecessary or arrogant. Who are we to judge what he might or might not gain from such insights?

The trouble is that most of us have encountered inter-faith

evangelism that is mocking, compares the worst failings of those of other faiths to our best ideals, believes the caricatures drawn by others rather than the testimony of believers themselves and refuses to listen to criticisms raised by those of other religions of our own faith. Such is indeed arrogant. It might also show a great lack of faith. Here I sympathize with Panikkar's call to go forward in confidence. If what I believe is true, then I can simply trust God to be at work as I and people of other faiths share their insights with each other. If I have entered into a process of double listening thoroughly, then my insights may well both inspire and challenge those I am in dialogue with.

The other side of this is that I too may find that the encounter raises questions I cannot answer and challenges things I thought I understood. Stackhouse is right to insist that we cannot truly enter into dialogue with someone of another faith unless we are sympathetic to it and are prepared to discover they might actually be right.[28] Even if I am not myself converted to the other faith I may well grow in my understanding of God from our sharing. In this way double listening as the basis for mission really is likely, in Donovan's phrase, to lead us to 'a place that neither of us have been before'. My belief is that that place will ultimately be the kingdom of God come on earth through the reconciling of all creation to God in Christ.

People of other faiths will offer their own view. I cannot prove who is right, I cannot be certain what I believe is indeed true; but that doesn't make it wrong for me to believe it and share my belief with others. It does mean that I will offer my beliefs humbly and without the language of certainty. I will expect them to do no less. Indeed, I think it is in sharing what we truly believe and hearing honestly the beliefs of others that we show real respect for those beliefs. If I respect those I am sharing with, I will seek to offer insights I think they may benefit from and challenge any of their ideas or practices I struggle with, and I will hope they do the same. To not do this suggests that all our sharing is some intellectual exercise about things that are not important. This is fine for someone simply trying to catalogue what people believe, but to the believer faith is far more important than that. Evangelizing people of other faiths as a deep sharing between friends in whom we recognize God at work, in which we too expect to learn more of God, is in fact possibly the greatest mark of respect we can give them.

Evangelism and conversion

In simple terms, conversion denotes changing from one way of relating to a faith tradition to another in which that faith is embraced as the person's own. The language of conversion is not restricted to a religious context; it can be used, for instance, when we have discovered for ourselves how good that new product really is and now buy it all the time. Biblically the word usually associated with conversion is *metanoia*, often translated 'repent'. A literal translation of this word would be 'change of mind', the word for mind used having the sense of 'perception' or 'understanding'. Seeing the world differently is not a bad translation of *metanoia*. In New Testament contexts, this word appears to be related to people realizing that they need to change the way they live, hence the idea of repentance as an admission of guilt. In such contexts a change of life was expected, not simply a change of belief.

Often conversion has been seen as an event; sociological study over the twentieth century has seriously questioned this model, suggesting that few conversions are really sudden, and most people come to that point due to prior experiences.[29] Equally, many who 'come forward' at evangelistic rallies are expressing an intensification of faith, not a new faith. I think it is helpful to remember that the monastics often speak of 'conversion of life', a process where one becomes Christ-like. Christendom turned the notion of sudden conversion into a model of entry into the church. This is a 'bounded set' view of Christianity in which one 'becomes a Christian' at some defined boundary point and thus enters the church. The boundary will vary; it might be saying a sinner's prayer, it might be baptism, it might be assenting to a declaration of faith. Figure 28 is a representation of this.

Figure 28 Bounded set? Or . . .

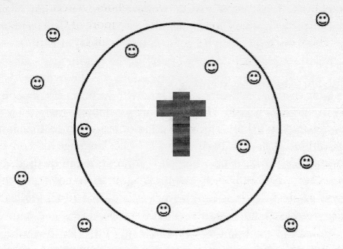

The question then is, 'Are you in or out?' Evangelism becomes the means of getting people into church membership, at which point the job is done. This tends to a 'smash-and-grab' approach in which evangelists are sent out to find people 'ready for harvest' and take them back to church. This model also produces a concept of 'pre-evangelism' in which people are made ready for conversion, then the evangelist comes along and reaps what others have sown.

The bounded set approach has unfortunate consequences that are contributing to the crisis in evangelism. It contains an inbuilt Christendom assumption that focuses on getting people to church rather than getting the church out into the world. This 'works' in a Christendom situation in which the country sees itself as Christian, but fails to engage with the foreign mission situation we now face. It also looks for places where sudden conversions are easy and plentiful as the right places to send evangelists. Following from this, the quality of evangelism is judged by the numbers who make a commitment; and as many evangelists are funded by giving, it makes sense to give money to support the evangelists with the most commitments.

Since most of those who have sudden conversions were raised in church, if you want a successful evangelistic ministry in the bounded set model the implication is clear: don't waste time on those without church backgrounds. This is, of course, not explicitly realized by those operating in this model, but the law of following numbers of conversions ties the two together, leading to apparent evangelistic failure if the numbers of people raised in church falls. This failure may not be in the gifting of the evangelist, likely to lose his or her funding, but in the model they are expected to work within.

Sociological evidence and the biblical emphasis on the process of becoming Christ-like suggest we should also see conversion as a process. This offers a model of church as a centred set, as illustrated in Figure 29. Here the key issue is not crossing the boundary but changing direction so that life is centred on Christ; this creates a set quite different from that created by the boundaries of church membership. Indeed, there will be those following Christ but who have not yet reached what we might perceive to be the key boundary. Here again we can draw on the idea of the gospel as a packet of seeds and

Figure 29 Bounded set? Or . . . centred set?

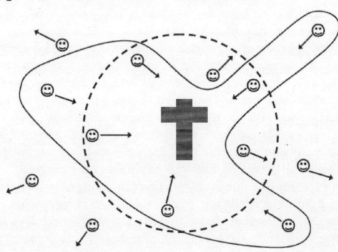

suggest that what different traditions have considered 'boundary issues' in deciding whether someone is or is not a Christian are actually questions about the order in which the seeds are planted in someone's life. In my view this order does not have a set sequence that is true for everyone, though there may be a series of patterns that often emerges. Rather the order is dictated by what God is doing in that person's life and where they are coming from. The bounded set approach mistakenly thinks that it is the flowering of a particular seed that marks conversion; instead we need to see conversion as a process in which all seeds come to flower in the right order for each individual.

Sometimes people seem to assume that there is a 180-degree turn at the start of the process and this is effectively the 'point of conversion'. That cannot be true if we believe both that the image of God in non-Christians leads many to do good, and that God is at work in them. For some the change in direction will indeed be radical; for others it will feel more like a small adjustment, or a slow turning through stages. Over time, however, even a small adjustment will lead down a path that is further and further away from that previously followed. As such we are always being called to adjust our path so that our lives may be better converted to Christ's pattern. Even the person with the radical story that looks initially like a 180-degree turn will find that actually they have further minor adjustments to make. This then has implications for the task of evangelism. The evangelist is not called to work at a 'point of conversion' but as a companion in the process of conversion. The effectiveness of the evangelist then needs to be measured not in terms of numbers crossing a boundary but on their ability to relate the Christian message to people where they are on the journey.

The need to discover today's Hellenists

Studies on network theory and belief tell us how resistant cultures are to outside influence.[30] Our social networks create strong pressures to believe what our network believes. Further to this, discussions about belief tend to follow patterns in each network that exclude dialogue with those outside it, often coupled with some level of taboo or embarrassment about such discussions. This is wonderfully illustrated in Nick Spencer's report of a non-Christian's disgust at merely overhearing some Christians discussing their faith in public.[31] Provided therefore the network connections can be maintained, beliefs are likely to remain stable. The loss of Christian belief represents the church's failure to maintain connection with shifting networks so that people are increasingly now raised within non-Christian ones. If this situation is to be reversed it requires people able to enter non-Christian networks, build relationships as outsiders and overcome the barriers erected against religion in those networks even to generate openness to Christian faith.

We need to find the Hellenists in our church, those who will be at home both in the church and in the networks beyond it. They are likely to have ministered or worked outside the church rather than be church leaders and pastors. It may be no accident that many cross-cultural missionaries in Britain are lay people, who have backgrounds other than theology or have been youth workers of foreign missionaries. It must be remembered that the Hellenists initially created controversy in the church and in the Jewish community, leading to the church's persecution. Today's Hellenists are likely to be no less controversial and may well look like enemies of the Christian tradition to those in Christendom as they prophesy against its temples and traditions.

We also need cross-cultural skills in the church to nurture those at different stages on the journey. Without these, too often a skilled cross-cultural evangelist will direct travellers towards the church, which then tries to stuff them into a predetermined mould. This leads to an artificial crisis between what God has done in someone's life and conformity to a cultural stereotype of what a good Christian is. This is why evangelists often find they cannot send people to any of their local churches and end up planting churches along cultural lines for those they are travelling with.

Double listening as the basis for contemporary apologetics and evangelism

Traditionally evangelism in a multifaith world has been viewed as a choice between three approaches: an exclusivist position, an inclusivist position and a pluralist position. From set theory the idea of bounded and centred sets has been used as descriptive of the process of conversion. Set theory also corresponds to these different understandings of mission. The bounded set approach corresponds to the exclusivist position; everything is either in or out. One could also have an 'open set', in which everyone is included, corresponding to the inclusivist position. Similarly one could have a multi-set model corresponding to the pluralist position. In advocating a centred set approach I have rejected all three traditional approaches for a fourth.

H. Richard Niebuhr, in his book *Christ and Culture*, offers five approaches that correspond well to the discussion above. Niebuhr's first two represent the extreme positions: 'Christ against culture', corresponding to the 'exclusivist', and 'Christ of culture', the 'inclusivist' approach.[32] The next two Niebuhr links together as expressions of 'Christ in the middle'. These appear to correspond to the modernist and the postmodernist approaches to pluralism, though it is extremely doubtful that Niebuhr, writing in the early 1950s, saw it this way. The first of these he calls 'Christ above culture', in which all of culture is 'summed up' and drawn to completion in Christ who is above all cultural expressions. The idea that Christ is 'above culture' fits the modernist notion of some objective position outside faith or culture from which all can be judged. Niebuhr's other representation of this third option is 'Christ and culture in paradox'. In this there is both a presence within and a conflict between Christ and culture, creating a tension that can't be resolved. This isn't quite the same as a postmodern pluralist approach, but is similar in that it seeks not to resolve the tensions between different cultures or faiths and Christianity.

Finally Niebuhr offers the model of 'Christ transforming culture'. This approach is both critical of culture and affirming of the seeds of the kingdom of God within it. There has been criticism of Niebuhr's approach as it has seemed to many very vague. Whether my approach is the same as his or not, the idea of transformation fits the centred set model and incarnational mission as the leaven within the culture. A transformational approach true to mission-shaped principles will both produce results that represent the diversity of each culture and in all cultures lead to changed lives that can only be achieved by the victory of Christ over sin and death.

I am confident that as people journey together in faith the Spirit will open a place for 'the sowing of each seed' in its right time. Therefore I believe that we can meet people where they really are and find new ways of communicating faith in each situation. We may well in the process learn new things about our own faith, discovering 'seeds' that had always been in the 'gospel packet' but not been used, and finding unexpected ways of using familiar 'seeds'. Ultimately the experience of God in the Christian tradition, my life and the lives of others gives me confidence to enter on a journey with those from all cultures and faiths without knowing what the end will look like. I trust the one I believe is in charge of the ending, who is at work seeking to bring all of us towards it, and who in the end is the one who alone brings faith and not the argument of any apologist, however skilled, nor the proclamation of any evangelist, however inspired.

Notes

1 This phrase is used as shorthand for the incarnation, life, teaching, death, resurrection and ascension of Jesus, and in a sense also bears in mind his second coming.

2 John Stackhouse, *Humble Apologetics*, Oxford University Press, 2002, pp. 73–5.

3 Karl Barth, *Church Dogmatics* 1/1, quoted in Dulles, *History of Apologetics*, pp. 305–6.

4 *Church Dogmatics* 2/2, quoted in Dulles, *History of Apologetics*, p. 306.

5 John Finney, *Finding Faith Today*, Bible Society, 1992.

6 Matthew Fox, *Original Blessing*, Bear & Co, 1983.

7 A common theme in Romans 1—8, for instance 7.14–25.

8 Hebrews 12.

9 See Romans 1, for instance, as well as the many Psalms that tell of the creation speaking of God.

10 See Alister McGrath, *Bridge-Building,* InterVarsity Press, 1992.

11 McGrath, *Bridge-Building,* especially pp. 9–74.

12 Stackhouse, *Humble Apologetics*, pp. 182–5.

13 Dietrich Bonhoeffer, *Letters and Papers from Prison*, SCM Press, 1981, p. 91.

14 Bonhoeffer, *Letters*, p. 124.

15 I'm not sure here if Bonhoeffer intends us to see such issues as irrelevant to a 'humanity come of age' or whether he simply wants to challenge the assumption that this is all our message is about.

16 Kevin Kinghorn, *The Decision of Faith*, T&T Clark, 2006.

17 Stackhouse, *Humble Apologetics*, pp. 149–60.

18 Published in Linton's *Poetry of America*, 1878.

19 Panikkar, 'The Dawn of Christianness'.

20 From the notes of Panikkar's 1989 Gifford lecture series, *The Rhythm of Being*, quoted by Gerald Hall in his address to the Australian Association of Study of Religion Conference 2003 (online at http://dlibrary.acu.edu.au).

21 Raimon Panikkar, *Intra-Religious Dialogue*, Paulist Press, 1978, pp. xxii f.

22 John Hick and Paul F. Knitter (eds), *The Myth of Christian Uniqueness*, Wipf and Stock, 2005, pp. 30–4.

23 Hick and Knitter, *Myth*, p. 32.

24 In Hick and Knitter, *Myth*, p. 209.

25 Panikkar, *Intra-Religious Dialogue*, pp. 103, 109.

26 As is acknowledged in the preface, Hick and Knitter, *Myth*, p. x.

27 Panikkar, *Intra-Religious Dialogue*, p. 111.

28 Stackhouse, *Humble Apologetics*, p. 101.

29 See, for instance, the helpful discussion in Sara Savage, 'A Psychology of Conversion – from All Angles', in Martyn Percy (ed.), *Previous Convictions*, SPCK, 2000. The whole book is about conversion in the contemporary world and is worth looking at to take these issues further.

30 See Rob Hirst, 'Social Networks and Personal Beliefs', in *Predicting Religion*.

31 Nick Spencer, *Beyond Belief*, LICC, 2003.

32 H. Richard Niebuhr, *Christ and Culture*, Harper, 1951.

13

Mission and the Legacy of Christendom

The challenge of inoculation

In many ways post-Christian culture in the West may seem like a foreign culture, but it is not the same as a society that has never encountered the Christian message. People today may know very little of the Christian faith, but they often assume they know more than they do, and their limited perceptions are in a sense enough to inoculate them against the real thing. This can work in a number of ways, from those who would describe themselves as Christian as a statement of British identity and little more through to those who reject Christianity because of the negative things 'everyone knows' about it. This is often influenced by the media both through reporting of news and history and through characters in soap operas and other dramas. All of this means that Christianity is not encountered as something new, but as something supposedly known and already rejected.

There is a list of common reasons for this rejection. Christianity is viewed as old-fashioned and irrelevant; as having a repressive, outdated morality; as being the cause of war; as being patriarchal, homophobic and authoritarian; as likely to persecute its opponents; as having a doctrine of creation that leads to abuse of the planet; as being judgemental and hypocritical. The history of Christianity tells us that many of these accusations have some grain of truth in them and you can usually find a Christian somewhere who will confirm a negative stereotype. As the Barna group puts it in their book *UnChristian*, we so often don't look like Jesus.[1] Looking at the church in the media, would people say of us, 'See how these Christians love one another'? If we come over as unloving among ourselves, why should anyone believe that we will love them? We also know that this is not the whole truth, and that there is also a positive legacy we can be proud of. If we rightly want to tell this other story we will only be able to do so if we are prepared to admit and ask forgiveness for the darker legacy of our faith. Indeed, my experience is that when we do this rather than seek to defend our faith, doors are opened. Equally if we want to call people to be followers of Jesus in the belief that he is the one who sets us free from sin and death, they are entitled to ask if this can be seen at work in our lives.

Nick Spencer's survey of the views of non-churchgoers found that while most people when asked to describe Christians resorted to the negative stereotype, if they were asked about Christians they knew, most said they were good, caring people.[2] We may be better witnesses than the stereotypes suggest! However, with active Christians making up about 10 per cent of the population, many British people will not, at least consciously, know anyone who is one.

The culture-gap in worship

When I worked as a youth evangelist in inner-city Nottingham in the early 1990s we did a survey of young adults' attitudes to church. Young adults who had never attended church told us they wanted the church to be there and that it was an essential part of the community. They were equally adamant that they didn't like churches that tried to be modern and 'trendy'; they ought to be traditional, have pews and traditional hymns. They saw them as places especially for old people and had no intention of going, except perhaps when they too were old.

The kind of worship that these young adults condemned as 'trendy', with music led by worship bands and developed by Christian rock acts, is the very thing often desired by others raised in the church. It is often assumed that this style of worship will also be attractive to those with no church background. However, while this music often seems very progressive in the church, in fact it is usually rather safe and old-fashioned in comparison to what is going on in the secular music scene. There are some very good Christian artists making excellent contemporary music in a number of styles, but worship music has a nasty tendency to sound as if the only genre it works with is the US soft-rock of the late 1960s and early 1970s, perhaps suspiciously the music of the generation now running our churches. Indeed, the dominance of this cultural style may well represent a Christian equivalent of the phenomenon of the domination of the New Age movement by exactly the same generational group. Although, with the increasing blurring of popular culture so that anything from the 1960s onwards might be listened to by anyone under 65, the pressure to be 'culturally relevant' in this way is far less than it was.

Contemporary spirituality has its own distinct cultural forms and these largely govern what many people view as spiritual. For such people the worship in the Christian tradition that is seen as spiritual is not all the kind of contemporary worship described above, but monastic offices or Taizé chants, lots of candles, meditation and icons. This leaves us with a dilemma. The very kind of church that is highly attractive to many Christian young people may offer nothing like the kind of worship that the non-churched would develop as an expression of faith. This reinforces the need to follow proper cross-cultural mission practice, allowing worship to be developed by the converts in their culture. The worship service should come late in cross-cultural mission, emerging from the life of a community of new Christian disciples. Unfortunately I have seen many fresh expressions that start with a worship service that people think the non-churched will like, but end up attracting other Christians or those with church backgrounds.

The barrier of language

One of the effects of so few people having a Christian upbringing is a loss of Christian language. The occasions that bring
people to church, if at all, are weddings, baptisms and funerals.
I wonder what a person with no church background would
make of the call, until recently found in the Anglican baptism
service, to 'resist the world, the flesh and the Devil'? Might
this not appear to suggest that Christianity was anti-ecological,
that it viewed the human body as evil and believed we were all
in danger from a guy with horns and red tights? Actually about
30 per cent of the population believe in the devil, a belief that
doesn't seem to be declining, so some at least might take the last
injunction seriously.[3] Their image of 'resisting the devil', however, might evoke horror films rather than Christian theology.
The language of sin, salvation, redemption and resurrection is
often not at all well understood. People know the words, but
they have become a kind of Christian jargon only understood
by the initiated. This may be a major reason why it is primarily
those from church backgrounds who respond to classic evangelistic preaching; much of it is simply incomprehensible to anyone else. We expect foreign missionaries to learn the language
of those they are sent to; the same is increasingly true for those
seeking to communicate the faith 'at home'.

Church buildings and spiritual tourists

As well as its more hi-tec manifestations, postmodernity is
also attracted to the premodern. We can see this in Paganism
emerging as a postmodern religion. In a similar way elements
of premodern Christianity are still highly attractive to the non-
Christian population. The significance of this should not be
overplayed; in a religious culture in which faiths are not seen
as complete systems but as combinations of different practices
that can be raided to form personal belief systems, the attraction of certain elements of Christian tradition does not represent an interest in Christianity itself. However, these points of

contact represent opportunities to open up other areas of the Christian faith for exploration, and as such are positive places for cross-cultural mission thinking.

A survey for English Heritage in 2003 found that 40 per cent of the population in our cities said that they visited church buildings as spiritual places.[4] Clearly they are not coming to worship services. Instead they will turn up at open churches, especially large churches and cathedrals in towns and cities, but also rural churches, to sit in the space, perhaps pray as many non-Christians do, and light a candle. These people are not looking to join a church, or an enquirers' group, and on the whole probably don't want people bothering them; they are engaging in a private spirituality. However, there are ways of offering more for them to experience within those parameters.

Most churches contain within their furnishings and architecture a lot of information about the Christian faith. Those raised in church will know the stories and beliefs these represent, but many visitors have no such background or knowledge. Helping the building speak to such people is a worthwhile exercise. Churches often have some literature available, but this is usually either geared to Christians, with information like service times and church groups, or in older churches focuses on the architecture, addressing history rather than spirituality. Churches could create a 'spiritual discovery' leaflet, telling the stories behind pictures, stained glass or statues, as well as the meaning of baptismal pools or fonts, crosses, altar tables and other pieces of church furniture. The text should offer story, brief description, and poetic or meditative material, rather than detailed doctrine or information on manufacture. They should allow an exploration of elements of Christianity, opening up the world of Christian spirituality and offering ways someone might explore Christian faith further; they should not be tracts ending with an invitation to commitment. Such leaflets could be greatly enhanced by prayers and poems creating reflection points around the building, together with similarly worded signage of key objects and places. An example of this is already produced by SGM Lifewords.[5] Larger tourist churches might also use imaginative art exhibitions, interactive audio-visual material and headset tours. A very creative way of doing this has been through audio-visual labyrinth installations.[6]

Many people entering churches are looking for places to pray or place prayer requests. These should be clearly signposted, with places to leave requests, and if possible people available who will take requests with offers of prayer if desired. This again would have to be done subtly, but many people are open to receiving prayer. Ambience is important: lighting should be gentle, candles and incense help create a spiritual atmosphere, and quiet spiritual music also adds to this. The type of music should fit the building, perhaps with monastic chant for the medieval, ambient electronic for the ultra-modern, but in every case meditative music, not loud praise. With appropriate staff or volunteers, times of prayer and meditation can be offered in tourist churches throughout the day. These need to be offered, not imposed; people should be invited to join in, not told to stop and be quiet, something I have heard in some cathedrals, which creates an impression that *we* are praying, as a way of telling others that this is our space, not yours.

The appeal of monastic spirituality

In 2006 a British reality TV show in which a group of non-Christian men joined a community of monks proved a big hit. Its success highlighted the interest in monastic spirituality present in the population, and made something of a media star of the abbot. It became a very public example of the growing interest in monastic communities among the non-Christian population. The difficulty for these communities is that this is not slowing the decline in people with monastic vocations, but increasing the demand for retreats and spiritual direction on the shrinking populations of these monastic centres. It may be that in time this will work through to more vocations, but that would run very much counter to a culture that is increasingly averse to such levels of commitment. However, others have drawn on this interest in spiritual direction in more postmodern ways, setting up life-coaching businesses or combining this interest with a focus on healing to create well-being centres.

In many countries there is growing interest in 'new monasticism'. This is an interesting development, taking place largely in Protestant churches that got rid of their monastic communities at the Reformation, and with it what had been the major mission force of Christendom. This post-Christendom rediscovery of monastic traditions may well have a very positive impact on global evangelism and re-evangelization. These range from new styles of religious community to people living out a rule designed to enable Christians to practise a spiritual life in the dispersed networks many operate within. They represent a move away from Sunday as the only expression of church in favour of weaving church into all of life: engaging with the 'excluded middle'. They also offer places of spiritual growth and commitment for those who are not called to a traditional monastic community. The original rise of monasticism was partly a reaction to the creation of nominal Christianity when it became a religion of state rather than of choice. There is a sense in which monastic life represents what Christians were actually called to prior to Christendom. In new monasticism this pre-Christendom commitment is being rediscovered. Alongside this, a number of mission agencies are also becoming new monastic communities, recapturing the vision of the early monastic missionaries as church planters and evangelists.

The embracing of Celtic culture

The interest in all things Celtic applies to Celtic Christianity too. It is also true that just as the general enthusiasm for our Celtic heritage is largely celebrating a highly fantasized view of it, the same can apply to Celtic Christianity. Celtic saints are 'in' because they are seen as separate from Christendom, eco-friendly, less dogmatic, and missionary. In short they represent to many people a lost Christian tradition that offers an attractive alternative to what they perceive as church. When compared to what we know of the genuine Celtic church, such views are inaccurate in many areas, and the strong ascetic element of Celtic Christianity is ignored. We have lots of 'Celtic' liturgy and talk of ecology, but not much more.

So far the creation of a contemporary Celtic Christianity has primarily been about a revival of church life, though groups like the Iona Community have strong programmes of social action as well as spiritual renewal. There are also crossovers into the New Age and Pagan market where Christian books on Celtic saints appear in bookshops alongside books of druidry and magic. I think there is a great mission potential here, especially for new monastic groups styled on the Celtic, if they follow in the steps of the first missionaries.

Notes

1 David Kinnaman and Gabe Lyons, *UnChristian*, Baker, 2007.

2 Spencer, *Beyond Belief*.

3 For instance, the Populus poll, April 2005 or the Communicate research poll, May 2006.

4 ORB survey, 2003, published in *Building Faith in the Future*, Archbishops' Council, 2004.

5 See the historic catalogue at www.sgmlifewords.com.

6 A good one used in many English cathedrals can be purchased from www.proost.co.uk. There is an online version at www.yfc.co.uk/labyrinth/online.html.

14

Good News in Today's Cultures

The atonement as good news in our contexts

A legacy of modernist approaches to evangelism is a gospel message that explains the mechanics of atonement through the death of Jesus. This tends to use the substitutionary approach developed by Anselm in the eleventh century as an answer to Jewish and Muslim criticism of the idea that God would become human and even worse suffer the humiliation of crucifixion. His response was a logical argument for non-Christians based on the need for God to satisfy both his justice and his love. In the sixteenth century Calvin, himself a lawyer, developed Anselm's argument in the framework of the law court.

We certainly can find biblical texts that support the substitutionary theory of the atonement; 1 Peter drawing on Isaiah 53 is the most straightforward, but the biblical writers have a much wider scope than this. The New Testament authors sought to understand Jesus' death in terms of their Jewish heritage. Jesus died at the Passover and turned the Passover meal into a commemoration of his own death. This evoked the very Jewish concept of salvation as liberation; the journey from slavery to the promised land became the liberation from sin and death and the promise of the coming kingdom of God through Jesus' death. The language of redemption, often coupled with the imagery of the slave market, also stems from this. The account of the veil of the temple being split as Jesus died and the language of him as the Lamb of God who takes away the sins of the world both point to the Jewish Day of Atonement. A goat was sacrificed for the sins of the people and its blood sprinkled on the temple, enabling the high priest to pass through the veil into the Holy of Holies and enter, for this day only, into the presence of God. The idea of Jesus dying in our place in the substitutionary model comes from here, but other imagery used by the New Testament authors draws on Jewish apocalyptic literature like that found at Qumran, which saw in this ritual a parable of the restoration of Eden brought about by a new Adam entering the true Temple in heaven and being restored to the image of God. The language of reconciliation, Jesus dying for our sin, being the great High Priest who opens up the way to God, and probably Jesus as the new Adam, also stem from the Day of Atonement and its apocalyptic development. Paul expands the atonement into a cosmic event in Romans 8 with the whole creation waiting to be set free and experience the liberty of the sons and daughters of God. As mentioned earlier, for Paul it is the world that is reconciled to God through Christ, not just individual human beings. This is to be expected if the atonement mends the broken relationships highlighted in Genesis after the expulsion from Eden.

Early church views of the atonement grew out of the scriptural imagery. One of the most common approaches was to view Jesus' death as the overcoming of the power of sin, death and the devil. Another, particularly associated with Irenaeus and still predominant in the eastern church, sees the whole of creation taken up in Christ's body on the cross, sin, death and evil transformed, and a new creation being born as Jesus rises from death. Slightly later the idea of Jesus' death as the ransom price to free us from slavery became popular in the West. It may be significant that freed slaves were important in the mission to non-Roman Europe in the latter half of the first millennium. Patrick had been a slave in Ireland, and Gregory and Boniface redeemed slaves from countries they were evangelizing, sending them back to their people as part of the mission team. Alongside this redemption imagery developed the idea that the price of Jesus' life was paid to the devil to whom we were enslaved. This was viewed as a trick played on the devil who in accepting Christ's life as the price for our freedom doesn't realize that death will not hold the sinless Jesus. It was this view in particular that Anselm was unhappy with, leading him instead to see Jesus' death as a price paid to God, not the devil; a view that then became predominant in the West.

John Stott, in his classic book *The Cross of Christ*, discusses a number of approaches to the understanding of the atonement, deciding that the substitutionary theory is the right explanation.[1] In the modern evangelical tradition Stott presents Jesus' death as an effective answer to the problem of individual guilt for sin. The way he assesses the other possible approaches is also very modernist. He assumes that they are competing theories, out of which only one can be right, though he notes biblical themes in all of them and dismisses none outright. He also assumes that we need to understand how the atonement works and that the Bible will tell us this. In terms of evangelism this fits the modernist understanding that conversion follows a change of belief, based on a comprehension of the need for forgiveness and of how God makes that possible through the cross.

There have always been those who have not taken Anselm's view, but more recently there has been a rising critique of the substitutionary approach to the atonement and its use in evangelism. In Britain in 2003 one such voice was that of Steve Chalke, a well-known evangelical church leader, speaker and evangelist. The following passage is indicative of this, and caused some controversy.

John's Gospel famously declares, 'God loved the people of this world so much that he gave his only Son' (John 3.16). How then have we come to believe that at the cross this God of love suddenly decides to vent his anger and wrath on his only Son?

The fact is that the cross is not a form of cosmic child abuse – a vengeful Father, punishing his Son for an offence he hasn't even committed. Understandably people both inside and outside of the Church have found this twisted version of events morally dubious and a barrier to faith. Deeper

than that however, is that such a concept stands in total con-
tradiction to the statement 'God is love'. If the cross is a personal act of violence perpetrated by God against humankind
but borne by his Son, then it makes a mockery of Jesus' own
teaching to love your enemies and refuse to repay evil with
evil. The truth is this, the cross is a symbol of love. It is a
demonstration of just how far God as Father and Jesus as
Son are prepared to go to prove that Love.[2]

In many ways what Chalke and others have done in pointing
out the potential unwanted consequences of the substitutionary
approach is very similar to what Stott did in showing that the
other models have consequences that are also unfortunate. The
earliest models, stemming from a world influenced by Plato, see
humanity, indeed creation, as one entity that Christ identifies
with and transforms, potentially downplaying the responsibility of the individual to God. The idea of the devil being bribed
by God, even in a trick, seems dubious. Chalke's suggestion
that there is something deeply unjust in a Father punishing
his Son for a crime committed by others is of the same ilk. If
all the models clearly express New Testament language, none
contains all the language and none is without problems as an
explanation of the atonement.

Should we reject all the models of the atonement and try to
work out a new one? I think not. Rather I think we need to
recognize that the Bible nowhere contains one coherent explanation of the atonement that we can propose as the correct
doctrine. Instead it expresses the truth that Christ's death and
resurrection solves the multifaceted human problem: it saves,
redeems, overcomes the power of sin, enables our justification, enables the birth of a new creation in which we are born
again, defeats the devil, and rescues us from death; and all
these things spring from the love of God in Christ Jesus. In
speaking of these the New Testament writers draw on a range
of imagery that connects with different aspects of Jewish and
Gentile culture; they are in that sense cross-cultural explanations. Particular biblical authors use a variety of 'theories of the

atonement' rather than consistently advocating one. There is not a tightly defined biblical theory of the atonement; there are instead many biblical ways of expressing its truth, drawing on imagery from the cultures the writers are seeking to reach.

The law court imagery of Calvin's version of substitutionary atonement was rational; it focused on the guilty conscience of the individual and offered a solution to that problem. As such it was a good biblical explanation for a modernist audience. It is far less persuasive to a postmodern audience. It is likely that other biblical imagery will be more effective. It is also no surprise in an age of objective scientific rationalism that Christians choose to argue that there must be one true explanation of the atonement and that we need to understand how it works in order to believe the gospel and come to faith. This influences the nature of the debate in Stott and, I think, in Chalke. It only makes sense to reject the historic theories of the atonement, all of which clearly draw on biblical imagery, if they are seen as objective and comprehensive explanations of the way the atonement works. If, however, the various theories are images we can use to explain the atonement, with no expectation that any one image is the bearer of a true and comprehensive explanation, then the questions raised against different models are not a problem. In this sense Chalke's description of the substitutionary theory as 'cosmic child abuse' becomes as much a mistaken approach to imagery of the atonement as an insistence that the substitutionary theory is the only correct explanation.

We desperately need to recover this full story of the atonement. Restricting it to the forgiveness of the individual has created for many a caricature of faith in which being a Christian becomes a selfish exercise in afterlife insurance. One can see how this has occurred in an age that focuses on the autonomous individual and tends towards a body–mind dualism in which a person comprises a mind with a body viewed as a machine it uses. Unfortunately this has led Christianity in some quarters to become a disembodied faith, only interested in saving souls. Not only is this a distortion of the faith that Christ and the apostles taught, it is deeply damaging in a world that needs to hear and experience a gospel that relates to environmental crisis, social breakdown, injustice, poverty, violence and suffering. The mission of God from creation to new creation is about all these things, and the atonement is as much about liberating creation as it is people from the effects of sin.

Good news for the questions people are asking

In 2003 a group of interviewers in Coventry diocese, under the leadership of the Revd Yvonne Richmond, sought to find out what was happening in the lives of ordinary non-churchgoing people. The results are published with analysis by Nick Spencer in *Beyond the Fringe*.[3] They offer a number of valuable messages for us, perhaps most of all in listing the six big questions people were searching for answers to.

The first was about destiny: what happens after death? The survey shows that people rarely have any thought of concepts like judgement.[4] Most see the soul as immortal. We go somewhere, heaven for some, reincarnation for others. Experiences are central; we are in the world of mediums, ghosts, near-death experiences and past-life regression. Few are looking for forgiveness as a way into heaven. Hell or a bad next life might be true but only human 'monsters' go there, not them or the ones they loved. For many the afterlife was about being reunited with loved ones. All of this expressed a longing for peace, a reconciliation of strained relationships, and a desire for a divine presence watching over people in this life and the next.

The best way to respond to this is to draw on the desire people are expressing to be at peace, to be reunited with those they care about, to be somewhere that is free from the problems of life. Here the vision of the kingdom, of a new heaven and earth without crying or pain, of the defeat of death and evil and of Jesus as the one who reconciles us not only to God but to each other, can be powerful. When people reflect on why the world they live in is not how they long for it to be, they often come to an awareness that their own human weakness is part of the problem and this creates an understanding of the need to change.

The second question was about meaning and purpose in life. The report notices that while people might feel there is no specific purpose in life, they often live as though there is. Here there was an interesting tension; people spoke of purpose in terms of living life to the full, being happy, or being successful, yet when asked who they admired they didn't cite multimillionaires, celebrities or sports stars. Rather they cited Mother Teresa, Gandhi, Jesus, Nelson Mandela and Martin Luther King, especially their quality of sacrifice for the sake of others. This highlights the struggle between the fallen and divine nature within us. Inside, most aspire to be like those figures of selfless sacrifice; people admire them because they know that is what is the best in humanity, but they don't think they can be like them.

Opening up the possibility that we *can* become like Christ is the best response to this. Indeed, it is essential that we have a gospel for this life and not just for entry into the next. The whole of creation is waiting for the sons and daughters of God to set it free from death, according to Paul.[5] We are not helpless in the face of the world's problems; we have been called to be part of God's plan to make this world the place we wish it were. If people are looking for purpose in their lives, this has to be attractive. Why, after all, do we love films in which the hero saves the world? We may not get to play the lead role, that is already taken; but we get to be part of the hero's action force. We too may face trials and hardships en route, but we expect that when we are trying to save the world. I think this vision has been desperately undersold; Jesus calls us to be part of his revolution at the cost of our own lives, and we've turned that into 'Come along to church every week and if you're lucky you might get to take the collection'.

Third, people marvelled at creation. It didn't make sense to see creation as 'just a product of evolution'; it spoke to them of being created and full of spiritual meaning. This again returns us to environmental concerns, and also points to creation as something that inspires deeper questions. It might also suggest the debate about science may not be as important as we have imagined. Indeed, there is clear movement away from science as explaining life's mysteries and from the scientist as public expert.

Wonder at creation is clearly a profitable place to explore faith. Environmental concerns are also high on many people's agenda. A vision of the kingdom that includes creation is needed. The language of the eastern approach to the atonement, which centres on Christ's incarnation in all creation, and the taking up of creation in him, may also resonate with the spiritual dimension in creation.[6] A very spiritualized ecology is sometimes encountered in more New Age circles. Contemporary Paganism is a more effective alternative here. Its major difference from Christianity relates to the vision of the kingdom. Paganism is about living with the world as it is now, learning to live well with all life, but not changing the way in which the world basically works. The Christian vision of the end of death and suffering is often viewed by Pagans as thus anti-ecological. Pagans often put Christians to shame on environmental issues. If people seeking a creation-centred spirituality are going to find the Christian faith attractive, we need to address this challenge in our own living.

Creation sparked the next question, about any possible spiritual force behind it. As we have seen, most people believe in God but there has been a marked shift away from the personal God of the Bible. People are seeking to make sense of their own spiritual experience without reference to a religious heritage. Many see Christianity as unspiritual, so they don't expect to encounter God among Christians or associate their spiritual experience with the Christian faith. In our experience-oriented age, talking about how Jesus opens the way to God will have little impact. People want to experience God for themselves. This is one of the reasons why praying for people is so important; it often gives them a tangible sense of God's presence.

I have used Ignatian meditation on Bible stories with non-Christians, which has proved very powerful. This works on stimulating the imagination; people become characters in a biblical story, often from the Gospels, and then in their meditation have a personal encounter with God or Jesus which involves a one-to-one conversation. Afterwards I have been aware not only of the impact of the experience on participants but also amazed at what God has said to people who are not Christians. If I have feared at times that they might 'make' God say whatever they wanted, this has not been the case.

Worship, particularly if it is reflective, can be a place of encountering God for non-Christians, as can retreats and holy places. Art and music can aid this too, together with nature. The evangelist should create space for such experience, helping people to explore its meaning, but remembering that being intriguing and open rather than using clear explanations encourages this. The problem is not that people in our day and age do not encounter God; it is that they do not recognize that it is God they are encountering. Like Paul in Athens, we must make the link.

Then there was curiosity about the supernatural realm, which leads us to much of the client-based style of religious practice associated with the New Spiritualities. In societies that are more open to the supernatural, people often come to faith after supernatural encounters, and there are stories of this beginning to happen in what had been the 'rationalist West'.

We must offer Christianity as a supernatural faith, but one in which the natural and supernatural are linked. The danger is that supernatural experience becomes like a drug, people always seeking the next fix. We need to show that God is at work to change lives, and connect the supernatural to the vision of the kingdom and the call to live as Christ did. Drawing the link between healing and salvation can be helpful here; both are part of the same process. God seeks to set us free from sin and death and call us to be citizens and missionaries of the coming kingdom, not just solve our immediate needs. We must also not avoid the issue of discernment. It is deeply mistaken for Christians to begin their witness to people exploring spirituality by listing all the things they think are of the devil. This gives far too much credence to the devil and not nearly enough to God, and often displays a lack of understanding about what is condemned. However, the other extreme, in which everything is viewed as good or coming from God, is equally unhelpful.[7] The essential thing here is to be sure of our motives. If we are cross-cultural evangelists our desire is to help people come to faith. This means we will be quick to listen and slow to judge. We will help people think through the possibility that there are evil spiritual realities and share our own experience rather than seek to frighten or condemn. Too often Christians seem to be seeking to win the argument rather than the person.

Last, people spoke of suffering, but not in the abstract way in which it can be seen as making faith impossible. Rather people felt that there was something wrong with the world, and suffering was a result of this. God might be implicated but often society was blamed. Again, people often come to see that they are in fact part of that society and this can then lead to an understanding of the need to change.

When this issue is raised it is important to discern if the person is asking a difficult philosophical question or telling you about their pain. The atonement in its full context of the mission of God has different ways of approaching this issue for different situations. Part of the answer is the supernatural dimension of healing, but healing in a holistic sense of body, mind and spirit, which can be offered both as part of a philosophical discussion and in prayer for those who suffer. Of course, the classic problem here is the question of why not everyone experiences instant healing. If the New Age therapist blames this on lack of spiritual awareness or karma, then Christians have their own version of this, blaming the victim, or the person who prays, for a lack of faith. Jesus seemed to think that faith as small as a mustard seed was enough, leaving me wondering what level of faith is too small, bar none at all, in which case you wouldn't be praying for them in the first place.

Salvation and the end of suffering is part of the vision of the kingdom yet to come, and part of the process of our transformation in Christ now. Small things may happen quickly, miraculously, but the whole process takes longer and is not complete until death and suffering are finally banished with evil and sin for ever. When we encounter people's pain, the conquest of suffering through the cross also shows God's solidarity with our suffering through his pain. God's love is very powerfully present when he overcomes suffering by taking it upon himself. Here too the wider picture tells us of new life beyond death, of hope after suffering. If Christ identifies with us in our suffering, it is so that we can identify with him in resurrection.

The interviewers moved on from this to ask people their views on church. Perhaps the most startling thing they discovered was that no one could understand why these things were connected. The church simply had no relevance to the big questions of life and was not seen to be addressing them. We need to wake up to the questions people are asking and listen for what God is saying to us through them.

The big questions raised in this survey are, of course, not exhaustive. Other people will have different questions, and there will be illustrations in each context that can be used to relate the differing parts of the gospel to those questions. Whatever the situation we encounter, the point is that we begin by listening and then speak about good news in response to the questions people are asking, not the ones we think they ought to be asking.

The problem of unity and diversity

If the New Spiritualities want to advocate diversity by denying any right path or true deity, the challenge for them, as we have seen, is how this avoids nihilism. The Nietzschean proclamation that 'God is dead', which spells the death of the transcendent and thus for the postmodernist also the death of objective truth, is coupled with the proclamation that 'all is the Will to Power' and that violence lies at the very root of creation. The only place that another vision can come from is, in my view, a transcendent deity. Yet such a God is seen as remote, dualist and certain to deny diversity.

Some have seen divine immanence as the only option for

Christian theology today. So Matthew Fox advocates panen-
theism, and eco-feminist Sallie McFague 'the world as God's
body' as a metaphor befitting an ecological age.[8] However,
a transcendent God does not have to be remote. In the Bible
creation is viewed as contingent upon God's sustaining power,
so God must be intimately connected with it.[9] Reading Fox
backwards, the claim, as the Greek syntax for *pan en theos*
allows, that the world is in God expresses the relationship
accurately while maintaining divine transcendence. Similarly,
instead of the world as God's body we might refer to it as
God's womb, bearing in mind that as with all metaphors it
has limits; it would be wrong to deduce that the world will be
'born' and 'grow up'. This pictures the intimacy of God with
creation and the dependence of creation on God's nurture, as
expressed for instance in Psalm 104. It is also a feminine image
not inconsistent with passages like Isaiah 66 or Jesus' description of himself as a mother hen, and this is helpful in an age
that sees Christianity as patriarchal.

Part of the problem, perhaps, is that transcendence and
immanence are often treated as spatial descriptions. This makes
sense in a world-view where heaven can literally be conceived
of as 'up', but not today where God, if spatially transcendent,
appears to be beyond the universe. Rather, as Ross Thompson
suggests, God relates to the universe as a game to its pieces or
music to its notes, and is thus not 'separate' spatially.[10] God is
present in the 'moves of the game' but is more than the sum
total of those moves. Pagans are right to see deity at work in
the balance of the eco-system but mistaken in identifying God
with that system. God is transcendent in being much more than
creation while still being present within it.

This view of transcendence does not place God at a distance
from creation, but in power over it, and thus raises accusations
that the Christian God is totalitarian. However, suggestions
that the eco-system, astrological evolution or the 'will to power'
dictate reality are of the same order; they are themselves meta-
narratives. The issue may not really be about the denial of the
'big stories', but the rejection of those that enable some to claim

superiority over others. It is therefore the idea that Christians are favoured by this transcendent God while others are told to 'become Christian or go to hell' that creates the problem. The Christian message is intended to be universally applicable; God is proclaimed as favouring all people equally and not as excluding some on the grounds of ethnicity, class or gender. This is the point of the Israelite claim that Yahweh is not a tribal deity, but God of the nations.

If there is only one transcendent God, can that God affirm diversity? For John Milbank, transcendence is vital not only for the denial of nihilistic conflict but for the affirmation of diversity. He notes that we can only maintain difference if there is something bigger than all the differences affirming them.[11] Without this, difference tends to a violent process of the assertion of one expression of diversity against another that cannot be countered by Pagan readings of nature as harmonious balance. Harmony and diversity can only be affirmed by opposing behaviour that violently asserts itself over others. There cannot be freedom for all diversities without conflict. Thus God must expose and judge that which engenders conflict and injustice in order to affirm diversity.

The philosopher Gilles Deleuze pictures the postmodern affirmation of diversity as an orchestra that reaches true musicality only at the point of dissonance. Only then are the musicians expressing themselves in freedom from the tyranny of the score. Milbank counters this by suggesting that true music follows the Baroque style. Here the virtuosity of each instrument is stressed, but without dissonance. By working within the rules of the music, each part is able to express itself, yet always within a total harmony. Baroque music used to leave the lines part unwritten because it was assumed that players would improvise and thus add their expression to that of the composer. In the same way God conducts creation towards a harmony that still allows each member to express his or her own individuality.

The Trinity as unity with diversity

The affirmation of diversity in harmony is not just demonstrated by God's character. In Christianity it is uniquely part of God's essence as 'three in one'. The western church has often stressed the unity over the diversity. The challenge today is to stress the other, without resorting to polytheism. The Trinity offers a model of God as intimate community out of which flows creation as diversity in harmony. The Old Testament also offers a plurality of perceptions of God in a number of metaphors. God is a rock, a warrior, a mother, a husband, a lion. Indeed, as we have seen, Yahweh replaces Canaanite polytheism not by denying the diverse attributes of El, Baal and Ashteroth but by incorporating them into 'himself'.

Allowing diversity but opposing conflict

The biblical struggle between God and chaos is in part an image of the struggle to overcome violence in creation. Revelation portrays Jesus as the final conqueror of the chaos serpent, but by refusing to use violence. In Revelation 5 he is pictured as 'the lion of the tribe of Judah . . . [who] has conquered, so that he can open the scroll'.[12] Yet this 'lion' turns out to be a lamb and his 'conquest' has come through his slaughter. The destructive evil of the will to power cannot be overcome by the use of power, only by its denial. This conquest through sacrifice is not just the means of Christ's ultimate triumph, but the pattern for Christians. Not that Christians must deny all roles of responsibility or leadership in society. Rather they need to recognize that the kingdom of God can never be achieved by force or conquest. Had this ethic been taken seriously at various points in the church's history, Christianity might not be viewed today as an oppressive metanarrative. Rather it might, following Milbank, be seen as the 'master narrative of non mastery'.[13]

The Body of Christ as the model of postmodern community

Because God is a community, humans in the divine image are also intended to work as community. In the first instance this should influence how we see the task of evangelism. The Christendom model has been of the lone evangelist travelling from place to place. This worked because the evangelist was not a church planter but a church recruiter, and not usually someone seeking to witness to God in the world but address an invited audience in the church. In theory it was the local church that modelled the life of Christian community in the local culture. In post-Christendom we need Christian communities to exist in the world as an essential part of Christian witness. We increasingly need to be sending small Christian communities with the intention that they will plant an inculturated church rather than lone evangelists calling the dwindling numbers of de-churched back to church.

Biblical descriptions of Christian community offer another important model of unity and diversity: the Body of Christ. If we look at Paul's first letter to the Corinthians, much of the material is about Christian community. In the image of the Body of Christ, Paul is appealing for tolerance of diversity. The body has different parts, and Paul clearly realizes that difference can lead to judgement and conflict, with one part of the body rejecting the others because they aren't like them.

This image works at a number of levels. It is Christ's body, the one in which he was incarnate. This now happens in the new Body of Christ, the Church. Jesus was incarnate as a Palestinian Jew in Jerusalem; now God is incarnate across the world in people of every age, gender, class, ethnicity and language who are called to fulfil the Great Commission that disciples should be raised up in every culture. In global terms Christ's body should express every form of cultural diversity possible; any culture in which there is no church is a call to the Body of Christ to become incarnate there so that such a church can grow. The focus on the Great Commission has often been on people groups with no Christian presence. In the growing global culture these people groups can no longer be defined by geography; there are now many such groups in nations with many churches. In our day the call to be the Body of Christ in mission is a call to a much greater cultural diversity.

The Body of Christ is also a local image; indeed, in 1 Corinthians Paul is addressing a local church about diversity within it. The issue of diversity and unity is not just something society faces as it both becomes more global and yet also more tribal, but is something that the church faces acutely within itself both locally and globally. At the global level a mission-shaped agenda will mean increased diversity in the church and this is already a contributing factor in global church disputes. In a globalized world culture, what Christians do in one place impacts on those in another. The image of the Body of Christ tells us that one part affects all the others, and of course reminds us that we cannot allow diversity to let one part injure another. Equally, as argued above, the reason a transcendent deity can guarantee diversity is that such a God can judge that some expressions of diversity are not to be permitted in order that others thrive and the kingdom of God is brought to birth. A call for greater diversity and greater tolerance of diversity cannot be an 'anything goes' approach.

Paul warns us that our natural tendency is to intolerance and the denial of diversity. This tension is nothing new; in modernity it expressed itself in the classic Protestant solution, an endless round of sectarian splits as people sought to form the true church. It was also expressed in the classic Catholic solution, to assume that it was already the true church and prevent much deviation from the central norm. In terms of Paul's imagery the problem of tension between different parts of the body has led to classic Protestant response in which the hand leaves the body, and a classic Catholic response in which the body rejects the hand. In current global disputes the same tendencies are clearly present. Neither approach enables the body to remain as it was intended, highly diverse in its expression yet in good fellowship across the wider church.

I think that Roland Allen's radical principle that only the local church can decide what it is to live the Christian life in its own culture is of great value. When the church abroad or the planting church tells the local expression what it should do to be authentically Christian it cannot do so objectively; it is likely to impose a solution from its culture in every culture it encounters. The only people who can discover how to be Christian in a particular culture are those living in it. For Allen this is not only about enabling the local church to take responsibility for expressing the faith in its context; it is also about trusting the Spirit to be at work in that church. A good example of this in practice was the decision of a number of western missions to allow the African church to decide whether it was acceptable to practise polygamy, recognizing the differences between western and African culture. As we saw with Paul, this doesn't mean that the global church should express no opinion, but the local church needs to explore its own expression with respect to wider church tradition. Unless we learn to adopt this kind of approach to other cultural expressions that raise moral issues, we will find the challenge of being the Body of Christ, practising unity and diversity, unachievable for us in a globalized yet diverse world.

Near the end of *Transforming Mission*, David Bosch argues that we need interculturation as well as inculturation in cross-cultural mission. In a diverse church there needs to be not only an understanding of the culture into which we have gone, but one between cultures. Part of the problem is that much evangelism and church planting material has been very good on thinking about culture and communication but sometimes not so strong on its ecclesiology. This has often led to a lack of thought about the way churches relate to each other, the sense that we are all part of the church globally. Because of this, nothing like enough attention has been paid to Bosch's insight. While we have rightly been exploring how to encourage indigenous churches in places where rather colonial models have existed, there has been very little thought at an international level of what it means to do cross-cultural mission in the countries that have been central to Christendom.

Evangelism and social change

If the mission of God is seen as transforming creation into the kingdom of God, and as part of that the restoration of humanity to the calling of Adam so that all creation be set free is vital,[14] then we must view evangelism and social action as inseparable. The goal of mission is not saving souls or growing the church but the transformation of creation. However, while people of any faith and none can do much that helps achieve such a vision, at a fundamental level the modernist assumption that humanity can solve the world's problems on its own is mistaken. Too many of the problems we face result from flaws in human nature. With much effort these may be controlled but they are never mastered; the central work of God in Christ is to set us free from their power entirely. Without this transformation the vision of the kingdom can never be fully realized. Jesus spoke of the kingdom and called people to be a part of it by becoming his followers. This is still the message we need to put across in our evangelism today. Evangelism is essential to the coming of the kingdom, as well as enabling people to become members of that kingdom, because a transformed humanity is part of God's mission plan.

If the kingdom is the end of mission, then it is difficult to see how the church can be expected to proclaim the kingdom in its evangelistic witness if it does not also work towards it in social action. Having said that, social action should not be undertaken in order to impress people for evangelistic ends; some social action campaigns connected to missions have come rather close to this. However, when churches and agencies have undertaken social action projects for their own sake and welcomed non-Christians as workers and volunteers, there has often been an evangelistic impact on those people. Sometimes this has been part of a vision for a project; several projects seeking to build Christian community have begun with a largely non-Christian community formed round the vision of a Christian for social change. On other occasions the effect has been quite unexpected. The mission of God focuses on the kingdom of God, and proclaiming that vision in ways that connect with each situation is the kind of 'good news' that attracts people to the Christian faith.

Notes

1 John Stott, *The Cross of Christ*, InterVarsity Press, 1986.

2 Steve Chalke, *Lost Message of Jesus*, pp. 182–3.

3 Nick Spencer, *Beyond the Fringe*, LICC and Cliff College, 2005.

4 Spencer, *Beyond the Fringe*, pp. 27–37.

5 Romans 8.

6 See also Ephesians 1, Colossians 1, and 2 Corinthians 5.

7 As already noted, David Hay's research shows that while still not one of the most common experiences he recorded, between 1987 and 2000 the largest increase was for the experience of supernatural evil rising from 12 per cent to 25 per cent. Clearly not all the supernatural experiences of those who don't go to church are positive.

8 Fox, *Original Blessing*, pp. 88–92; Sallie McFague, *Models of God*, SCM Press, 1987, pp. 59–69.

9 Colossians 1.15–17; Hebrews 1.3; John 1.

10 Ross Thompson, *Holy Ground*, SPCK, 1990, pp. 245ff.

11 John Milbank, 'Problematizing the Secular', in Phillipa Berry and Andrew Wernick (eds), *Shadows of Spirit*, Routledge, 1992, p. 41.

12 Revelation 5.5.

13 John Milbank, *Theology and Social Theory*, Blackwells, 1990, p. 6.

14 Romans 8.

15

Inculturation or Syncretism in the Emerging Culture?

How incarnate can a missionary actually be?

Paul's famous dictum was to become 'all things to all people', borne out in his differing approach in the Jewish synagogue to the Gentile market place. However, there are limits to the extent that we can be incarnational with integrity. Jesus scandalized the religious authorities by spending time with those whose lifestyles were outside accepted morality, but he didn't adopt their lifestyles. Such limits are there in cross-cultural mission. Work with those in the sex industry or addicts are obvious examples. We also need to face the issue of what it means to do cross-cultural church planting when the culture of those we are among is part of what they need saving from. I suspect that church plants here will be bridges, one foot in the culture but the other in a place that enables people to develop out of the culture without having to make a radical culture shift.

In working among those of other religions there are areas where we cannot share in the practices of that faith. However, there is much about a cultural expression of faith that we can adopt, and also places where we can share in religious and spiritual expression. So we saw in both the Celtic monks and the Jesuit missionaries the adoption of the appearance and style of the local non-Christian religious leaders while expressing an indigenized Christian faith. This debate surfaces in Muslim outreach where it is recognized that culture, ethnicity and family life are all united with religion; thus some advocate that people can become Muslim followers of Jesus rather than officially convert to Christianity. Experience suggests that this can be a difficult tightrope that can mean maintaining faith and community with other such believers without others suspecting that you have left Islam.

Is mission-shaped church simply consumerism?

John Hull is not alone in criticizing the advocacy of different cultural expressions of church in the *Mission-shaped Church* report as an unthinking accommodation to consumerism. How can one tell if a church is a cross-cultural expression of faith or the result of consumer culture compromising faith? The problem is that both can look the same at first glance. The style of the church will not tell us if it is mission-shaped. The crucial question is, how did this church get here? Christians who become part of a local culture, spend time doing double listening, seeking to find out what God is doing there, share faith within that culture so that people become Christians and plant a church within that culture, these Christians express mission-shaped principles. If on the other hand a local church looks at a manual on new ways of being church, decides that it likes the idea of starting something, picks the type it feels would best attract the local population and sets it up, then you have a piece of consumer marketing of church that has little to do with mission-shaped principles. Such a church is unlikely to attract the desired locals, who have had no hand in birthing it. No effort has been made to enter their culture either, rather it has been assumed that local Christians already know what the local non-Christians want. The result is often that it becomes a new consumer choice for local Christians who leave other churches to go to this new option. At best it may attract people back to church as well as provide an expression of church that might stop others leaving, and both of these are positive. Rarely, however, will it attract those who have had no connection with church already.

In their book *Gone for Good?*, Francis and Richter recognize that in our multicultural world there will be no 'one-size-fits-all' church. They advocate what they call the 'multiplex church', which offers a series of different expressions to choose from, rather like a cinema offers a range of movies.[1] Pete Ward argues in *Liquid Church* that contemporary people require designer approaches to religion, and that churches should seek to provide choices of style of church and religious products that enable people to feed their own spiritual lives.[2] Both are right to point out that our culture will not be favourable to an 'only one way to do church' approach. However, both are leaning towards consumer marketing rather than expressions of church that faithfully represent the Christian tradition. A 'liquid church' may easily become whatever the consumer wants regardless of the Christian tradition. The multiplex showing a range of films is offering a set of predetermined choices rather than enabling inculturated expressions. To stay with the film metaphor, a mission-shaped approach would instead be a local film festival at which anyone can show their own films, rather than a multiplex which simply offers you a choice of other people's.

Another issue is the tendency for Christians to view consumerism as something to oppose while not seeing the way it shapes the church already. Like any aspect of culture, if we are to apply mission principles there will be areas of consumer culture that create openings for an inculturated church and others where we need to be counter-cultural. In the religious market place it is wise to think carefully how our 'products' look to our potential 'customers'. Faithful cross-cultural mission requires us to support a diversity of Christian expressions that reflect different cultures. This doesn't justify an attempt to market anything people will buy as Christianity. Indeed, this can easily end up suggesting consumer capitalism is itself a Christian goal. This seems to be what has happened in the USA, according to Smith and Denton.[3]

In a consumer culture it is impossible to police the marketing of faith, but we can't assume that what sells must be what's right. Further to this, while we need markets, much free market culture is based on an appeal to human greed and competition, glorifying the Nietzschean 'will to power'. We need to challenge this model, which creates aspirations only the few can obtain and uses the competition this creates to drive the economic engine at enormous cost, both to those keeping up with the rat race and especially to those always at the bottom destroyed by the process. People need saving from that which is destructive in their own lives, and so what people want and what is Christian are not the same thing.

Are different cultural expressions of church compatible with Acts?

If we are called to plant churches in different local and network cultures, the fear is that we will create lots of independent homogeneous churches rather than a local church that expresses the imagery of the Body of Christ. This is why Hull suggests that *Mission-shaped Church* promotes church apartheid. However, the reality is that local churches that seek to be all-age and multicultural too easily become only for families with children and slightly multicultural. An insistence on one multicultural expression of church has tended to actually exclude many of the cultures it has hoped to embrace. They can also end up blending different cultures into a flabby soup, rather than allowing each to be celebrated, creating a church culture that is not within anyone's culture.

Do we have to choose between church unity and cultural diversity at the local level? The reason this can seem the case is that, as at the global level, there has not been enough focus on the catholicity of the church or inter-culturation. A proper attention to these would enable expressions of church planted in different local and network cultures to operate not as independent churches but as congregations within a broader church. So there would be a congregational level organized according to cultural expression, and different congregations would then relate at a local church level. This level cannot operate as the primary worship service and maintain the cultural diversity hoped for in the different congregations. Rather the image, as suggested in response to Francis and Richter's idea of the multiplex church, would be that of festival: a chance for the different congregations to share their stories, experience each other's cultures and participate in their worship, rather than attempt to create a common act of worship that actually prevents inter-culturation taking place.

Christianity as a client-based religion?

For the last 1,000 years, most people in Christian nations just had one religious choice: whether or not to practise the Christian faith they were raised in within churches that by and large saw everyone as members regardless. Today people in the same countries can explore hundreds of expressions of religion and spirituality within a society that prizes consumer choice very highly. Choosing Christianity is thus far less obvious than it used to be. We are, whether we like it or not, in a religious market place along with every other expression. This is very obvious to me when running Christian stalls at Mind Body Spirit fairs, and I often come across church leaders who feel that Christians shouldn't be at such events at all, because they are then granting legitimacy to the other religious expressions in that market place. This is simply a refusal to realize that we are in that market place already, simply by existing in contemporary culture. Unless we wish to withdraw altogether from the world, we have no option. Indeed, when there is a common belief that there is truth in all religions but no one religion is exclusively true, we are likely to find that people are using bits of the Christian faith as part of their own pick-and-mix variety, and we have no control over this.

One of the main reasons for the rise of client-based religions in the West is that they suit secular lifestyles. The New Age approach is also strongly geared to a consumer approach to religion. It would be very easy to create a 'new age' Christianity geared to meeting the personal needs and aspirations of believers. Such a church would make few demands on its members save that they keep it going financially, but would offer them contact with a God who wanted to heal their illnesses, make their relationships happy, ensure their careers were successful and enable them to feel positive about themselves. The truth is, of course, that something like this does indeed happen in some charismatic churches, especially those attracted to various forms of prosperity teaching. I believe that God is interested in our lives and does answer prayer, sometimes in miraculous ways. However, the problem arises when Christianity is offered as a life-enhancement package with a guarantee of even more in the life to come. This is not at all the way Jesus or Paul talk about becoming a Christian; they both state that it should be challenging and a call to service and sacrifice. The trouble is that our culture naturally promotes these health and wealth aspirations, and Christians are not immune to them.

The charismatic movement is a child of the postmodern generation of the 1960s just as much as the New Spiritualities are. That it has reawakened much of the church to the more supernatural side of the faith is a considerable blessing to us in our re-enchanted world. However, theologically the charismatic movement has often seen itself as at war with its postmodern cousins, viewing them as demonic opponents rather than faiths to relate to in cross-cultural mission. This can prevent charismatics both from offering their much-needed gifts in mission and from spotting how they might become New Age themselves. Such syncretism is a strong temptation for churches today because it will make them attractive and thus numerically successful.

Environmental issues are at present understandably high on people's agendas. The church of the twenty-first century needs to engage with this, and has a poor past record in this regard, though increasingly this is not the case. Here too there is a potential risk of syncretism, most likely if creation blessing is stressed while at the same time denying the need for creation to be saved from the power of sin and death. That I think Matthew Fox has already done this, creating what might be called a contemporary Pagan Christianity, points to the reality of this danger.[4] The problem is not the recovery of a creation blessing tradition in Christianity; this is much needed and Fox has been of great benefit in advocating this. Rather it is the loss of the concept of salvation from sin that is the mistake. Once this is denied, creation spirituality becomes rather Gnostic; it is about the awakening of understanding of our duty to creation. It also becomes relativistic, an expression of a shared spiritual journey in which Christianity is really no different from any other faith. The call of Panikkar and Hall away from Christianity as a religion that seeks to convert, and towards a Christianness that is about living well in the world, could be an expression of this. Finally it is likely to become Pagan in that creation is viewed as needing no change, and thus what is natural is also what is good. The Christian imagery of the kingdom of God is rejected by Pagans on precisely these grounds; it implies a need for creation to be different. A creation-centred Christianity that denies the need for salvation from sin may thus become a faith geared to living well in this world, but lack the means to enable people to do this and with no hope of the kingdom of God to come in its midst.

Retreat from cultural change

During times of change and challenge it is attractive to some that faith can offer a safe place to escape to. The danger is that this encourages us to equate defending past expressions of faith with defending the faith in general. Our current faith traditions are expressed within modernist terms, and the danger is that their current modernist expression is seen as the only true expression. Christians are in danger of thinking that defence of the faith and defence of modernity are the same thing for this reason. The New Testament makes it clear that Christianity is to its core a faith that is expressed afresh within new cultures. We have perhaps been deluded by the long Christendom interlude into equating Christianity with establishment and traditionalism. Things have changed so comparatively little that we have lost touch with the idea that Christianity is an incarnational, ever-changing faith. As the protective edifice of Christendom crumbles, trying to crawl back under its remaining walls is not an option; learning again as a missionary faith to live in a world not of our choosing and be born into that world anew is the only authentically Christian way forward. This way forward will carry with it the insights of all Christian traditions in what Brian McLaren helpfully calls 'a generous orthodoxy'.[5] To be orthodox is in this sense rightly seen not as 'doing it as we've always done' or 'expressing belief as we've always expressed it', but as living afresh the timeless story of God's mission in the world centred on the Word made flesh living in human society, an inculturated expression of God.

Notes

1 Francis and Richter, *Gone for Good?*, pp. 310–16.
2 Pete Ward, *Liquid Church*, Paternoster Press, 2002.
3 Smith and Denton, *Soul Searching*.
4 Fox, *Original Blessing*, 1983.
5 Brian McLaren, *A Generous Orthodoxy*.

16

Mission in Today's Temples and Market Places

What is going on?

The point of this chapter is to mention some of the innovative ways people are doing mission-shaped evangelism in our culture. Treating these initiatives as if they are blueprints for success would be to fail to understand mission-shaped principles, so responses need to emerge from listening to each situation and cannot be predetermined. The hope is that these examples might inspire creative thinking and help an increased openness to the kind of responses possible.

Retail mission

Shopping is arguably the new religion of the developed world, and shopping centres our new temples; if Paul came today he would see them as places for mission. Certainly one Anglican priest, realizing that his local Asda/Wal-Mart was the main meeting place of his area, decided that this was where he would plant church. Being from the Anglo-Catholic tradition, he held Mass in the lobby of the store around opening time on Sundays, with the manager's co-operation. This was broadcast over the loudspeaker system. Those who came stayed for breakfast in the store café, adding a social dimension to the service, during which time the priest was available to staff and shoppers. Elements of this have been catching on; Christmas carols have been broadcast across the national store network, and many other Asda/Wal-Mart stores now have chaplains.

A number of shopping centres have chaplaincy teams and prayer rooms on site. Chaplains relate especially to the shop-workers, building relationships and offering support, but they also hold events in the centre such as lunchtime meditations. Some shops are taken over at various times of the year, like Christmas, to provide spaces for reflection, prayer and explor-ing faith. Cafés and well-being centres have been created in such settings.

In a different approach, shops have been set up that have no obvious Christian connection, as both a 'tent-making' industry and a way to meet people. Mike Frost and Alan Hirsch tell of one case.

> The Subterranean Shoe Room in San Francisco is one such example. San Francisco is a city full of people who wouldn't normally be found in church due to alternative lifestyles and liberal beliefs, therefore conventional churches struggle in their evangelism. This shoe store is owned by a southern Baptist church planter/evangelist who realised a different way of connecting with people was required in this context. Because of his love for shoes as well as needing an income, he has opened the store selling new and retro (restored second-hand) shoes.
>
> Those who browse unsure of what they are looking for are invited to share a bit about themselves so he can tell them what kind of shoe might suit them. Many people there-fore open up their lives to him. After hearing them out, he then recommends just the right shoe. He says as a church planter, he spent ninety percent of his time with Christians. Now as a shoe salesman, he spends ninety percent with non-Christians, just the kind of people you don't find in church. He has found a way to incarnate the message of the gospel to a group of people normally hostile to Christianity.[1]

A similar example came from a local post office, where the Christian proprietor became known as a good listening ear. At the centre of a small community the shop was used by everyone, a place all could become known and gain from that faith-inspired input.

This approach could have many applications: bars and cafés are obvious places, but any business with high levels of customer service and contact time would work. Perhaps one effective idea might be to run a hairdressing salon, a place where everyone talks about what's going on in their lives while the stylist is doing their hair.

Car boot sales

Many people in Britain are out shopping on a Sunday morning rather than in church; a good number of these are at car boot sales.[2] These have sprung up in car parks and show grounds around the country. People sell things from the back of their car or on a makeshift stall, while others come to pick up a bargain. In reality these are as much social events as trading events. If the people are there then that's where the church needs to be. A group of Church Army students decided to take the idea of stalls run at Mind Body Spirit fairs into a local car boot sale; they created a place where people could be prayed for, and reflective literature was available to take away. People were open and happy to connect in what might seem an unlikely environment. They demonstrated the great openness to prayer that many non-Christians show today.

Nightclubs

A Baptist church in Hereford, situated among clubs and pubs, found that it was suffering from a litter problem on Sunday mornings. They formed a team of litter-pickers, members who began to clear up the mess on Saturday nights and who found they chatted with clubbers in the process. Now the church opens its foyer in the evening to those out on the town and has become an integral part of Hereford nightlife. Around 200 people visit the church every Saturday night between the hours of 11 p.m. and 3 a.m. for the warmth of the foyer, a free hot drink, and a place to talk. The main body of the church is open for anyone who wants to sit quietly or pray with another. Services now also happen at Easter and Christmas.

Church Army have provided evangelists as nightclub chaplains who provide support for people in the night-time economy, both staff and clubbers. They also act incarnationally within the clubbing community, building relationships and forming community. The aim is for such communities to become churches in the culture. These projects have found that they need to create space outside the clubs to meet, socialize and explore faith issues in a setting not specifically aimed at Christians. One example is Solace in Cardiff, a joint Anglican–Baptist church plant connected to one of Church Army's nightclub workers, Wendy Sanderson.[3] They have used local pubs and clubs as places to socialize and meet for open discussion, run music events and events geared solely for their Christian community.

Some Christians have set up their own nightclubs or become club promoters as part of mission in this culture. This has been a mixed experience; the sheer economics of running a nightclub have been prohibitive. Promoting a night in a club run by others has been more successful. A key issue is to decide what is being attempted here: is this DJ worship, or a 'secular' club night run by Christians seeking to create good atmosphere and build relationships? In the long run both may be desirable, but if the club is intended to be a place of mission contact, then the second is probably the priority, the worship coming later when there is an established Christian community.

Extreme cycling

Most extreme sports have a distinct culture and a dedicated following. Extreme cycling is one such example. Like most extreme sports it tends to be focused on young adult age groups; there are male and female riders, and sizeable spectator followings at both national and international events. Rezurgence is a group of Christian riders who rent space at national events to

build relationships with fellow riders of a variety of disciplines
– BMX, Downhill, and Endurance. They serve drinks, offer a
bike wash-and-repair service, provide a place for riders to relax
or chat and a prayer zone. To maintain respect, they vigorously
compete at as many levels as possible. Their website describes
them as follows: 'Rezurgence are not priests on bikes or vicars
in hoodies as some would like to think. We are simply a mix of
riders that follow Christ – and some who don't – unity what a
great thing. We are about riders for riders – a community that
supports riders – end of story.' Their view is that a rider's pursuit of 'the ultimate experience' might be connected to a spiritual searching. A study by Eric Brymer has shown that many
of these experiences parallel those found in activities such as
meditation.[4]

Surfers and skaters

Legacy XS youth centre in Benfleet, Essex grew out of an
initially small youth group meeting in a vicarage in 2001.
Through relationship building numbers grew and a trip to
Soul Survivor Christian youth event saw 12 members become
Christians; a youth congregation, Legacy, was started, led by
around half a dozen 'leaders' who nevertheless saw themselves
as members of the community first and leaders second. The
group became aware that they were having little impact in the
wider community and wanted to create a drop-in space others
could use. They hit on the idea of a skate park, something that
local young people had been asking for. Working with young
people in the area, a skate park was created in an old army
hut. Now the Legacy XS youth centre hosts both the Legacy
Sunday congregation and a drop-in centre for all young people
in the area, focusing on both school work and fun. A café, a
computer gaming room, a pool table and other activities make
the centre attractive while Sunday worship sees a congregation
of up to 80 young people worshipping and growing in their
faith, some of them as a result of attending Legacy XS in the
week. Importantly, skateboarding isn't just an activity, it forms

part of the worship. People ride during songs, or to drumming, or they use the ramps for prayer, making this one of the more unusual examples of inculturated worship.

Mind Body Spirit fairs

Fairs at which therapies, spirituality, mediums, psychics and fortune tellers, crafts and arts and other aspects of holistic life-styles are promoted have become a global phenomenon. They can be large-scale events in major cities or small local gatherings. In a number of countries Christian groups hire stalls at these events, and in Britain I have been among those training such groups across the country for the last few years. This has involved quite a cross-cultural journey for some entering this field for the first time. Several groups from charismatic evangelical churches began by trying to stop the fairs altogether, before they realized that they needed to be inside, sharing faith with the large numbers exploring spirituality. Groups like these are experienced at praying for people but often have to work hard at learning the culture and the language; those who fail to do this can find they are ejected for being offensive. This is not about having to censure what Christians believe, it's about the style and language with which belief is presented.

In essence, these stalls create a spiritual space and opportunities for prayer, talk and reflection. Healing prayer is essential, but beyond that a number of creative approaches have been tried by different groups. People like things to take away and reflect on: prayer cards, stones with Celtic crosses, and small books with meditations are popular, and a number of products are being developed for this purpose. Scripture Union have begun to produce a series of small books under the title *Wise Traveller*, which contain creative reflections on life themes, also very applicable in this context. Other resources have been developed by the groups themselves. In the UK, Journey Into Wholeness, based in Colchester, has developed a series of leaflets geared to the Mind Body Spirit context. Dekhomai, from the Greek verb 'to accept', operates at the two biggest fairs in

London and Manchester; they have a series of meditation cards and an activity creating prayer beads.[5] One of the most sophisticated groups is the Community of Hope in Australia. They run a large stall geared to Christian versions of 'personal readings'. Unlike some other readers at the fairs, these are not fortune telling, but ways of exploring a person's spiritual journey and the place of the Christian faith within that. These include using gem stones, love languages, personality profiling and even tarot cards, drawing on the Jewish and Christian mysticism that lies behind the cards' images. If that last incarnational approach seems a step too far, other groups use a pack of cards called the Jesus Deck. Developed as a Sunday school Bible teaching tool, there are four suits, one for each Gospel, containing well-illustrated cards of the different stories in each. In effect these are used for a creative applied Bible study, opening up biblical insights for those used to images rather than text.

The challenge in this context is to move from what are becoming established mission presences to places where community can be formed, requiring ways to meet on neutral territory outside the fairs, followed by church planting in this culture. The reality in the UK at least is that many of those involved do not have the resources for this and so co-operative ventures between groups are likely to be needed.

Nature and its seasons

I remember the Pagan academic Graham Harvey telling me that Paganism was about reclaiming rights and rites; rights for a new religion to celebrate its faith and rites marking the times and seasons of nature and human life.[6] He felt that the church had taken the rituals out of life, which is a view I share. Some Christians are putting them back. A remote rural church in a Somerset benefice was under threat of closure. Taking the opportunity to do or die, it altered its pattern of services from a monthly traditional Morning Prayer to seven festivals a year. The new focus on seasonal celebrations revealed a desire to connect with church. Now instead of a congregation of four, over half the village population, around 40, attend services and the church is once again at the heart of the community. The seven services include some more novel choices of festival such as Clypping, a medieval custom of hugging the church. A pet service is also popular. The churchyard is managed for wildlife and is known in the village, through notification in the parish magazine and by word of mouth, as a 'quiet space'. People come from further afield to see displays of seasonal flowers such as snowdrops and orchids, and to be quiet, look and listen. Christmas can attract up to 120 people.

Online

There are three basic approaches to online mission: evangelism through chatrooms and interactive sites; websites that enable exploration of the Christian faith; and online churches. i-church is one such church, run by the Diocese of Oxford and led by a web pastor together with a team of pastoral assistants. The intention was to create a new spiritual community using the internet, a network church for people who were not members of a local church as well as a place for existing church members who travel or cannot get to their local church. This particular project seemed to attract people because it was authorized by the Church of England; they felt secure in signing up to it and had an idea of the basic doctrines. However, the level of interest was too much to cope with in the early stages; people approaching church on the internet seemed to both demand and expect a far greater level of one-to-one contact time than would be expected in a more traditional parish church. From time to time i-church has had to be closed to new members to cope with the interest. In i-church's experience so far, an early lesson to learn is that such work needs more resources than were first imagined. Bearing in mind the attraction of the Anglican label, the question to be asked is whether such a project attracts existing Christians rather than the non-churched. Also there is the question of whether off-line meetings will result, as is the case with a number of Christian online forums.

There are a number of other online churches, all very much in the learning stage. They clearly connect with a need, but how they connect to the mission of the church is still not clear.

In the UK the work of Bruce Stanley, also a life coach, is enabling the exploration of Christian faith on the internet through his own site Embody, the Christian enquiry site Re Jesus, and the production of the online Labyrinth.[7] These sites are responding to the way the internet works as a resource for many today. They are interactive, offer a range of opinions and ways of exploring faith issues, encourage feedback and seek to reflect other internet content. They are not online sermons or tracts, both of which are one-way communication inviting no discussion or exploration. Research at the University of Manchester on the use of the internet by New Religious Movements to gain adherents suggested that websites were not a way people joined a faith, but were very useful for those wanting to explore a faith, which might be part of a process of becoming a member of a faith community later.[8] Websites intended to be part of Christian evangelism need to take this into account, which those mentioned here appear to do.

For me the most important area of evangelism is in social networking sites and discussion forums. In places like Habbo Hotel and Second Life, which generate virtual online worlds, Christians can create characters and places in which to meet people.[9] These enable online relationships to be created in exactly the same way relationships can be created off-line. With less flexibility, and perhaps more ease, other sites such as Facebook[10] contain numerous discussion forums in which faith agendas can be explored, as do sites like Yahoo.com groups, forumgarden.com, theforumsite.com or spiritualforums.com. Alternatively you can find specific interests via Google. Finding discussion is easy; finding good discussion less so; it's always worth looking at discussion boards before getting involved. There are also some warnings to heed. All sites involve potential deception because you meet people as they want to present themselves, not as they actually are. In one sense this is helpful; people are more open to new ideas than they might be in a face-to-face meeting. Conversely people are less inhibited and can be far more aggressive and unpleasant. Take into account that there are no inflections of voice or body language, and misunderstanding happens very easily. In spite of this, behind every forum name or avatar is a real person with real feelings who you are really communicating with.

If you want to be a positive Christian presence online, how you communicate is often a lot more important than what you communicate. Always assume the best of others, assume you have misunderstood when offended or angered, be courteous, and check your facts, so that you don't become a source of the endless rumour and gossip that goes around. Behave as you would face to face and then remember to be even gentler and thick-skinned. Unfortunately you will find some extraordinarily unpleasant Christians online, and you may have to undo their enormous damage. Needless to say, Christians don't have a monopoly of bad behaviour online, and some sites seem to be totally dominated by people destroying each other. Find places where good discussion happens and people seem open, not just wanting to score points, and remember to behave as you would in other cross-cultural situations. Lastly, remember that two or three people may be posting in any discussion, but a few hundred could be reading it.

Festivals

I have been part of a team for the past ten years running a venue at the Glastonbury festival called Elemental. This was set up by a group from Bristol consisting of artists, DJs and other creative Christians. Greg and Clare Thompson, who run Elemental, also helped run Rubiks Cube Drum 'n' Bass nightclub and café; they have a Christian community centred within and around their home and are part of the core team behind Love Bristol community projects.[11] The Glastonbury venue is a large marquee run by 50 volunteers, so this is not the kind of scale most will copy, but the principles have been used elsewhere. A welcoming space is created with sofas and drinks for sale at a good price; the walls become an art gallery; there is live music and DJs; hospitality extends to foot-washing and hair-washing, both very popular at an often muddy festival; spirituality is woven through the day with simple acts of worship, meditation workshops, story-telling, prayer offered for all who want, Jesus Deck readings and other ways of engaging with people's spiritual journey. Late-night discussions and performances round off the day late into the next morning. There are a number of other groups at Glastonbury festival among the 200,000 people, together with a whole range of spiritualities in the healing fields in particular.[12]

Eden People in Guildford sprang out of a group involved in Elemental.[13] They have tailored the same approach to local community festivals. Using a much smaller venue, the same mix of welcome, care, reflection, prayer and creativity is used on a more local scale. Inspired by this kind of approach there is also a Christian venue at the V festival. In the USA the nearest thing to Glastonbury is the Burning Man festival, and there too Christians have a presence.[14]

At Merseyfest 2005, the Liverpool diocesan children's adviser and her team set up a children's prayer tent shaped like a caterpillar in the Family Zone. Four people were on duty constantly with a welcome and passport table outside the entrance. Over 850 caterpillar prayer passports were given out to children, mostly non-churched, during a 12-hour period, who went into a tent with interactive prayer stations. Parents brought their children in the hope that it was a crèche, but were gently persuaded to make the journey with their children. Coloured stickers were collected at each prayer station that made up a butterfly. Coloured footprints and instruction cards led them to meet with God. Some children returned on the Sunday to repeat the experience.

Health and fitness

Gyms and fitness centres have begun to talk about 'well-being' and 'wholeness', and a Christian charity has started work within this culture. Fit Lives began in Woking seven years ago, when its founder, a tennis coach, realized that his tutees wanted to talk to him about deeper things in life than tennis elbow.[15] Now a management team is trying to make its work more widely accessible. Their mission is to help local churches demonstrate the love of God in practical ways within the community of health clubs. Christians with skills in fitness, health and relaxation spend up to eight hours a week in their respective clubs, with the blessing of the local management. They help to run classes and clubs, and act as a spiritual support to club members, through chatting in the gym or at the coffee shop. The classes themselves do not plug Christianity specifically, but the work often feeds members into more overtly Christian courses also held at the club. From these, spiritual exploration can grow.

In addition, some clubs offer yoga and tai chi, as well as hypnotherapy, and activities such as tarot card readings and angel therapy are sometimes available. Fit Lives doesn't actively oppose this, but tries to create a positive Christian alternative. Many of the group's co-ordinators act as chaplains to the fitness centre, and work with staff as well as clients. For the club managers, whose job it is to keep the club members coming back, the idea of having someone around to act as a chaplain is potentially appealing and if handled sensitively this generates support from staff. There are plans to plant new churches out of these contacts.

Community service work

A Methodist church on an estate in Sheffield went out onto the streets in 2000 with a questionnaire. They asked their neighbours what mattered to them, and what the church could do to help. Most people didn't recognize that the church could play a role in local issues and were surprised at the question. The church discovered that the most pressing local needs were litter-picking, a drop-in centre for the elderly, and youth activities. It also realized that any response would need to come from all the local churches and so an ecumenical prayer group was formed. At the same time local shopkeepers were keen to lease their premises to the churches for community ventures. Recognizing an opportunity, the churches set up the Terminus Café.

The café is self-financing and includes a charity shop; it opens three days a week to around 60 visitors a day. Its Christian remit is made clear by a monthly service, Worship at the Terminus, at 4.30 on a Thursday afternoon. Bible study groups happen at varying times and venues to suit the differing needs of local residents. Café staff open and close the day with prayer, and this is visible through the window. In 2004, as a result of witnessing this, visitors began to ask for prayer. A prayer board is now situated in a discreet part of the café and one-to-one prayer is available. Volunteers from across the church and community now staff the café, and the Terminus Initiative has been created to cover the café, an asylum-seekers' befriending service and a credit union. Other café initiatives include a Tuesday night youth café where young people can hang out and play computer games.

An Anglican Baptist cell church on a new Northampton-shire estate that lacked a church building or medical centre was made aware of a need among young mums for companionship. The health visitor from the nearest general practice noticed that a number of young mothers on the estate, Grange Park, were being diagnosed with post-natal depression. In 2003 she approached the estate's vicar and his wife. They decided to open their home for two hours on Thursday mornings to any young mum who would value the chance to meet others and consult the health visitor. The aim was to build community so that the women could grow in confidence, discover friendship, and find support. Talking Point now offers an informal, welcoming setting. Good-quality coffee and cake is available in the sitting-room which has cushions, blankets and inviting toys, while any older siblings are provided with easy activities in the kitchen. Between 12 and 18 women at a time take advantage of this purely social service. As a result of this contact with the church, a few mothers asked to have their babies baptized.

Two of them attended an Alpha course and have been instrumental in developing this work on the estate.

With Talking Point and an estate toddler group established, an informal monthly session for children and their mums called Stepping Stones was set up. Held on Tuesday mornings in the community centre hall, this offers an interactive telling of a Bible story followed by a time of reflection. Around 25 adults bring children each month, both members of Talking Point and others from the estate. Festivals see an increase in attendance to around 100 adults. One Tuesday a month includes breakfast and this attracts another 25 adults. The team asked the women who attended Stepping Stones to view it as a pilot project and after three months they were given the opportunity to fill in a questionnaire and comment on how to take it further. Around a third of regular Stepping Stones members responded that they would like something for adults as well. As a result, 16 women gathered at the vicarage for a 'pizza and pud' evening followed by a discussion. Many had been to the vicarage through Talking Point, which made it a familiar venue.

The motto of the leaders is always to tell people what you are going to do; don't have any hidden motives. This has led to the women involved choosing their own course of Christian discipleship and being able to participate in the work at any level. Five or six husbands meet separately with the vicar either socially in the pub or for an express version of Alpha over beer and pretzels in each other's homes.

In Essex, Safe Haven is a spiritual home for people who live with mental illness. Held monthly on a Tuesday evening in Waltham Abbey church, the hour-and-a-half-long gathering attracts up to nine people across the adult age range. Other meeting places have been explored, but it was found that those who attend prefer the 'spiritual' feel of the church. It offers a safe place for each person to explore their spiritual journey in a framework which is Christian, but accepts people where they are; around three-quarters of those who attend regularly have no church or Christian background. Some people come each month, others when they can. It is facilitated by a minister with background and experience as a counsellor with people with mental illness. Other group members also help to facilitate the meetings. Meetings are simple, beginning with a meditation followed by a time of quiet. People then indicate by placing a lit candle in the middle of the group that they are ready to share their thoughts.

Mission in the home, street and neighbourhood

In 2003 an Anglican minister moved to a growing new housing estate in Witney, Oxfordshire, to start a community project funded by the Diocese of Oxford. She spent the first three months of her new role 'getting to know people' in local churches and the school. At the end of those three months, she sent a newsletter to every house identifying herself as a community worker and inviting residents to a meeting with the local planner. Around 50 people from the 250 houses then established on the estate turned up. This residents' meeting continues to take place once every three months, attracting 50 to 80 people at a time to its community discussions around wine and cheese. It is particularly valued by newcomers to the estate, which has since grown to 960 houses.

The estate is home to a huge cross-section of people. Social housing, young families, home-based workers and early retirees all live together on what in its early years was a building site as well as a place in which to build community. Through the community project, Discovery Days, these different types of people are able to come together in relevant groups at different social and Christian-themed events. Events are advertised in a monthly community newsletter written by the minister and delivered by volunteers. Various activities have been formed following an indication of need; an encounter with a young mother looking for someone to talk to led to a mother-and-toddler group being set up, which attracts around 40 women each week.

Other regular events are run by Discovery Days. Families meet for Sunday tea and Christian-based activities; men meet

for football; readers meet in a book group; home-based workers meet for lunch. Christians on the estate meet in one of two
weekly small groups, while a second kind of Discovery group
happens for seekers. More generally interested residents of the
estate may attend Breathe, a social evening with wine, chat, and
the possibility of moving through a series of stations provoking
reflection on a life issue. Christians are present at all the different events and activities, whether social or Christian-focused.
The evangelism present in different events is described in terms
of a scale of 10 to 1, on which individuals may be at the Christian end, or the disinterested end. Events are advertised placed
along that line, so that people can choose where they fit. By
listening to the needs of the different groups of people within
the community, Discovery Days offer a chance for everyone to
experience faith and friendship.

The Lighthouse on an Urban Priority Area estate on the out-
skirts of Bristol arose out of the prayers of two local women,
members of different churches. Their vision for the estate was
the provision of a relaxed environment where people could
come together to share food and share their lives. Following
the arrival of a new female minister on the estate, the women
are able to invite their own contacts to a regular gathering at
her church-provided house. The Lighthouse meets for a meal at
6.30 on Friday evenings. The focus is around the sharing of one
another's lives with all their various problems and situations,
a care that continues outside the meetings and throughout the
week. Numbers vary from 12 to 40, with most attending not
being Christians. Men and women, old and young, children
with parents, all come because they find something special. The
Lighthouse has been described by them as a 'life-saver', somewhere with 'warmth' and a place where 'we find God'.

The leaders are open about offering prayer for people, and
members have begun to ask for more Christian content to the
evenings, a result of the Christian welcome and strength of
relationship offered at the Lighthouse. Videos and interactive
learning are used rather than acts of worship. Some members
choose to attend a monthly Sunday evening service in a local

community centre, an event that leaders describe as 'a maturing expression'. Through the offering of a safe space, a new community has formed that gives local people a place to experience Christian love.

Schools

A project named Sorted in Bradford began from the work of a Church Army evangelist sent to live in a non-affluent area of the city and work with local young people. Initially connections were made through skateboarding, and a skate park was set up. This provided a good local facility and enabled a number of contacts to be made. However, the breakthrough came when the evangelist became part of the chaplaincy at the local church-run state school. Rather than teaching religious education or taking acts of worship, he set up lunchtime clubs and spent time in the playground getting to know the pupils. From this he was able to offer support and friendship, and relationships were built. A Friday evening social club was set up; as well as providing a place to hang out, play games and socialize, it offered some low-key faith input. As young people began to be interested in exploring faith further, a worship service and a discipleship evening have also been added. Recently a number were baptized by the bishop within a service created by the group. One of the key elements of the project is to have it run not by adult volunteers, who are present, but by the young people themselves. So part of the discipleship is helping the young Christians take on leadership roles in all aspects of the project. In the longer term it is hoped that they will be able to run the project entirely.

Learning the lessons

The stories in this chapter are only a small cross-section. There are, however, ten key principles present in them that can be drawn on in any situation.

1 Any 'place' where people meet is somewhere Christians can meet people and a church be planted in the 'local' culture.

2 If there are Christians already present, help them if possible to become the missionaries to that culture.

3 If Christians need to 'move in' they must not be a dominating presence, and need to become at home in the culture or have a clear and welcomed chaplaincy role.

4 The first thing Christians must do is listen, following the double listening process.

5 Christians need to be where people are, joining in their activities rather than inviting them to church events.

6 Christians should only set up projects and events the community ask for or clearly need, and not duplicate secular groups.

7 The place to begin is not with worship, but with social activities and social projects with no explicit faith content.

8 More explicitly Christian activities need to grow out of the questions of the non-Christians and they need to own them.

9 The most effective projects when fully established operate at three levels: (1) Build relationships in the wider community on their territory. (2) Create or find places where Christians and non-Christians build relationships and explore issues and questions of lifestyle, faith and spirituality on neutral territory; these may be joint social action projects as well as such activities as book clubs or pub groups. (3) Establish discipleship groups explicitly aimed at those who want to explore and deepen Christian faith. This last stage may include faith exploration courses like Alpha as well as groups for committed Christians; it is also here that 'locally' birthed worship should happen. Many mission projects try to jump from the first stage to the third and miss the vital second stage. For many non-churched people without this neutral second stage the journey from local culture to Christian community is too great. It is interesting to note here the observation that Celtic monastic communities had a similar structure. As we have seen, some projects may have many ways of expressing each level.

10 Once the three levels have been established, two principles are vital to maintain them. First, all levels are open and can be attended by anyone regardless of where they are on their spiritual journey. This enables people to find the level they fit and try out other levels. It also means that there is no sense of a hidden agenda or secret inner group. Second, it is important to ensure no level loses its intended character even in response to those who attend. One must remain guests in the territory of others at the first stage; there must be no increase or decrease in the Christian content of level two; nor any attempt to water down the Christian content of the third stage to make it easier for explorers to attend. As long as this is done, anyone can be part of the community being built at a level that suits them and all are enabled to move from a purely social relationship to committed Christian discipleship within the community's life.

Notes

1 Michael Frost and Alan Hirsch, *The Shaping of Things to Come*, Hendrickson Publishers, 2003, p. 23.

2 The equivalent in the USA is garage sales, but as boot sales take place in fields or large car parks with many others doing the same, they take on a sort of market stall feel.

3 www.solace-cardiff.org.uk

4 Eric Brymer, *Extreme Dude: A Phenomenological Perspective on the Extreme Sports Experience*, University of Wollongong, Australia, 2005.

5 http://dekhomai.co.uk

6 Author of a very good exploration of contemporary Paganism: Graham Harvey, *Speaking Earth: Listening People*, Hurst & Co., 1997.

7 www.embody.co.uk/, www.rejesus.co.uk/ and www.yfc.co.uk/labyrinth/online.html.

8 Delivered in a paper on INFORM day at LSE, London, 2000.

9 www.habbo.co.uk/ and http://secondlife.com/

10 www.facebook.com/

11 www.lovebristol.org/

12 www.glastonburyfestivals.co.uk/information.aspx?id=139

13 www.matrixtrust.com/group/group.aspx?id=2981

14 See articles by John Morehead at www.lop45.org/forum/forum/
uploads/JohnWMorehead/2006-10-12_173333_JohnsEssay1.doc and
www.lop45.org/forum/forum/uploads/JohnWMorehead/2006-12-05_
001039_Burning_Man_Missional_Apologetic_Paper.doc. All linked
from his blog, http://johnwmorehead.blogspot.com/

15 www.fitlives.co.uk/

17

A Mission-Shaped Christianity for a Post-Christendom World

A new reformation

As we listen to both the global culture of today and its local and non-local expressions it could be suggested that our world is going through the kind of major cultural change that occurred at the passing of the ancient world into the classical, or the classical into the medieval and the medieval into the modern. As the shift from the modern to what we call the postmodern occurs, a reminder that its identity is still being formed, there are some global messages for the church. We are currently rooted firmly in modernity and ill-equipped to express Christ faithfully in the emerging culture. As a consequence of this, the spread of postmodern culture around the world brings with it a decline in the church, or its transformation into a veneer under which a non-Christian spirituality is expressed. If there are apparent exceptions to this, it is perhaps because culture is not changing uniformly across different nations and in some places religious identity is woven into political struggles that maintain its place.

As we look at the history of God's mission, such large-scale changes have led to similar changes in the church: at their best, freshly incarnating Christ's Body in the world renewing gospel witness; at their worst, adopting elements of the 'spirit of the age' that have distorted the faithfulness of that witness. In a time of such change we are also called to a radical transformation of the church, to a new reformation. The challenge will be to enable this to be a faithful incarnation in these new cultural expressions and avoid the dangers of both traditionalism, a refusal of incarnation, and syncretism, an uncritical incarnation. This new reformation requires not only a death and resurrection of the church so that it becomes mission-shaped, but also a vision for the same transformation in the world. Because both of these require a transformation of people, a mission-shaped evangelism is an essential part of this reformation.

Evangelism after Christendom is . . .
. . . Not getting people to church but getting people to be Church

Christendom enshrined the notion that all citizens were Christian and thus members of the church. Getting people to church where they might encounter God and receive instruction to enable them to live out their faith became the aim. More recently, both in a renewal of the need to evangelize people within Christian nations and in reaction to declining church attendances, the call 'back to church' has had a new emphasis. Belonging to a church is intended to be part of our Christian life, but going to church is too easily seen as all of that life. The prime calling of the church is to be part of God's mission; in our neighbourhood, at work, with friends and relations, during our leisure activities and in our various networks. We need to be Church as Christ's Body in the world. The incarnation showed us God in human form and enabled us to discover God's love and vision for us: encountering God in human flesh is still the best means of enabling people to make these discoveries. It is a very high calling and one we will keep falling short of; but that too, if handled with openness and a genuine desire to be Christ-like, is a positive witness. Indeed, it helps people to imagine how they might also follow Christ as fallible human beings.

Further to this, we need to realize that while beautiful buildings and paid minsters can aid our spiritual life, they are not essential to it. We need to be able to concentrate on building communities; communities that incarnate what all might be in

God's kingdom. If an essential part of evangelism is to model transformed communities, evangelism is the task of the whole church, within which those called to be evangelists enable that ministry as the lead explorers of Christian community in each culture. This also means that the essential unit of cross-cultural evangelism will be small missionary communities, incarnations of the Body of Christ in each culture, the leaven in the dough that can work through it as the kingdom spreads.

. . . Not taking God to people but seeing what he is already doing in their lives

Recognizing that God is present everywhere in culture and at work in people's lives is essential for cross-cultural evangelism. Not seeing this leads to much of what people find offensive in evangelistic practice. Behaving as if we are taking God to people tends to make us judgemental, stops us listening, encourages a formula-selling approach to evangelism and, if God is at work in that person already, will often mean that far from working with the Spirit we are working against the Spirit, preventing people from growing towards Christ rather than helping them.

When we expect God to be at work in people's lives, evangelism is transformed. We begin by listening; we become interested in people's spiritual journeys and see the image of God in them. Instead of 'sniffing around trying to catch them out' we seek to meet with them at their best, assuming that God will be there too. We hold the attitude of Jesus, who would not snuff out a smouldering wick or break a bruised reed; we find out what God is doing and join in.

We also expect God to teach us through others. Evangelism becomes a process of journeying together towards God. This is not a form of pluralism; it is not that whatever path a person takes is guaranteed to make them Christ-like. In Christ all *can* do this, they have within them the seeds and shoots of that journey, but not all *will* do this. Learning from others is essential for cross-cultural evangelism; the person who is at home in the culture is the only one who can discover what it is to be a follower of Christ in that culture. Indeed, we need to trust God's Spirit to be at work in all people seeking to lead them to Christ, and also in guiding the church that comes to birth on that journey. Churches controlled by church bodies from outside the culture are prevented from becoming mature, and tend to be inauthentic expressions of church.

... Not first about getting people into heaven but getting heaven into people

In the western church too much emphasis has been placed on getting into heaven to the detriment of how we are called to live on earth. This can be traced back to the roots of Christendom and the theology of Augustine and has continued with different emphases through the medieval and modern periods. In Paul's Acts sermons, the day of judgement is often mentioned, but the emphasis is on 'we must change the way we live'. Paul doesn't ignore forgiveness and the afterlife at the final judgement, but emphasizes that because we have died with Christ to sin and been raised with him to new life we are not just forgiven sin, we are set free from its power so we can change the way we live. Ultimately we are to become like Jesus and in this show ourselves to be indeed the Body of Christ on earth.[1] This is why Jesus insists that not all who call on him will enter the kingdom, only those who do what God requires. Similarly in the final judgement story of the sheep and the goats he emphasizes that his true followers are those who have lived lives consistent with his character.[2] The point, of course, is not that we can become perfect by our own efforts, but that those in Christ are set free from the power of sin and are enabled by the power of the Spirit to live transformed lives. This is not to expect instant perfection of Christians, but to suggest that anyone who is not becoming more Christ-like is not in Christ and Christ is not in them.

An emphasis on getting heaven into people rather than people into heaven alters our evangelistic message. Perhaps most importantly it radically alters the reasons offered for becoming a Christian. The worst outcome of proclaiming a partial gospel of forgiveness and heaven is that while it is good news for those asking questions about the next life or feeling the weight of guilt, it provides a very questionable motive for following Christ; it encourages us to do so purely for selfish ends and to treat faith as an insurance policy. Add the further inducement of prosperity teaching and it is not surprising if many churches the world over contain too many people displaying little of the fruit of the Spirit in their lives.

Preaching a gospel based on the next life encourages a response based on self-preservation; it also encourages the evangelist to use the coercive threat of hell to maximize the effect. I think this may partly be why hell has become a controversial topic. There is something rather distasteful about the followers of a religion based on forgiveness, love for enemies and a repeated injunction not to judge others, indulging in the idea of a gruesome punishment awaiting those others. Turning this into a message that is supposedly 'good news', trying to scare people into the kingdom and in the process appealing to the very self-interest that Jesus actually calls his followers to deny, compounds the problem. The answer is not to rid the Christian world-view of the ideas of hell or the final judgement. To do this makes the coming of the kingdom of God something uncertain because God is not prepared to act to remove evil from the world. However, like Peter we can trust that God is patient, wanting all to be saved. Sadly, some seem wedded to self-interest and life choices that continually take them away from the kingdom. Attracting people to follow Christ by proclaiming a vision of the kingdom and calling us to be transformed as part of that vision is a far stronger message, likely to attract followers who really will die to self and live for Christ. Ironically, would not those who come to faith for fear of hell or to ensure entry to heaven after death risk coming under Jesus' warning that those who try to save their lives will lose them?

As we saw from the Coventry study, many people have self-interested goals for their own lives yet admire those who have chosen a path of living for others. It's just that they don't believe they could ever do that. Amid the suspicion of power and the cynicism about truth there is also a desire for genuinely holy people; people who will not just speak of an alternative vision for life but live it out. It is this that makes Jesus attractive to many who would not wish to see themselves as Christians. This is partly why the postmodern West is once more looking for a miraculous faith, one in which healing occurs in body, mind and spirit. This needs to be part of our missionary practice, but without forgetting that in our day we will find ourselves like Paul in Ephesus, one among many miracle-workers. If we are Christ's Body then the work of God's Spirit should be self-evident in our lives.

The good news is not just that there will be a day when the kingdom of God comes in full, and mourning and crying and sickness and death pass away, and that will be a day of judgement on the evil that causes such suffering. The good news is also here and now, that if we turn towards that kingdom and desire to live as its citizens, the power of God can change us. We too can be the people we admire; heaven can come here and now within us and spread from us to those around.

... Not saving people from the world but allowing God to transform them as part of a plan to transform the world

Paul's argument in Romans moves from forgiveness to changed lives, but this is still not its climax. It is not just individual lives or even human communities that are to be transformed, but the whole of creation. The whole creation waits for the sons and daughters of God to be revealed so that it may be set free from the power of sin and death and become all that God intended it to be.[3] The mission of God begins with the act of creation, drawing order out of chaos, and ends with new creation in which that chaos is finally no more. This is another reason why Adam becomes a focus of the Romans account. The first Adam, as the one in God's image, was charged with doing what God had been doing, subduing the chaos and filling the earth with life. Instead he was mastered by sin and death. The second Adam, Jesus, breaks the power of sin and death and becomes the first of a new humanity, able to fulfil Adam's calling to bless creation and work with God in the coming of the kingdom throughout it. This is why creation longs for the sons and daughters of God to be revealed.

People today are deeply aware of the way we are damaging creation, and the church has been one of the institutions blamed for this. While some of this criticism has been unfair, the church has sometimes embraced theologies that see the world as evil, something to be saved from, not something to be saved. Here too there is a need to widen our gospel message, to include the whole scope of the mission of God.

One of the issues we will rightly be judged on is how we live with creation as well as each other. Christians should be at the forefront of environmentalism, and not afraid to challenge the lifestyle choices that witness to the kind of self-interest we are called to deny as followers of Christ. However, the great strength and appeal of contemporary Paganism is that not only does it call us to live responsibly with all living and non-living things, it celebrates that life and re-sacralizes it. The celebration of life often seems lacking in the church; the root of this is that strain of theology that sees the body and the world as sources of temptation and evil to be resisted. Jesus often pictures the final destination we are called to as a party to which all are invited. Creation is also invited to the party when Christ comes again and is now part of the community of celebration we are called to be, rejoicing at the revealing of the sons and daughters of God.

Your kingdom come, your will be done, on earth as it is in heaven

When the disciples ask Jesus to teach them how to pray, the first thing he tells us to ask for is God's will to be done and God's kingdom to come on earth as it is in heaven. This request could sum up the vision for the mission of God; proclaiming that this prayer is even now coming true and that all can be a part of this cosmic event is the heart of our evangelistic message. How this vision works out in each place and culture is part of what we are called to discover as cross-cultural evangelists. Mission-shaped evangelism requires us to once again embrace the full message and practice of the mission of God. This is a work not just of calling to faith, but discipling in faith; of church health, not just church planting. Mission-shaped principles are not just for the initial stages in this; they are needed at every stage of the journey. This is why a call for a mission-shaped evangelism rightly also requires a call for a mission-shaped church.

Jesus' call to become part of the vision of the kingdom is challenging, it requires us to lay down our lives, but also promises us true life, life lived to the full. While it is true that some people will respond to evangelism because of guilt, or an awareness that their lives are a mess, many will not, although they may well be deeply attracted to a call to the kingdom, to an inspiring vision and a real challenge. This is why the crucial issue in evangelism is a call to life transformation.

If it is true in any place or time that the calling to follow Christ is a calling to a vision of the kingdom, it is especially so at times of major cultural change. Whatever in hindsight the failings of Christendom are, part of its success was a vision for society after the collapse of Rome, embodied in the vision of Augustine. We might wish this vision had not identified the political state with the religious community. However, what might the alternative have been had the church not stepped into the vacuum? A likely scenario was descent into inter-tribal violence, a collapse of sanitation and welfare, a breakdown of trade and food supplies and a world in which people were the continuous victims of marauding bands of desperate warriors and settlers seeking to take their land, livestock and people. This is what happened on the northern fringes of the former empire, but the cross-cultural evangelists of the monastic move-ment were able to draw the Germanic and Celtic people into the vision of the kingdom too.

I believe we live in such a time again. What we call post-modernity is a culture not yet fully emerged from the collapse of modernism. Because of the reach of modern capitalism and the collapse of the Communist bloc, the empires of the Cold War are disintegrating or changing and this is an increasingly global phenomenon. This change may not yet be strongly evident in the less developed nations, but it is spreading there too. The challenge for the church is that part of this change seems to be a collapse of Christianity. It is easy to respond to this by fighting for survival, but I think the time we live in calls for a much bolder strategy. Like Augustine, we are called to give birth to the vision of the kingdom in our day and thus actually shape the culture emerging from the collapse of modernity.

I have characterized the issues facing our global culture after modernity as a crisis of unity and diversity and the difficulty of not descending into a Nietzschean cycle of violence and conflict. Not everything can be reduced to this issue, but even those that have other causes are often influenced by it. Take, for instance, climate change. Industrialization may be the root cause of this problem, but the issue of unity and diversity gets in the way of tackling it. How do we balance the desire of developing nations to grow economically, thus increasing their carbon footprint, with the need to curb emissions? Do the developed nations deny them the route they have already taken to development? The biggest polluters are still the developed nations, but can their governments cut emissions without requiring their citizens to accept lower living standards? What politician in these democratic countries would advocate such a policy? Who, if anyone, would vote for it? Then there are other players investing in new technology; perhaps trying to create renewable energy, which is a great idea until the wind farm is proposed for your backyard. There is the issue of bio-fuels, very good for the petroleum and motor industry whose goal is not cutting carbon emissions but staying in business as fossil fuels deplete, but is their production good for the environment? What about food miles? Stopping food imports and buying local seasonal products may well cut the carbon contribution of food transport, but what of the developing economies it would ruin as they lost their sources of international revenue? And how do you ensure a fair comparison between the energy used to bring tomatoes from Africa with that used to grow them in a greenhouse in England? Is this really an environmental policy or a trade protection policy bolstering western farmers at the expense of their poor foreign counterparts? And what supermarket will refuse to stock foreign or out-of-season food and risk losing their customers to a rival? There are various mechanisms trying to solve this, such as trade summits, emissions reduction talks, the United Nations, but all tend to be held hostage to the most unco-operative larger member. The trade is handled by the international markets; they may be good methods for distributing goods, and are locally influenced by consumer choice, but the consumer has much less influence on more complex global issues. Indeed the market enshrines the notion of competition to gain maximum self-benefit, and this gets in the way of the necessary actions being taken.

There are many other issues of conflict in the world. The break-up of the former Yugoslavia and inter-ethnic war, once again becoming an issue as Kosovo declares independence; tensions between Arab Muslim and African Christian in sub-Saharan Africa; tribal violence in Kenya following elections; the problem of asylum-seekers and illegal immigrants; gang culture on the streets of the world's cities; issues about the right to die for terminally ill patients; the rights of those seeking abortions, balanced with the rights of the disabled who might have been aborted; medical experiments and ethical concerns; the growth of GM crops; the queues at petrol stations following rumours of a shortage. Of course, the conflicting needs of different groups are nothing new. The problem is that we have lost the over-arching frameworks to moderate them, particularly when they increasingly cross the boundaries of political authorities. As a people we are also less inclined to bow to the system, wanting our voice to be heard and our culture to be celebrated. This leads to much popular politics happening on an issue basis. People don't ascribe to the big visions and ideologies of political parties but campaign instead for the handful of issues they feel passionate about.

Our world desperately needs a vision of what it is to be a global family able to embrace cultural, economic and ethical diversity yet without impingeing on the good of other disparate groups. We also need to find ways to rise above our tribal interests to seek what is good for other groups and the creation we share. There are those outside the Christian faith working for this, but what of the Church? Might the vision of the Body of Christ and of a God who is a community, seeking to embrace the world yet doing so through weakness, love for enemies and care for the marginalized, sick and poor, have something powerful to offer? Might the worldwide Church model this life across the world and inspire others to join them on the journey to the kingdom? Sadly, at present the Church itself is struggling to embrace its own diversity in the increasingly close global community it finds itself in. We know that this is not easy, as not all expressions of diversity can be allowed without others and the whole Body suffering; but are we even trying to embrace this vision or simply trying to ensure that our bit of the Body wins and drives out the others? We do not need a new or renewed Christendom, we need a new vision of the kingdom that inspires the Church to be a powerful witness in the world God's mission seeks to save. That the kingdom can come on earth as it is in heaven.

In the early chapters of Acts, the way the believers lived deeply impressed many through the love and care they showed one another. Since then the Church has spread from Jerusalem, through Judea and Samaria to the ends of the earth. As it spread, missionaries, from the Hellenists, through Paul, Justin, the Celtic monks, the Jesuits and pioneers of cross-cultural mission, have learned to let the mission of God that seeks a church in every culture guide them in their mission-shaped evangelism. This has brought greater and greater diversity to the Church, although much of it has been suppressed by Christendom. As Christendom fades, the challenge is to affirm that diversity, and ensure a renewed call to mission-shaped evangelism in the new 'foreign cultures' of former Christian nations, a call to find out what God is doing in all creation and nurture into life the seeds of the kingdom. This must not be a church preservation pro- gramme or a church growth programme; it is a call to witness to the kingdom of God expressed incarnationally in each place in both our message and our lives. In that increasingly diverse expression of faith we must develop afresh ways of living out what it is to be the global and local Body of Christ, embracing diversity within unity. Not just for the Church's sake, but for a world living in a vision vacuum, waiting, though it does not know it, for the sons and daughters of God to be revealed.

Notes

1 See especially Romans 3.21–26; 5; 6; 7.14—8.17; 8.28–30.
2 Matthew 7.21–27; 25.31–46.
3 Romans 8.18–27.

Resources

From the author

Hollinghurst, S., *New Age, Paganism and Christian Mission*, Grove, 2003.

Hollinghurst, S., *Coded Messages*, Grove, 2006.

Hollinghurst, S. (et al.), *Equipping Your Church in a Spiritual Age*, CBTI, 2005 (obtainable as a PDF via the Sheffield Centre).

The Sheffield Centre www.churcharmy.org.uk/sheffieldcentre/

Blog http://onearthasinheaven.blogspot.com

Mission thinking and resources

Bosch, D., *Transforming Mission*, Orbis, 1991.

Croft, S. (ed.), *the Future of the Parish System*, Church House Publishing, 2006.

Dulles, A., *A History of Apologetics*, Ignatius Press, 2005.

Grove Books Evangelism series www.grovebooks.co.uk

Hunter III, G. G., *The Celtic Way of Evangelism*, Abingdon, 2000.

Long, C. H. and Paton, D. (eds), *The Compulsion of the Spirit: A Roland Allen Reader*, Eerdmans, 1983.

Meta Vista www.meta-vista.org

Mission-shaped Church, Church House Publishing, 2004.

Proost (creative resources) www.Proost.co.uk

SGM Lifewords www.sgmlifewords.com

Shape Vine www.shapevine.com

Share online guide www.shareguide.org

Sheffield Centre www.churcharmy.org.uk/sheffieldcentre/

Stackhouse, J., *Humble Apologetics*, Oxford University Press, 2002.

Understanding contemporary culture, spirituality and mission in this context

Brown, C., *The Death of Christian Britain*, Routledge, 2001.

Davie, G., *Europe: The Exceptional Case*, Darton, Longman and Todd, 2002.

Davie, G. (ed.), *Predicting Religion*, Ashgate, 2003.

Greene, C. and Robinson, M., *Metavista: Bible, Church and Mission in an Age of Imagination*, Paternoster, 2008.

Heelas, P. and Woodhead, L., *The Spiritual Revolution*, Blackwell, 2005.

Francis, L. J. and Richter, P. J., *Gone for Good?*, Epworth, 2007.

McLaren, B., *A Generous Orthodoxy*, Zondervan, 2006.

Murray, S., *Post-Christendom*, Paternoster Press, 2004.

Partridge, C., *The Re-Enchantment of the West*, T&T Clark, 2004.

Rankin, P., *Buried Spirituality*, Sarum College Press, 2005.

Savage, S., Collins-Mayo, S. and Mayo, B., *Making Sense of Generation Y*, Church House Publishing, 2006.

Smith, C. and Denton, M., *Soul Searching*, Oxford University Press, 2005.

Stories of mission (with and without analysis) and mission projects/groups

Brown, M., *How Christianity Came to Britain and Ireland*, Lion, 2006.

Church Army www.churcharmy.org.uk

Donovan, V., *Christianity Rediscovered*, SCM Press, 2001.

Encounters on the Edge (quarterly booklets from the Sheffield Centre) www.encountersontheedge.org.uk

Fit Lives www.fitlives.co.uk

Fresh Expressions www.freshexpressions.org.uk

Love Bristol www.lovebristol.org

Matrix Trust www.matrixtrust.com

Oliver, J., *Night Vision: Mission Adventures in Club Culture and the Nightlife*, Canterbury Press, 2009.

Wessels, A., *Europe: Was it Ever Really Christian?*, SCM Press, 1994.

Resources also accessible to non-Christians

Dekhomai www.dekhomai.co.uk

Embody www.embody.co.uk

Labyrinth Online www.yfc.co.uk/labyrinth/online.html

Resources

Re:Jesus www.rejesus.co.uk

Richards, A., *Sense Making Faith*, CBTI, 2007, also www.spiritual journeys.org.uk

Wise Traveller booklet series, Scripture Union, 2007, also www.wise traveller.org.uk

Index

abortion 91
Abraham
  Paganism and 102–3
Acts of the Apostles
  circumcision and 119
  community of Christians in 255
  Jewish believers 115, 121–2,
    128
  miracles and healing 125
  Paul in Ephesus 126
Africa 94, 254
  local cultures 214
  mixed religious practice 95
  new Christendom 74–80
  traditional religion 75, 78
afterlife 44–5, 202, 203
Albania 69
Alexandria 128
All Hallows Eve 150
Allen, Roland 1–2, 113, 128,
    163–4
  local churches 214
Alpha courses 161, 238, 242
Ambrose, Bishop of Milan 133,
    138
American Church Research
  Project 13
American Religious Data Archive
  (ARDA) 82–3
Anabaptists 143, 155, 157
angels, cross-cultural 118
Anselm 198, 200
Antioch 121

Gentile and Jewish
  church 119–20
apologetics 174–5, 187–8
Apology (Justin Martyr) 132
Aratus of Soli
  Phainomena 123
Aristotle 134
Artemis/Diana 125
Ascension 114
asceticism 144–5, 147, 196–7
Ashteroth 103, 104
Assyrian Catholic Church 145
atheism 43–4
Athens 122–3, 126
atonement
  cultural contexts of 198–205
  Paul on 199
Augstine of Canterbury 147–8
Augustine of Hippo 133, 253
  church and state 252
  City of God 142–3
  defends church 141–4
Australia 56–8
authority
  authoritarianism 190–1
  modernity vs
    postmodernity 35–6

Bacon, Francis 27
baptism
  Anabaptists and 155
  conversion and 182
  Donatist controversy 141–2

Index

Index

Index

Martin of Tours 138–9, 147
Mary, mother of Jesus
 Isis and 128, 138
Matthew, Gospel of
 authority of disciples 112
 baptism 113
 Great Commission x
Mayo, Bob 52
 *Making Sense of Generation
 Y* (with Savage and Collins-
 Mayo) 49–50, 56
media
 New Spiritualities in 41–4
 reality within 25
Medici family 154
meditation 205–6
Medium (television) 42
Melchizedek 103, 105
Michelangelo Buonarotti 153
Milan, edict of 136
Milbank, John 210, 211
miracles and healing 125, 159,
 250
Miss World riots 75
Mission-shaped Church
 report ix, xii, 1, 167, 169,
 218, 220
mission-shaped evangelism 252,
 255–6
 meaning of ix
 rationalist paradigm 162–3
 see also cross-cultural mission;
 evangelism
modernist culture
 capitalism and 38
 exclusivness 187
 experts and 36–7
 inculturation of
 Christianity 160–1
 'Late' 26
 mission and 158–62, 168–9
 overarching explanation 35
 people as good 61

rationality 37
 shifting into postmodernity 25
 texts and scholarship 32–3
monasticism 252
 appeal of 195–6
 becoming Christ-like 182–5
 as counter-culture 144–5
 medieval Britain 147, 148
 rejected by Protestants 155
morality
 conscience and 160
 secularism 159
Murray, Stuart 137, 142, 143
music 210
*The Myth of Christian
 Uniqueness* (Hick) 176–7, 178

nation-states
 church and 252
 church's relation with 141–4
 ethnos 117–18
 secularism 81–2
Nero, Emperor 132
New Guinea 68
New Spiritualities
 beliefs 44–8, 57–8, 84–8
 in Britain 54–5
 Celtic Christianity and 197
 client-based 221–2
 connection to Christianity 50
 counter-culture to
 mainstream 50–2
 East European countries 69
 environment and 60, 205
 European Values 73
 feminine power and 61–2
 fuzzy fidelity 72
 generational groups 48–58, 192
 Mind Body Spirit fairs 230–1
 online 233
 in popular culture 41–4
 in postmodern culture 62–3
 recognizing encounters 59–60

Index

Index